Privacy in the Information Age

Privacy in the Information Age

Fred H. Cate

BROOKINGS INSTITUTION PRESS
Washington, D.C.

Library of Congress Cataloging-in-Publication data

Cate, Fred H.
  Privacy in the information age / Fred H. Cate.
     p. cm.
  Includes bibliographical references and index.
  ISBN 0-8157-1316-9 (cloth : alk. paper). — ISBN 0-8157-1315-0
(pbk. : alk. paper)
  1. Privacy, Right of—United States. 2. Computers—Law and
legislation—United States. 3. Data protection—Law and
legislation—United States. 4. Privacy, Right of—Europe. 5. Data
protection—Law and legislation—Europe. 6. Computers—Law and
legislation. I. Title.
KF1263.C65C38 1997   97-21114
342.73'0858—dc21   CIP

9 8 7 6 5 4 3 2 1

The paper used in this publication meets the minimum requirements of
the American National Standard for Information Sciences—Permanence
of Paper for Printed Library Materials, ANSI Z39.48-1984

Typeset in New Century Schoolbook

Composition by AlphaWebTech
Mechanicsville, Maryland

Printed by R.R. Donnelley and Sons Co.
Harrisonburg, Virginia

THE BROOKINGS INSTITUTION

The Brookings Institution is an independent organization devoted to nonpartisan research, education, and publication in economics, government, foreign policy, and the social sciences generally. Its principal purposes are to aid in the development of sound public policies and to promote public understanding of issues of national importance.

The Institution was founded on December 8, 1927, to merge the activities of the Institute for Government Research, founded in 1916, the Institute of Economics, founded in 1922, and the Robert Brookings Graduate School of Economics and Government, founded in 1924.

The Board of Trustees is responsible for the general administration of the Institution, while the immediate direction of the policies, program, and staff is vested in the President, assisted by an advisory committee of the officers and staff. The by-laws of the Institution state: "It is the function of the Trustees to make possible the conduct of scientific research, and publication, under the most favorable conditions, and to safeguard the independence of the research staff in pursuit of their studies and in the publication of the result of such studies. It is not a part of their function to determine, control, or influence the conduct of particular investigations or the conclusions reached."

The President bears final responsibility for the decision to publish a manuscript as a Brookings book. In reaching his judgment on competence, accuracy, and objectivity of each study, the President is advised by the director of the appropriate research program and weighs the views of a panel of expert outside readers who report to him in confidence on the quality of the work. Publication of a work signifies that it is deemed a competent treatment worthy of public consideration but does not imply endorsement of conclusions or recommendations.

The Institution maintains its position of neutrality on issues of public policy in order to safeguard the intellectual freedom of the staff. Hence interpretations or conclusions in Brookings publications should be understood to be solely those of the authors and should not be attributed to the Institution, to its trustees, officers, or other staff members, or to the organizations that support its research.

For my parents,
who have often wondered
but never doubted

Foreword

The government, business, and even private citizens can, and routinely do, collect data on individuals. The information that can be easily stored and used is enormous. Consequently, an intense debate has erupted about the impact of that information on personal privacy. Unfortunately, that debate has become largely polarized between the advocates and opponents of further government intervention to protect privacy.

According to information law scholar Fred H. Cate, effective protection for personal privacy requires balancing competing interests. Knotty questions about intellectual property, the application of the First Amendment, economics, multinational regulation, and data security and encryption inevitably arise in the quest to protect personal privacy.

History, culture, and varying legal systems also influence the extent of privacy protection. Member states of the European Union, for example, must comply with a directive that greatly restricts data collection and use, not only within Europe but throughout the world if the data originate in a member state. In contrast, privacy protection in the United States is complex and decentralized. The laws and regulations governing the use of personal information are many and varied, usually pertaining to a specific industry or issue. This sectoral approach results in a patchwork of uneven, inconsistent, and often irrational privacy protection.

Self-help, mutual agreements, market-based accommodations, group action, technological solutions, and adherence to voluntary codes of practice, Cate says, are usually more effective in protecting privacy and more consistent with other democratic ideals than government intervention. He believes the government still plays an important role in protecting privacy, but, he concludes, that role should extend only to articulating principles for information privacy, adjudicating disputes about privacy rights, facilitating discussion, education, and cooperation, and leading multinational negotiations to resolve conflicts among competing national privacy laws.

Legal regulation of privacy should be limited to facilitating individual action in those situations where the lack of competition has interfered with private privacy protection. In those situations, the law should provide carefully circumscribed, basic privacy rights, the purpose of which is to facilitate—not interfere with—the development of private mechanisms and individual choice as the preferred means of valuing and protecting privacy. Individual responsibility, rather than regulation, is the principal and most effective form of privacy protection in most settings.

Given the importance of the topic addressed in Cate's book, in April 1997 the Brookings Institution invited senior industry leaders, government officials, and privacy scholars to a conference, Privacy in the Age of Electronic Commerce, organized by Robert E. Litan, director of the Economic Studies program. The participants reviewed Cate's manuscript, and a summary of their discussion is reprinted in appendix C. This volume is richer for the contributions of those participants.

Theresa Walker edited the book, Cynthia Iglesias verified it, Inge Lockwood proofread it, and Deborah Patton prepared the index.

This project was supported by the Brookings Center for Law, Economics, and Politics, which received financial support from Bell Atlantic Corporation, CITIBANK, Compaq, Data General Corporation, Hewlett-Packard Company, John and Mary R. Markle Foundation, MasterCard International, NCR Corporation, Nomura Research Institute, Ltd., Pfizer, Inc., Pharmaceutical Research and Manufacturing of America, Silicon Graphics

Computer Systems, the Starr Foundation, Sun Microsystems, Inc., Texaco Foundation, Unisys Corporation, Visa U.S.A., Inc., and Wyeth-Ayerst International. The Brookings Institution is grateful for their assistance.

The views expressed in this book are solely those of the author and should not be ascribed to the individuals or organizations acknowledged above, or to the trustees, officers, or staff members of the Brookings Institution.

Michael H. Armacost
President

September 1997
Washington, D.C.

Acknowledgments

I have benefited substantially from the generous assistance of many people. In particular, I would like to thank David Flaherty, Duncan MacDonald, P. Michael Nugent, Joel Reidenberg, Marc Rotenberg, Paul Schwartz, and Alan Westin. I doubt if any of these scholars will be satisfied with my conclusions, but they have each shared generously of their time and expertise. In addition, W. Scott Blackmer, Peter Gray, Robert E. Litan, Duncan MacDonald, Marc Rotenberg, Paul Schwartz, and Alan Westin read prior drafts of this volume and provided detailed comments, for which I am deeply grateful.

I appreciate the thoughtful suggestions of the participants in the Brookings Institution's conference, Privacy in the Age of Electronic Commerce. The opportunity to have such a distinguished and knowledgeable audience review one's work is rare. I am grateful to the participants, the Brookings Institution, and Robert E. Litan, director of the Economic Studies program, for this privilege.

I also appreciate the aid of two excellent research assistants, Molly Moran and April Sellers, and a talented and tolerant secretary, Mary Michelle Yager.

Finally, I am indebted as always to my wife, Beth, for her willingness to listen, insightful comments, excellent editorial skills, and everything else.

Contents

xi

CHAPTER ONE

Introduction

"**P**rivacy" is among the most hotly debated topics in Washington and other national capitals today. Almost 1,000 of the 7,945 bills introduced in the 104th Congress addressed some privacy issue, and this level of political activity is reflected throughout much of the world, especially in Europe, where members of the European Union are busy implementing the *Directive on the Protection of Individuals with Regard to the Processing of Personal Data and on the Free Movement of Such Data*. Privacy is the subject of thousands of scholarly and popular books, articles, position papers, reports, Internet web pages and discussion groups, and newsletters. The debate over privacy protection has spawned an astonishing array of industry and academic conferences, working groups, public interest and lobbying efforts, public surveys, and news stories.

This recent surge in attention to privacy is the result of the rapid spread of information technologies into every facet of life. Exponential increases in computing power and dramatic decreases in the physical size and price of computers have created a frenzied cycle in which both individuals and organizations increasingly use computers, spawning phenomenal growth in and dependence on computer-based services, and resulting in greater demand for and use of computers.

The result is that more data than ever before are made available in digital format, which is significant because digital information is easier and less expensive than nondigital data to

1

access, manipulate, and store, especially from disparate, geographically distant, locations. And more data are generated in the first place, because of the ease and very low cost of doing so and because of the high value of data in an increasingly information-based society. Data often substitute for what would previously have required a physical transaction or commodity. In electronic banking transactions, for example, no currency changes hands, only data. And recorded data, such as a list of favorite web sites or an automatically generated back-up copy of a document, also make the use of computers easier, more efficient, and more reliable. Finally, our computer technologies and services tend to record what might be characterized as "gratuitous" data, such as the web sites we have visited.

As a result, others know more about you—even things you may not know about yourself—than ever before. According to a 1994 estimate, U.S. computers alone hold more than five billion records, trading information on every man, woman, and child an average of five times every day. Just one industry—credit reporting—accounts for 400 million credit files, which are updated with more than two *billion* entries every month and facilitate 1.5 million credit decisions every day.[1] The ramifications of such a readily accessible storehouse of electronic information are astonishing. Consider this catalog from the *New York Times Sunday Magazine* of the data that are routinely collected about you:

—Your health history, your credit history, your marital history, your educational history, and your employment history.
—The times and telephone numbers of every call you make and receive.
—The magazines you subscribe to and the books you borrow from the library.
—Your travel history. . . .
—The trail of your cash withdrawals.
—All your purchases by credit card or check. In the not-so-distant future, when electronic cash becomes the rule, even the purchases you still make by bills and coins could be logged.
—What you eat (no sooner had supermarket scanners gone on line—to speed checkout efficiency—than data began to be tracked for marketing purposes). . . .
—Your electronic mail and your telephone messages. . . .
—Where you go and what you see on the World Wide Web.[2]

The proliferation of computers, our increased dependence on them, and their effect on the volume of data generated and recorded and on the ease and comparatively low cost with which those data are collected, manipulated, and stored, has prompted increased concern about privacy. That concern includes serious questions about how greater privacy protection might interfere with other values we care about and with the services that computerization has afforded. Marc Rotenberg, director of the Washington-based Electronic Privacy Information Center, has observed that "privacy will be to the information economy of the next century what consumer protection and environmental concerns have been to the industrial society of the 20th century."[3]

Yet for all of the passion that surrounds discussion about privacy, and the recent attention devoted to electronic privacy, surprisingly little consensus exists regarding what "privacy" means, especially with regard to the variety of contexts in which privacy issues are raised; what values are served, or compromised, by extending further legal protection to privacy; what values are affected by existing and proposed measures designed to protect privacy; and what principles should undergird a sensitive balancing of those values, particularly in light of privacy's many definitions, contexts, and sources of legal protection.

This book is an effort to address those four issues in the context of computerized information, and to facilitate a meaningful, specific dialogue toward, at best, identifying areas of common agreement or, at the least, narrowing those areas of hopeless impasse. The analysis that follows draws on the extensive published research of scholars concerned with privacy and related subjects, business and government reports, material from privacy advocacy groups, laws and reported judicial decisions, and conversations with many leading scholars and commentators in the field. This analysis does not attempt to reinvent modern privacy law but rather to make sense of an astonishingly large and diverse array of often conflicting material, in an effort to address coherently the issues identified above.

Chapter 2 provides an overview of the technologies that are provoking the current privacy debate and a discussion of the range of legal issues that these technologies raise. Chapter 3 briefly examines the central elements that make up a definition of privacy and the values served, and liabilities incurred, by each of those components. Chapter 4 addresses the regulation of privacy in Europe. U.S. regulation is treated in greater detail in chapters 5 and 6 because it is more varied and less well-settled than European law. Chapter 7 identifies four sets of principles for protecting information privacy. The principles recognize the significance of individual and collective nongovernmental action, the limited role for privacy laws and government enforcement of those laws, and the ultimate goal of establishing multinational principles for protecting information privacy.

CHAPTER TWO

Electronic Information Networks

The practical ability to create, manipulate, store, transmit, and link digital information is the single most influential innovation of the twentieth century. Computers and the networks that connect them have rapidly become a dominant force in business, government, education, recreation, and virtually all other aspects of society in the United States and throughout the world. The International Telecommunication Union predicts that by the turn of the century information services and products—already the world's largest economic sector—will account for $3.5 trillion in revenue.[1]

The role that such information plays throughout the economy was forcefully recognized in the Clinton administration's *National Information Infrastructure Agenda for Action*: "Information is one of the nation's most critical economic resources. . . . In an era of global markets and global competition, the technologies to create, manipulate, manage and use information are of strategic importance to the United States."[2] According to Anne Branscomb, author of *Who Owns Information?* "Information is the lifeblood that sustains political, social, and business decisions."[3] During the 1980s, U.S. businesses alone invested $1 trillion in information technology, and since 1990 they have spent more money on computers and communications equipment than on all other capital equipment combined.[4] U.S. consumers last year

5

spent more money on personal computers than on television sets and sent more mail by computers than by the U.S. Postal Service.[5]

The vast majority of information in the industrialized world today is electronic. Text is composed on word processors, stored in computer memories, transmitted via local networks, telephone lines, and satellites, and recorded on printers, facsimiles, and computer monitors. Images and sounds are captured by cameras, scanners, microphones, and other sensors, stored on tape or disc, broadcast over the air or through coaxial cables or optical fibers, and displayed on television or computer screens or heard on radio. Data and voice signals are collected by telephones, computers, and remote sensors, and transmitted via pairs of copper wires, optical fibers, and satellites, or beamed through the air. Documents are printed, photocopied, facsimiled, scanned, and increasingly stored electronically.

Consider the growing market for financial services—banking, securities and commodities trading, letters of credit, currency conversions, loan guarantees. What is a global financial system, but, in the words of Charles Goldfinger, a "network of information"?[6] As a result, banks in the United States and elsewhere are investing heavily in information technologies; Hong Kong's giant Hongkong and Shanghai Banking Corporation, for example, has a $1 *billion* information technology budget.[7]

No form of communication other than face-to-face conversation and handwritten, hand-delivered messages escapes the reach of electronic information technologies. As those exceptions indicate, no communication that bridges geographic space or is accessible to more than a few people exists today without some electronic component. And the dominance of electronic communication is growing at an astonishing pace.

The Internet is perhaps the best example. As of January 1997 this ubiquitous and most familiar information network connects more than 16 million hosts—computer systems or networks, each of which may connect thousands of separate machines—in 190 countries.[8] In January 1996, the Internet connected 9.47 million hosts; four years earlier, there were fewer than 1 million.[9] The growth in commercial on-line services—the bellwether of future financial stability for the Internet—is equally dramatic. In January 1997, almost 4 million Internet hosts were designated ".com" for commercial.[10] Eighteen months earlier, fewer than half—1.74 million—of those companies were present on the Internet.[11] In 1994, only 774,735 hosts were designated ".com."[12] This growth is paralleled by the volume of advertising on the Internet and the inclusion of Internet addresses in traditional print and broadcast advertising, and by the number of commercial transactions taking place via the Internet. These figures tend to underestimate the size of the Internet, but they provide a reliable benchmark for its growth: the Internet has been doubling in size every twelve to fifteen months.[13]

But the Internet is only one tangible example of the explosion of digital information that includes other national and global networks, company computer and telecommunications systems, electronic mail (e-mail), computer bulletin boards, portable telephones, digital facsimile machines, voice mail, nationwide paging services, interactive television, video telephones, and countless other technologies.

Information Technology Issues

The continuing proliferation of information technologies and services has presented many legal issues, which are the subject of extensive ongoing discussion among government officials, business leaders, academics, and others. These issues may be divided generally into five categories.

Intellectual Property

The first category includes matters dealing with the ownership of electronic information and the application of existing intellectual property laws to the Internet. The technologies involved may distort the application of existing law. For example, U.S. copyright law permits one user to give to another a physical copy of a copyrighted book, but the law prohibits that user from transmitting an electronic copy of that same book. Similarly, digital technologies may alter a legal calculus: what constitutes "fair use" and is therefore permitted under U.S. law without the copyright holder's permission, depends in part on whether there is a market for the portion of a work copied. As computers create markets in smaller and smaller fragments of works, uses that were fair in print may cease to be so in the context of digital information. The medium may make enforcement easier or more difficult. It is often easier to detect and prevent the copying of a computer file than of a book but often harder to know who performed the illegal copying. And information technologies may raise entirely new issues altogether, such as who owns the content of an electronic database.

Application of the First Amendment

A second set of issues posed by information technologies concerns the application to electronic expression of the First Amendment to the U.S. Constitution and other national and multinational guarantees of freedom of expression.[14] In the United States, the Supreme Court, beginning with its earliest free expression cases, has found that the protection afforded by the First Amendment depends on the medium of communication involved. When traditional media, such as newspapers, books, and pickets, are involved, the Court has interpreted the First Amendment to prevent the government from restricting expression prior to its utterance or publication or merely because the government disagrees with the sentiment expressed,[15] from making impermissible distinctions based on content,[16] or from compelling speech or granting access to the expressive capacity of another[17] without demonstrating that the abridgement is narrowly tailored to serve a compelling governmental interest.

When the government sought to impose similar restrictions on newer media, however, such as sound trucks, telephones, or broadcast television, the Court has assumed that "differences in the characteristics of new media justify differences in the First Amendment standards applied to them."[18] In *Kovacs* versus *Cooper*,[19] a case involving a New Jersey statute forbidding the use of a "loud and raucous" sound truck, Justice Robert Jackson wrote in support of the ordinance's constitutionality:

> I do not agree that, if we sustain regulations or prohibitions of sound trucks, they must therefore be valid if applied to other methods of "communication of ideas." The moving picture screen, the radio, the newspaper, the handbill, the sound truck and the street corner orator have differing natures, values, abuses and dangers. Each, in my view, is a law unto itself.[20]

What is the law applicable to digital information, which shares characteristics of many different media? This issue has been at the heart of recent disputes in the United States over legislation attempting to regulate sexually explicit expression on the Internet. The government has argued that the Internet is like over-the-air broadcasting and therefore subject to the same restraints as broadcasters. First Amendment advocates have argued, and so far the courts have agreed,[21] that the First Amendment should apply to the Internet with the same force with which it applies to print media. The resolution of this question goes to the heart of the scope of free expression to be permitted through digital expression.

Economic Issues

How electronic information networks are paid for and how hospitable they are to commerce are also issues. At present, most publicly available forms of two-way communication, such as telephone and mail, are regulated by national governments. Often, these regulations set forth the terms under which service must be provided, establish basic principles of nondiscrimination among customers, and govern, either directly or indirectly, the rates that may be charged and the profits that may be taken.[22] The Internet is a notable exception. Although a user may pay a fee to a local Internet service provider to gain access to the Internet, no charge is assessed for using the Internet itself, and there is no regulation of its economic health or quality of service. The Internet is unique among media of communication in not levying a charge based on distance, duration, time, or message size. A telephone call from

Washington to London is subject to regulated tariffs based on the duration and time of the call. But an electronic message, or even a digital telephone call, transmitted through the Internet is "free" to the user.

Three features of the Internet may help to explain this anomaly. First, the Internet was originally funded by the U.S. government. The Internet began in 1969 as an experimental project of the U.S. Defense Department's Advanced Research Project Agency (ARPA). Originally called ARPANET, the network linked computers and computer networks owned by the military, defense contractors, and universities conducting defense-related research. The network was later expanded to allow researchers around the country access to powerful supercomputers located at key universities and research laboratories.[23] The government paid for the ARPANET, therefore diminishing any incentive for developing cost recovery and pricing mechanisms.

Second, from its inception, the network was designed to be a decentralized, self-maintaining series of redundant links among computers, capable of rapidly transmitting communications and rerouting them automatically if one or more individual links were damaged or otherwise unavailable. The goal was to allow defense research and communications to continue even if portions of the network were damaged by nuclear blast. To achieve this resilience, ARPANET both encouraged the creation of multiple links among the computers on the network and allowed messages to be broken down into separate "packets," each of which carried the address of its destination so that they could be routed separately from sender to receiver. Thus a message might travel over any number of redundant routes to its destination, and different portions of the message might travel over different routes. The choice of route for each packet was—and is—made automatically at each network intersection.[24] This automatic routing of Internet messages, the network's capacity for routing different parts of messages over different pathways, and the existence of so many pathways have impeded the development of pricing based on distance, duration, time, or message size.

Finally, although the government no longer directly finances the Internet—successor to ARPANET—as such, the bulk of the computers and networks that constitute the Internet today are owned by individual businesses, educational institutions, and other organizations, including government agencies. Financing of the separate components is accounted for separately by the diverse groups that own them. As a result, the considerable variety of funding sources for what constitutes the Internet today has helped to stall pressure to charge for using the Internet.

These same three features, however, have prompted questions about the long-term stability of the Internet and interest in facilitating the rapid deployment of Internet-based commercial services as a likely source of future financial support. Commercial services have largely been limited to promotional and information roles until effective means of paying for goods on-line are developed. Credit cards have thus far proved an ineffective solution, because of fears that data will be intercepted. As a result, while some users provide credit card information on-line, many on-line service providers allow the user to order via the Internet and then call via the public telephone network to provide payment information. Providing for secure on-line payment systems is critical to commercial use of the Internet and to its long-term financial stability.

Multinational Impact and Regulation

The legal issues posed by information networks concern the multinational character of those networks. Digital information is inherently global: it respects no boundaries. Branscomb has written, "The very existence of information technology is threatening to nation states."[25] And Joseph Pelton has noted that information technologies and services may well be "rendering the nation state obsolete."[26]

Whether in a wire or optical fiber or beamed from a satellite or microwave dish, information—particularly electronic information—is ubiquitous. Unlike a truckload of steel or a freight train of coal, television and radio signals, telephone, facsimile, and modem communications are difficult to pinpoint and almost impossible to block, through either legal or technological means. "Digital information flowing in cables or moving through space will be, in effect, a single, homogenous stream. . . . It will become increasingly impossible to maintain any of the traditional distinctions between transmissions carrying news, entertainment, financial data or even personal phone calls."[27]

As a result of its inherently transnational character, information has been the subject of some of the earliest multinational agreements, treaties, and organizations. Binational postal treaties were concluded as early as 1601 between France and Spain and 1670 between France and England.[28] The Postal Congress of Berne in 1874 established a multinational postal regime—administered today by the Universal Postal Union—seventy-four years before the General Agreement on Tariffs and Trade was opened for signature.[29] This global framework is so comprehensive, and the practical difficulty of separating domestic and international mail so great, that UPU regulations today set the terms for domestic as well as international service.

Electronically transmitted information also prompted multinational agreements almost immediately upon its commercial deployment. The telegraph was first employed commercially in the early 1840s, and by 1849 bilateral and multinational agreements were in place to facilitate and regulate its transnational use.[30] In 1865 Napoleon III called an international conference in Paris to address technical standards, codes, and tariffs for the telegraph. The twenty countries attending negotiated the first International Telegraph Union, which later combined with the Radiotelegraph Conference to form the International Telecommunication Union. In short, by the time the telephone appeared on the scene in 1876, there already existed an eleven-year-old structure for dealing with multinational electronic communication.

Governments have been less far-sighted in dealing with the implications of the current information revolution, however. While talks are under way in some multinational forums, such as the World Intellectual Property Organization and the European Union, concerning the issues presented by multinational networks, national law continues to be the principal recourse for regulators. As a result, information networks and databases are subject not only to the laws of the jurisdiction in which they are located but also to the laws of the jurisdiction in which they are received. For information resources available via Internet, that involves 176 separate national legal regimes, as well as state or territorial laws.

Privacy, Security, and Encryption

Finally, new information technologies include the privacy of individuals, the security of data in the computer or on the network, and the availability of encryption software to protect data in the event they are intercepted. In this context, privacy refers to controlling the dissemination and use of data, including information that is knowingly disclosed, as well as data that are unintentionally revealed as a by-product of the use of the information technologies themselves.[31]

Security refers to the integrity of the data storage, processing, and transmitting systems and includes concerns about the reliability of the hardware and software, the protections against intrusion into or theft of the computer equipment, and the resistance of computer systems to infiltration by unpermitted users, that is, "hacking." Encryption is the practice of encoding data so that even if a computer or network is compromised, the data's content will remain secret. Security and encryption issues are important because they are central to public confidence in networks and to the use of the systems for sensitive or secret data, such as the processing of information touching on national security. These issues are surprisingly controversial because of governments' interest in preventing digital information from being impervious to official interception and decoding for law enforcement and other purposes. In the United States, encryption software is treated as a "munition" and therefore is subject to government regulation.[32]

The Digital Data Explosion

The issues in the five categories identified above are raised not only by the Internet but also by a wide range of other information technologies and services. Moreover, the importance of those issues and the urgency of resolving them are exacerbated by the fact that more data than ever before are being made available and in digital format. There are at least four reasons for this surge.

First, information is easier to generate, manipulate, transmit, and store than ever before. Consider two simple examples. In the first, a student who was writing a paper before the widespread availability of word processors had to write or type each draft by hand, a laborious and time-consuming process that discouraged multiple drafts. Prior drafts required physical space to store and, once stored, they were of value only to the extent the writer could locate the specific text he or she wanted quickly and predictably. Sharing drafts over geographical space required mailing a copy or the original. One then had to wait for a response. In the modern world of word processing software and e-mail, multiple drafts are easier to generate and can be stored indefinitely and in virtually infinite number, accessed quickly and precisely, and shared instantaneously via e-mail.

For the second example, consider a business wishing to record information about its customers. Previously, such information had to be collected and recorded by hand, and then stored in physical files that required extensive personnel time to maintain. Even then, the data contained in those files were of little use for mass marketing purposes because of the difficulty of correlating the necessary information from a large number of discrete files. Today, even the smallest business can maintain a computerized database of customers or potential customers, updating the information in those electronic files automatically from electronic transaction records, public information sources, or private information suppliers, such as credit bureaus. Marketing to those customers can be accomplished with the push of a button because of over-the-counter software that will search for specific data or collections of data and then generate address labels, e-mail, or even digital telephone calls to the selected individuals.

The second explanation for why more data are collected, and in electronic format, is the dramatically lower cost of collecting, manipulating, storing, and transmitting electronic data. Through the Internet and e-mail, even the most penurious student can access or distribute volumes of data that were unimaginable in a precomputer age. This is not to suggest that sophisticated information processing systems are inexpensive, but rather that they perform the services they offer at far lower cost than would be possible without those electronic systems.

Third, in an increasingly information-based society electronic information is valuable in its own right and in comparison with the same data in a nonelectronic format. Would a business be willing to pay more for a digital copy of a list containing the names and addresses of potential customers, which may be used again and again and used interactively with other data sets, or for a set of printed labels, which may be used only once? The Internet affords many similar examples, but none better than the World Wide Web, which allows a user to use her mouse to click on a highlighted term and have a computer then automatically take her to the site or text or service linked to that term. The same intelligence contained in this "hyperlink" could be conveyed with only a listing of the address of the linked site or the person to be contacted, but that would not be nearly so convenient or useful as being taken there automatically with one click of a button.

The greater value of digital information is not justified only in terms of its convenience and lower cost. Electronic data often substitute for what previously would have required a physical transaction or commodity. For example, the Internal Revenue Service today encourages taxpayers to file tax returns electronically. The IRS also prefers to pay refunds electronically directly into taxpayers' bank accounts and is even experimenting with filing by touchtone telephone. In some contexts, electronic data have effectively put an end to physical transactions. For example, virtually all settlements of payments among banks are accomplished through the transfer of electronic data: almost no currency and less and less paper change hands. As a result, not only are more digital data generated but they are relied upon more frequently and more completely.

Finally, computer systems and networks contribute to the existence of more information because of characteristics of the technologies and software necessary to their use. For example, most modern word processing programs automatically generate back-up copies of documents at regular intervals to protect against accidental erasure; most system administrators regularly back up their entire networks to tape or disk on a regular schedule. Because of the large volume of data involved, programs that access information via the Internet "cache" some or all of that information to the hard drive. And virtually all e-mail systems create multiple copies of a message—at least one in the sender's computer and one in the receiver's, and usually more. Computer technologies and services even record what might be characterized as gratuitous data—data that are captured for no immediately apparent reason. Often uses will later develop for such data, but recording each web site a user visits on the Internet or the keystrokes used in a computer session tends to reflect the interest of programmers and designers to record data simply because their equipment and software can do so.

As a result of these four reasons, and others, we are witnessing an explosion in digital data, which is dramatically raising the costs of failing to address the issues that new information technologies pose. As every facet of society relies more heavily on electronic information technologies and data, the ramifications of no solutions or poor solutions to those issues become more significant. The more heavily U.S. businesses invest in and depend on specific information technologies, and the more expectations as to the legal framework in which those systems operate are solidified, the more difficult and costly it will be to change behaviors.

The Context for Current Issues

The five sets of issues presented by information technologies—exacerbated by the proliferation of digital data—do more than threaten the stability of the information society; they also form the backdrop against which any single issue must be viewed. To be sure, these categories overlap, but they also intrinsically relate to one another; any effort to address one category of issues will necessary affect, and be affected by, the others. It is therefore impractical to consider any single category—including the privacy issues posed by digital information—without considering the interrelationship among all of the categories. Although some of that interaction may be complementary, the vast majority will bring the specific issues into conflict with one another and with other values of the society.

For example, heightening intellectual property protection for digital information will necessarily threaten First Amendment interests in the free flow of expression. Decreasing such protection, however, will undermine the willingness of businesses to make valuable information available in electronic format and ultimately encourage publishers and others to use technological means to protect their works, thereby further offending the First Amendment interest in access to information. The application of other nations' laws to these and other issues poses fundamental constitutional questions, because both the First Amendment and the guarantees for, and restrictions on, copyright protection are contained in the U.S. Constitution.

This potential for conflict becomes especially clear when one looks at the privacy, security, and encryption issues posed by information technologies. Greater privacy protection and the use of encryption software threatens the activities of the press and others who are serving important First Amendment interests, as well as the interest of the society in effective law enforcement and national defense. Reduced protection for privacy, however, could result in government intrusions that compromise other constitutionally protected values. Security and encryption are essential to the commercial use of information technologies and services, but access to consumer information and the opportunity to market strategically to consumers are also critical to modern business practices. And, as is discussed in greater detail in chapters 4, 5, and 6, the interaction of privacy protection with the multinational characteristics of most digital information systems is especially problematic in light of the wide divergence among national privacy laws.

The complexity does not diminish the importance of attempts to resolve the issues posed by the Internet and other digital information services, but it does suggest the need for precision and sensitivity. Lawmakers often tend to focus on only one issue at a time. This mode of action may be politically necessary, but it is nonetheless regrettable. In digital information, the issues are so closely linked, and the ramifications of efforts to address any one of them so widely felt, that the context of the broad range of issues assumes new importance.

CHAPTER THREE

Privacy

Despite the attention given to privacy, especially recently, surprisingly little agreement has occurred on what privacy means. In his sweeping survey of the history of privacy law in the United States, Ken Gormley identified in the literature four understandings of privacy: "an expression of one's personality or personhood, focusing on the right of the individual to define his or her essence as a human being" (Roscoe Pound and Paul Freund); "autonomy–the moral freedom of the individual to engage in his or her own thoughts, actions, and decisions" (Louis Henkin); "citizens' ability to regulate information about themselves, and thus control their relationships with other human beings" (Alan Westin and Charles Fried); and the "essential components" approach, in which scholars identify certain essential components, such as "secrecy, anonymity and solitude" (Ruth Gavison).[1]

These four approaches are clearly intertwined. The information an individual chooses to disclose about herself under the third definition of privacy above—focusing on control over information—will certainly reflect upon the personality or identity that she chooses to portray, thereby implicating the first concept of privacy. The fear of compulsory disclosure may very well influence her freedom to engage in independent action, thereby implicating the second concept of privacy. In short, more than one of these understandings may undergird a claim to privacy.

Moreover, even these four broad understandings of privacy fail to capture the full range of meanings given the term. For example, as is discussed in chapter 5, the U.S. Supreme Court has often treated privacy as the right to exclude others from intruding into the physical space surrounding an individual. As a result, an individual's privacy is at risk if the government invades her physical space, even if by so little as a "spike mike" the size of a thumbtack thrust through an exterior wall.[2] An individual's privacy is not at risk according to the Court, however, if the government searches her trash bags awaiting collection on a public sidewalk.[3]

Arnold Simmel has focused on the normative, rather than descriptive, aspect of privacy:

> Privacy is a concept related to solitude, secrecy, and autonomy, but it is not synonymous with these terms; for beyond the purely descriptive aspects of privacy as isolation from the company, the curiosity, and the influence of others, privacy implies a normative element: the right to exclusive control to access to private realms.[4]

The desire for privacy "does not exist in isolation, but is part and parcel of the system of values that regulates action in society."[5] Seen in this light, privacy is a struggle for control between the individual and society.

Randall Bezanson, too, has written about privacy as a contextual concept, but he has identified the historical roots of privacy not as an antisocial aspiration but rather as a social instrument, the boundary of which "is a reflection of, and indeed is dictated by, social habits and institutions."[6] According to Bezanson, at its origin in American jurisprudence, the right to privacy encouraged the disclosure of sensitive information to others within a given social grouping or class by penalizing its distribution outside of that intimate association. Protection of privacy therefore "represent[ed] an effort to maintain social organizations and values that were threatened by urbanization."[7]

Paul Schwartz has gone even further to advocate an understanding of privacy as participation in society and therefore essential in a democratic system:

> Privacy conceived as relating to the human capacity for participation is more helpful than the concept of informational seclu-

sion in structuring data protection law. The privacy as participation approach finds that limitations on the processing of
personal information are necessary because individual decisionmaking in a democratic society takes place *without* and *within*
the life of the community. Indeed, the health of such a society
depends on the functioning of each person's individual capacity
for decisionmaking.[8]

Francis Chlapowski has written of privacy as property—"personal information is not only an aspect of personality, it is also an
object of personality"—citing to John Locke's claim that "every
Man has 'property' in his own 'person,'" and therefore "enjoys a
right to control and dominate the products of his person."[9] This
definition highlights the intrinsic and complicated intersection
between privacy and property. As a practical matter, the possession of property facilitates greater privacy through the acquisition of high walls, physical seclusion, and guards, attorneys, and
other staff who are paid to be discreet and protect the individual's
privacy. Conversely, poverty historically has led to less privacy,
particularly where families share common dwellings with thin
walls and little, if any, physical separation. A homeless person
living on a street or in a homeless shelter has less privacy than an
individual occupying a private home. Moreover, the laws that
protect property effectively protect privacy as well, by allowing
property owners to call upon the state to evict trespassers and
prosecute intruders.

David Flaherty, data protection commissioner for British Columbia, has provided a descriptive listing of information-related
privacy interests reflected in the literature:

—The right to individual autonomy;
—The right to be left alone;
—The right to a private life;
—The right to control information about oneself;
—The right to limit accessibility;
—The right of exclusive control of access to private realms;
—The right to minimize intrusiveness;
—The right to expect confidentiality;
—The right to enjoy solitude;
—The right to enjoy intimacy;
—The right to enjoy anonymity;

—The right to enjoy reserve; and
—The right to secrecy.[10]

The specific meaning of any understanding of privacy—
personality, autonomy, control of information, specific enumerated elements, protection of physical seclusion, property, or instrument of social control, as illustrated in chapters 4, 5, and 6 in
this book, is determined almost entirely by the context in which
it is derived and applied. This is not surprising, given the conclusion of anthropologists that privacy is a socially created need.
"Without society there would be no need for privacy."[11] The demand for, and contours of, privacy differ significantly depending
upon the level of development in a society. As a creation of
society, therefore, it should come as no surprise that privacy is
largely defined within the context of the society itself.

We shall certainly see each of these understandings reflected
in the claims of privacy advocates and lawmakers in Europe and
the United States. As a matter of general definition, however, for
a volume concerned with privacy issues presented by digital
information, the definition of privacy created by Alan F. Westin
in his pathbreaking study, *Privacy and Freedom*, is most applicable. Westin defined privacy as "the claim of individuals, groups,
or institutions to determine for themselves when, how, and to
what extent information about them is communicated to others."[12] Except when otherwise noted, this is the meaning given to
"information privacy" throughout this volume. The key elements
of this definition are its focus on control of information—for
whatever reason—and its ascription of the right of privacy to
individuals and institutions alike.

It must be observed that Westin's definition of information
privacy is exceptionally broad, certainly too much so to define the
boundaries of a legal claim for invasion of privacy. As Tom Gerety
has commented, "In the legal context, this [definition] simply
includes too much. . . . When taken as the delineation of a legal
concept, it confounds every attempt to cabin the right to privacy
with prudent and plausible remedies. . . . Surely privacy should
come, in law as in life, to much less than this."[13] That is a
significant caution which should be kept in mind in any consider-

ation of claims to legal rights to privacy. But a broad definition is appropriate because it must cover a wide variety of claims for protection. As used in the following pages, information privacy is a social value—and for its staunchest proponents an aspiration— but not itself a legal right.

The other significant aspect of Westin's definition is its inherent neutrality. The information that individuals, groups, or institutions choose to communicate to others may be true or false, significant or trivial, meaningful or misleading. Information privacy does not depend on the content or merit of the information at issue. As a result, protecting privacy may sometimes impose great costs, for example, when it prevents a prospective employer from learning the falsity of an applicant's resume, as well as serve critical social and political values.

Values

Why should any society recognize a right of "individuals, groups, or institutions to determine for themselves when, how, and to what extent information about them is communicated to others?" This inquiry is particularly important in light of the fact that privacy is not an end in itself but rather an instrument for achieving other goals. "Pure" privacy is no more desirable than no privacy. In fact, the obsessive quest for privacy has been called a symptom of clinical neurosis.[14] Rather, privacy is a tool needed to achieve some result. A society's interest in protecting privacy reflects that society's interest in the result, not in privacy.

What are the essential roles that privacy plays in achieving desirable results? Westin has identified four values applicable to individuals and to organizations that informational privacy serves. His categories provide a useful framework for identifying the benefits served by privacy.

Autonomy

Individuals and institutions alike require some degree of personal or organizational autonomy to function:

The most serious threat to the individual's autonomy is the possibility that someone may penetrate the inner zone and learn his ultimate secrets, either by physical or psychological means. This deliberate penetration of the individual's protective shell, his psychological armor, would leave him naked to ridicule and shame and would put him under the control of those who knew his secrets.[15]

This value, reminiscent of the understanding of privacy as autonomy itself, recognizes that privacy is vital to the development of each individual. "Who can know what he thinks and feels if he never has the opportunity to be alone with his thoughts and feelings?"[16]

The need for private space to develop, and reflect on, ideas and opinions is critical in a democracy. The exercise of independent judgment, according to Westin,

requires time for sheltered experimentation and testing of ideas, for preparation and practice in thought and conduct, without fear of ridicule or penalty, and for the opportunity to alter opinions before making them public.... Without such time for incubation and growth, through privacy, many ideas and positions would be launched into the world with dangerous prematurity.[17]

Organizations, like individuals, often require privacy for independence and integrity—what Westin has labeled "organizational autonomy." Organizational autonomy includes the need for one organization to keep secrets from another in a competitive market, as is, in fact, required by antitrust laws and protected by trade secret laws; to govern itself independently, within the limits set by law; and to support its members' collective privacy (it would make no sense to accord an individual the right not to disclose the organizations to which she belongs, but to require organizations to disclose the names of their members). Even government institutions in the United States, which are subject to extensive openness and disclosure obligations, are nonetheless permitted, and in some cases required, to conduct certain activities in private. Private institutions have no less need for privacy, and, in fact, a competitive market requires considerable secrecy for their activities.

Release from Public Roles

Privacy is necessary for individuals because it provides an opportunity for emotional release—the chance to be out of the public eye, to not be "on," and to express anger, frustration, grief, or other strong emotion without fear of repercussion. "Such moments may come in solitude; in the intimacy of family, peers, or woman-to-woman and man-to-man relaxation; in the anonymity of park or street; or in a state of reserve while in a group."[18] The consequences of denying opportunities for such privacy can be severe, ranging from increased tension and improvident expression to suicide or mental collapse.

Organizations, too, require time out of the public eye to facilitate frank, relaxed communication, experimentation, and individual risk taking within organizational governance. Constant scrutiny can cause organizations never to get away from public posturing and image control. Westin writes about this need for release from public roles:

> Given [the] penchant of society for idealized models and the far different realities of organizational life, privacy is necessary so that organizations may do the divergent part of their work out of public view. The adage that one should not visit the kitchen of a restaurant if one wants to enjoy the food is applied daily in the grant of privacy to organizations for their staging processes.[19]

Robert Luce wrote almost three-quarters of a century ago about this value of privacy when applied to legislative discussions:

> Behind closed doors nobody can talk to the galleries or the newspaper reporters. . . . Men drop their masks. They argue to, not through, each other. . . . Publicity would lessen the chance for concessions, the compromises, without which wise legislation cannot be secured. Men are adverse to changing their positions or yielding anything when many eyes are watching.[20]

Self-evaluation and Decisionmaking

Privacy provides individuals with an opportunity for self-evaluation. Solitude and the opportunity for reflection are essential to creativity. Individuals need space and time in which to process the information that is constantly confronting them, especially as society grows more information dependent. Privacy, according to Alan Bates, allows the individual the opportunity to "assess the flood of information received, to consider alternatives and possible consequences so that he may then act as consistently and appropriately as possible."[21] Privacy also recognizes the interest of the individual "in the proper timing of the decision to move from private reflection or intimate conversation to a more general publication of acts and thoughts. This is the process by which one tests his own evaluations against the responses of his peers."[22]

Privacy is essential for group evaluation and decisionmaking in the institutional setting. If every conversation among organizational leaders or between leaders and their staffs, if every draft memo, if every proposal for action were public, frank discussion would be severely inhibited and thoughtful decisionmaking undermined. This value obviously relates closely to the preceding two, and it is supported by a wealth of experience. In the United States, for example, the law provides for the absolute secrecy of jury deliberations and judicial conferences among judges, at least until final action is taken. Premature disclosure threatens the accuracy of the outcome and the efficiency with which it is reached. Even subsequent disclosure may have some effect, as suggested by the fracas over the decision by the Library of Congress to release Justice Thurgood Marshall's papers after his death.[23] The advice of law clerks to their judges and staff aides to their legislators is kept secret. The U.S. Constitution was drafted in private; in this century, the Cuban missile crisis was resolved in private. Presidential historian Michael Beschloss has written that throughout the latter episode, "Kennedy repeatedly benefitted from a cocoon of time and privacy. . . . In the culture of 1962, Kennedy had the leisure, with full consultation of his advisors, to make a thoughtful decision that most historians would now find to be wise."[24] The effect of public scrutiny could have been disastrous. Privacy is necessary for responsible decisionmaking.

Limited and Protected Communication

The final value of individual privacy identified by Westin is the opportunity it provides for limited and protected communication, thereby avoiding "the situation in which each individual was utterly candid in his communications with others, saying exactly what he knew or felt at all times," which he characterizes as "the greatest threat to civilized social life."[25] This value of privacy recognizes that individuals require opportunities to share confidences with their family, friends, or close associates. The information may be particularly valuable to the person to whom it is disclosed, and the opportunity for private communications may facilitate a response that is important to the original speaker.

Organizations share the need for limited and protected communications—to receive advice from institutional advisors such as attorneys and accountants, and to facilitate the disclosure of information by customers, clients, and others. This interest extends beyond the individuals' interest in the privacy of their communications, to encompass the institution's interest in having access to the information necessary to conduct its activities. Therefore, a bank seeks privacy for the financial information it possesses about its customers, because that information is necessary to the bank's activities and customers would be less willing to disclose that information if the bank could not legally protect against its disclosure. A university controls access to its faculty's assessments of its students not only out of concern for its students' individual interest in privacy but also because of its institutional interest in candid and accurate assessments, which might be withheld if those assessments were not protected from disclosure. A newspaper or a government agency might promise a source of information anonymity in order to obtain desired information.

This explains why in the United States most states exempt from their defamation laws communications to law enforcement officials, courts, or even close business associates, and why most states protect from disclosure conversations between attorneys and their clients. These are precisely the types of communication society wishes to encourage. Protecting the privacy of the parties involved in the disclosure is another way of facilitating these important communications.

Costs

While privacy is a necessary element of quality life in modern society, one must also acknowledge that privacy imposes real costs on individuals and institutions. Judge Richard Posner has written:

> Much of the demand for privacy . . . concerns discreditable information, often information concerning past or present criminal activity or moral conduct at variance with a person's professed moral standards. And often the motive for concealment is . . . to mislead those with whom he transacts. Other private information that people wish to conceal, while not strictly discreditable, would if revealed correct misapprehensions that the individual is trying to exploit.[26]

The opportunity to mislead is inherent in legal protection for "the claim of individuals, groups, or institutions to determine for themselves when, how, and to what extent information about them is communicated to others."[27] Privacy therefore facilitates the dissemination of false information, for example, when a job applicant lies about his previous employment, by making discovery of that falsity more difficult or impossible. Privacy similarly protects the withholding of relevant true information, as, for example, when an airline pilot fails to disclose a medical condition that might affect job performance. Privacy interferes with the collection, organization, and storage of information on which businesses and others can draw to make rapid, informed decisions, such as whether to grant credit or accept a check. As these examples suggest, the costs of privacy may be high. Those costs include both transactional costs incurred by information users seeking to determine the accuracy and completeness of the information they receive, and the risk of future losses resulting from inaccurate and incomplete information. Privacy therefore may reduce productivity and lead to higher prices for products and services.

The price of privacy is measured in social and psychological, as well as economic, terms. Psychologist Sidney Jourard has observed that "the wish for privacy expresses a desire to be an enigma to others or, more generally, a desire to control others' perceptions and beliefs vis-à-vis the self-concealing person."[28] Yet as individuals build social and professional relationships, choose whom to trust and on whom to rely, they have a legitimate interest in not having their perceptions and beliefs concerning others manipulated through misrepresentation. Privacy also may threaten physical safety. In light of the evidence concerning recidivism among child molesters and other sexual offenders,[29] protections against disclosure of past offenses interfere with the public's ability to learn the information necessary to protect itself. What parent would not want to know if her child's babysitter had been convicted for child abuse?[30] Similarly, what store owner would not want to know whether a clerk was a kleptomaniac? What patient would not want to know whether his physician had a history of malpractice? What man or woman would not want to know if a potential sexual partner had a sexually transmitted disease? What airline would not want to know if its pilots were subject to epileptic seizures? Yet the interest in not disclosing that information is precisely what privacy protects.

Moreover, even when the information disclosed is not inherently significant or in the context of a relationship where health or safety is at stake, there is nonetheless value in curiosity. For example, in the United States, aggressive, prying exposés have established *60 Minutes* as the nation's longest-running investigative journalism program. Popular comedies such as *Candid Camera,* the public's preoccupation with the criminal and civil trials of O.J. Simpson, real-life crime programs such as *COPS* and *Rescue 911*, and movies, books, and articles about real people and events display the intensity of popular interest in the lives of other people. The widespread existence of the tabloid press, gossip, and public taste for stories about others—whether tales of uncommon courage or of unmitigated scandal—suggest that this curiosity is not limited to the United States.

As Judge Posner has noted, "casual prying" is not only a common feature of everyday life, it "is also motivated, to a greater extent than we may realize, by rational considerations of self-interest. Prying enables one to form a more accurate picture of a friend or colleague, and the knowledge gained is useful in one's social or professional dealings with him."[31] Even the term "idle curiosity," according to Judge Posner, is "misleading. People are not given to random, undifferentiated curiosity." For example, "gossip columns recount the personal lives of wealthy and successful people whose tastes and habits offer models—that is, yield information—to the ordinary person in making consumption, career, and other decisions. . . . [They] open people's eyes to opportunities and dangers; they are genuinely informational."[32] Protection for privacy, therefore, not only interferes with the acquisition of information that has a particular, identified significance, it also impedes a voyeuristic curiosity that is widely shared and that serves valuable purposes for both individuals and society.

Despite its benefits, privacy may be seen as an antisocial construct. It recognizes the right of the individual, as opposed to anyone else, to determine what he will reveal about himself. As a result, privacy conflicts with other important values within the society, such as society's interest in facilitating free expression, preventing and punishing crime, protecting private property, and conducting government operations efficiently. To the extent that legal protections and social mores concerning privacy interfere with the acquisition and use of personal information, privacy may even conflict with the interest of the persons whose privacy is being protected. If a customer wants credit in a retail store, but the law prohibits the store owner from obtaining or verifying the credit information necessary to extend that credit, the customer is inconvenienced, even though she may be willing at that moment and for that purpose, to consent to the disclosure of her credit information. If she requires emergency medical attention, but privacy laws interfere with the hospital obtaining her medical records, she may face greater risks than mere inconvenience. Instant credit, better targeted mass mailings, lower insurance rates, faster service when ordering merchandise by telephone, special recognition for frequent travelers, and countless other benefits come only at the expense of some degree of privacy.

The Privacy Balance

Privacy is not an absolute. It is contextual and subjective. It is neither inherently beneficial nor harmful. Rather, the term connotes a complex aggregation of positive and negative attributes. Moreover, the privacy interests at stake in any given situation may vary from the profound to the trivial, and that valuation will depend significantly on who is making it. For example, if privacy protects the combination to my safe or the location of a key to my house, it is extraordinarily valuable to me and, in most circumstances, to society more broadly, which shares my interest in avoiding theft and other criminal conduct. If privacy allows me to avoid the inconvenience of junk mail, it is somewhat valuable to me, but less so to others, who benefit from the subsidy paid by bulk mailers and from the ability to target advertisements for products and services. If, however, privacy permits me to avoid paying taxes or obtain employment for which I am not qualified, it may be very valuable to me, but extremely costly to society as a whole. It is clear, therefore, that neither privacy values nor costs are absolute. One individual's privacy interests may conflict with another's, with the interests of society, or even with others of his own interests. What is needed is a balance, of which privacy is a part. Determining what that part is in any specific context requires a careful evaluation of subjective, variable, and competing interests.

As Westin has written, "Each individual must, within the larger context of his culture, his status, and his personal situation, make a continuous adjustment between his needs for solitude and companionship; for intimacy and general social intercourse; for anonymity and responsible participation in society; for reserve and disclosure."[33] Societies have accommodated those competing values and protected them within their legal systems in very different ways. The following chapters examine the two ends of the spectrum of privacy protection—Europe and the United States.

CHAPTER FOUR

Privacy Regulation in Europe

Although legal protection for a "right of privacy" originated in the United States, Europe was the site of the first privacy legislation and has been the source of most comprehensive privacy regulation.[1]

National Data Protection Laws

In 1970 the German state of Hesse enacted the first data protection statute; Sweden followed in 1973 with the first national statute. Today, Austria, Belgium, the Czech Republic, Denmark, Finland, France, Germany, Hungary, Iceland, Ireland, Italy, Luxembourg, the Netherlands, Norway, Portugal, Spain, Sweden, Switzerland, and the United Kingdom have broad privacy or data protection statutes.[2]

These omnibus laws are often supplemented by other laws and regulations that apply to specific types of processing activities for specific subject matter. European data protection laws are notable generally for four features: typically they apply to both public and private sectors; they apply to a wide range of activities, including data collection, storage, use, and dissemination; they impose affirmative obligations (often including registration with national authorities) on anyone wishing to engage in

any of these activities; and they have few, if any, sectoral limitations—they apply without regard to the subject of the data.[3]

Beyond these four broad similarities, however, national data
protection laws in Europe diverge significantly, largely based on
the responsibilities and power given to the central data protection authority by the national data protection law. In Sweden and
France, for example, the Data Inspection Board and National
Commission on Informatics and Liberties, respectively, are comparatively powerful and charged with overseeing a wide range of
data processing activities. They have sweeping authority to grant
or deny authorization for public and private data processing
activities.[4] As the title of the CNIL suggests, the French data
protection board's mandate is perhaps the broadest in Europe.
Besides overseeing data protection, the CNIL has established
separate subcommissions on freedom to work, research and statistics, local government, and technology and security.[5] The
structural independence, power, and scope of the Swedish and
French data protection boards, however, do not necessarily mean
that these authorities have proved highly effective in protecting
citizens' privacy. On the contrary, these very features often lead
to too little funding to accomplish so many tasks. The result,
according to Commissioner Flaherty, is a "very bureaucratic approach to data protection for the public *and* private sectors
[which] bogs down in paperwork and the registration of data
banks to the neglect of audits, the investigation of complaints,
and the conduct of meaningful public relations."[6]

At the other extreme, Germany's data protection law creates
an effectively advisory data protection system at the federal
level. The German federal data protection commissioner is part of
the Ministry of the Interior and under the authority of the minis-
ter. The role of the commissioner is to "advise, admonish and
assist the government."[7] The commissioner can submit formal
complaints about information processing activities to the responsible federal ministers, but the power to impose legally binding
resolutions of those complaints rests elsewhere. This does not
mean that the German data protection system has proved ineffective, but rather that federal protection is only one part of an
integrated federal-state (Länder) system and that it has had to

depend on political persuasion and public pressure to protect personal privacy.

Other European countries lie somewhere between Swedish and French "regulatory" data protection systems and the German "advisory" system. The diversity of those national data protection systems, and the perceived inadequacy of many European regimes, has prompted greater attention to multinational approaches to protecting privacy.

Multinational Data Protection Measures

Enactment of data protection laws by individual European nations has been paralleled and, in some cases, anticipated by multinational action. In 1980 the Committee of Ministers of the Organization for Economic Cooperation and Development (OECD)[8] issued *Guidelines on the Protection of Privacy and Transborder Flows of Personal Data* (guidelines).[9] The guidelines outline basic principles for both data protection and the free flow of information among countries that have laws conforming with the protection principles. The guidelines, however, have no binding force and permit broad variation in national implementation.

One year after the OECD issued its guidelines, the Council of Europe promulgated a convention, *For the Protection of Individuals with Regard to Automatic Processing of Personal Data*.[10] The convention, which took effect in 1985, is similar to the guidelines, although it focuses more on the importance of data protection to protect personal privacy. The convention specifies that data must be obtained and processed fairly; used and stored only for legal purposes; adequate, relevant, and not excessive in relation to the purpose for which they are processed; accurate and up-to-date; and stored no longer than necessary.[11] The document gives individuals the right to inquire about the existence of data files concerning them; obtain a copy of that data; and have false or improperly processed data corrected or erased.[12]

The convention requires each of the member countries (now twenty-six) to enact conforming national laws. By 1992, however, when debate over the more detailed European Union data protection directive, discussed below,[13] overtook the convention, only ten countries—Austria, Denmark, France, Germany, Ireland, Luxembourg, Norway, Spain, Sweden and the United Kingdom—had ratified the convention, while eight—Belgium, Cyprus, Greece, Iceland, Italy, Netherlands, Portugal and Turkey—had signed without ratification.[14] The Council of Europe subsequently urged all European Union member states to ratify and implement the convention when it endorsed the European Commission's proposal for a data protection directive. By 1997, all of the fifteen EU member states (except Greece, which is currently considering a privacy bill) and Switzerland have national legislation consistent with the convention.

Nevertheless, the resulting protection for personal privacy is far from uniform, for at least three reasons. First, some of the national data protection legislation existed before the adoption of the convention. Second, the convention was not self-executing and therefore permitted each country to implement its national laws conforming to the convention's terms in very different ways. Finally, the convention did not include definitions for important terms, such as what constitutes an "adequate" level of data protection; as a result, member countries were left free to adopt their own, inconsistent definitions in their national legislation.

Data Protection Directive

As a result of the variation and uneven application among national laws permitted by both the guidelines and the convention, in July 1990 the commission[15] of the then-European Community (EC) published a draft *Council Directive on the Protection of Individuals with Regard to the Processing of Personal Data and on the Free Movement of Such Data.*[16] The draft directive was part of the ambitious program by the countries of the European Union[17] to create not merely the "common market" and "economic and monetary union" contemplated by the Treaty of Rome,[18] but also the political union embodied in the Treaty on European Union signed in 1992 in Maastricht.[19]

The shift from economic to broad-based political union brought with it new attention to the protection of information privacy. On March 11, 1992, the European Parliament[20] amended the commission's proposal to eliminate the distinction in the 1990 draft between public and private sector data protection and then overwhelmingly approved the draft directive. On October 15, 1992, the commission issued its amended proposal; on February 20, 1995, the Council of Ministers[21] adopted a *Common Position with a View to Adopting Directive 94/ /EC of the European Parliament and of the Council on the Protection of Individuals with Regard to the Processing of Personal Data and on the Free Movement of Such Data.*[22] The directive was formally approved on October 24, 1995, and will take effect three years later.[23]

Scope and Definitions

The directive is extraordinarily comprehensive. It requires each of the fifteen EU member states to enact laws governing the "processing of personal data."[24] The directive defines "processing" broadly as "any operation or set of operations," whether or not automated, including but not limited to "collection, recording, organization, storage, adaptation or alteration, retrieval, consultation, use, disclosure by transmission, dissemination or otherwise making available, alignment or combination, blocking, erasure or destruction."[25] "Personal data" are defined equally broadly as "any information relating to an identified or identifiable natural person."[26] This would include not only textual information but also photographs, audiovisual images, and sound recordings of an identified or identifiable person. Moreover, the directive is not limited to *living* natural persons.

As a practical matter, the directive does not apply in only two contexts: activities outside of the scope of EC law, such as national security and criminal law, and the processing of personal data that is performed by a "natural person in the course of a purely private and personal activity."[27]

In addition, the directive authorizes a number of exemptions or derogations from specific requirements under limited circumstances. The broadest of these exemptions—article 13—permits member states, in narrowly defined situations, to restrict the obligations and rights concerning four of the directive's requirements: those pertaining to data quality, the information to be given to data subjects, the access of data subjects to data about themselves, and the registers of data processors and processing activities.[28] Those contexts in which derogations or exemptions from these obligations and rights are permitted include, in addition to areas such as national security and criminal law where the directive does not apply, "an important economic or financial interest of a Member State or of the European Union, including monetary, budgetary and taxation matters" and "the protection of the data subject or of the rights and freedoms of others."[29] Other, more narrow provisions that permit member states to derogate from a specific requirement are addressed in the following pages in the context of the discussion about each of those requirements. Except for these limited exclusions, the directive applies to all processing of personal data.

Basic Protections

National laws enacted in compliance with the directive must guarantee that "processing of personal data" is accurate, up-to-date, relevant, and not excessive. Personal data may be used only for the legitimate purposes for which they were collected and kept in a form that does not permit identification of individuals longer than is necessary for that purpose.[30] Personal data may be processed only with the consent of the data subject, when legally required, or to protect "the public interest" or the "legitimate interests" of a private party, except when those interests are trumped by the "interests of the data subject."[31] The processing of data revealing "racial or ethnic origin, political opinions, religious beliefs, philosophical or ethical persuasion . . . [or] concerning health or sexual life" is severely restricted and in most cases forbidden without the written permission of the data subject.[32]

Disclosure to Data Subjects

Data processors must inform persons from whom they intend to collect data of the purposes for the processing; the "obligatory or voluntary" nature of any reply; the consequences of failing to reply; the recipients or "categories of recipients" of the data; the data subject's right of access to, and opportunity to correct, data concerning her; and the name and address of the "controller."[33] The processor must provide the same disclosure to individuals about whom data have been collected without their consent.[34]

Access to, and Opportunity to Correct, Personal Data

The directive requires member states to enact laws guaranteeing individuals access to, and the opportunity to correct, processed information about them. At a minimum, those laws must permit data subjects "to obtain, on request, at reasonable intervals and without excessive delay or expense, confirmation of the existence of personal data relating to them, communication to them of such data in an intelligible form, an indication of their source, and general information on their use."[35] Member states may limit this right of access only to protect national security, defense, criminal proceedings, public safety, a "duly established paramount economic and financial interest of a Member State or of the [European] Community," or a similar interest.[36] Even in these limited cases, the processor must provide access to a third party charged with acting on behalf of the data subject.[37]

National laws under the directive must also permit data subjects to correct, erase, or block the transfer of "inaccurate or incomplete data,"[38] and the opportunity to object at any time "on legitimate grounds" to the processing of personal data.[39] The directive requires that data subjects be offered the opportunity to have personal data erased without cost before they are disclosed to third parties, or used on their behalf, for direct mail marketing.[40]

Data Security

The directive also establishes basic requirements for protecting personal data from "accidental or unlawful destruction or accidental loss and against unauthorized alteration or disclosure or any other unauthorized form of processing."[41]

Registration of Data Processing Activities

In keeping with most European data protection legal regimes, the directive requires that data processors—called "controllers" in the directive—notify the applicable national "supervisory authority" before beginning any data processing.[42] Member states' national laws must require that the notification include, at a minimum: the name and address of the controller; the purpose for the processing; the categories of data subjects; a description of the data or categories of data to be processed; the third parties or categories of third parties to whom the data might be disclosed; any proposed transfers of data to other countries; and a description of measures taken to ensure the security of the processing.[43] Controllers must also notify the supervisory authority of changes in any of the above information.

The directive requires each supervisory authority to investigate data processing that "poses specific risks to the rights and freedoms of individuals."[44] For certain routine processing that does not pose a significant threat to individuals' rights, such as producing correspondence or consulting documents available to the public, the directive permits member states to simplify or even eliminate the notification requirements.[45] Each supervisory authority is required to keep and make available to the public a "register of notified processing operations."[46]

Restrictions on Automated Decisionmaking

In a significant departure from most prior data protection laws, the directive requires member states to "grant the right to every person not to be subjected to an administrative or private decision adversely affecting him which is based solely on automatic processing defining a personality profile."[47]

In the *Explanatory Memorandum* issued with the amended draft directive, the commission offered three clarifications of this requirement. First, to be prohibited by the directive, the decision must be adverse to the individual; "the simple fact of sending a commercial brochure to a list of persons selected by computer" does not constitute an adverse decision.[48] Second, the commission stressed that the provision applies only to decisions taken "solely" by automatic processing; "what is prohibited is the strict application by the user of the results produced by the system."[49] For example, national laws must forbid an employer to reject an applicant solely based on the results of a computerized psychological evaluation. Third, the provision applies to processing that uses "variables which determine a standard profile." The use of automated processing to determine facts about a specific individual and then make an adverse decision against her, for example, to determine an individual bank balance and then refuse to provide cash because the account holder is overdrawn, would not be forbidden.[50]

The directive also requires that every data subject be "informed of the reasoning applied in any automatic processing operation the outcome of which is invoked against him."[51]

Supervisory Authorities

Under the directive, each member state must establish an independent public authority to supervise the protection of personal data.[52] Each "supervisory authority" must have, at minimum, the power to investigate data processing activities, including a right of access to the underlying data, as well as the power to intervene to order the erasure of data and the cessation of processing, and to block proposed transfer of data to third parties.[53] The supervisory authority must also be empowered to hear complaints from data subjects and must issue a public report, at least annually, concerning the state of data protection in the country.[54]

Liability and Remedies

The directive requires that member states' laws provide for civil liability against data controllers for unlawful processing activities,[55] and provide "dissuasive" penalties for noncompliance with the national laws adopted pursuant to the directive.[56] In addition to requiring the supervisory authority to enforce those laws and to hear complaints by data subjects, the directive mandates creation of a "right of every person to a judicial remedy for any breach of the rights guaranteed by this Directive."[57]

Restrictions on Transborder Data Flow

Perhaps the most controversial provision in the document is the requirement that member states enact laws prohibiting the transfer of personal data to nonmember states that fail to ensure an "adequate level of protection."[58] The directive provides that the adequacy of the protection offered by the transferee country "shall be assessed in the light of all circumstances surrounding a data transfer," including the nature of the data, the purpose and duration of the proposed processing, the "rules of law, both general and sectoral," in the transferee country, and the "professional rules and security measures which are complied with" in that country.[59] The prohibition is subject to exemptions when (1) the data subject has consented "unambiguously" to the transfer; (2) the transfer is necessary to the performance of a contract between the data subject and the controller or of a contract in the interest of the data subject concluded between the controller and a third party; (3) the transfer is legally required or necessary to serve an "important public interest"; (4) the transfer is necessary to protect "the vital interests of the data subject;" or (5) the transfer is from a "register which according to laws or regulations is intended to provide information to the public and which is open to consultation either by the public in general or by any person who can demonstrate legitimate interest."[60] The directive forbids member states from restricting the flow of personal data among themselves because of data protection or privacy concerns.[61]

European Privacy Concepts and Principles

The data protection directive marks the high-water mark of legal protection for information privacy. It is distinguished by its breadth in the data, activities, and geographic area to which it applies. It is very much a European product, reflecting the tenor of predecessor national data protection laws and the economic demand for a larger, more unified European Union. It reflects much more, however, that is equally indicative of its European origins.

Privacy as a Human Right

First, the directive's terms, and the process from which it resulted, reflect a commitment to privacy as a basic human right, on par with the rights of self-determination, freedom of thought, and freedom of expression. Article 1 obligates member states to protect the "fundamental rights and freedoms of natural persons, and in particular their right to privacy with respect to the processing of personal data."[62] This is a new and in many ways revolutionary approach to privacy. One of the EU's most distinguished data protection experts, Spiros Simitis, formerly data protection commissioner in the German state of Hesse and chair of the Council of Europe's Data Protection Experts Committee, characterized this innovation as follows:

> Contrary to most other documents and nearly for the first time in the history of the Community, the Commission in its draft said that the need for the Directive is based on the need to protect human rights within the Community. This is why, when we speak of data protection within the European Union, we speak of the necessity to respect the fundamental rights of the citizens. Therefore, data protection may be a subject on which you can have different answers to the various problems, but it is not a subject you can bargain about.[63]

The implications of characterizing privacy as a fundamental human right are both numerous and profound, as suggested by Simitis's comment. Because this approach raises the value placed upon protecting privacy, it justifies sweeping regulation, such as that contained within the directive, and considerable costs imposed on individuals, private sector institutions, and governments required to comply with its terms. The British Bankers' Association has calculated the cost of a single institution providing one customer with "a simple and straightforward report" containing the basic information required under the directive at "in excess of £150." The BBA concludes that the total cost of one major bank complying with the directive "runs into millions."[64] Governments face similar costs in administering the required registration systems and carrying out the other responsibilities of the supervisory authority necessitated by the directive. The ultimate costs will be borne by taxpayers and consumers; the directive therefore operates as a tax on European citizens and institutions, justified by the high value placed upon privacy. Moreover, to the extent articles 25 and 26 are enforced to apply the directive's terms to non-European data users, the tax will be borne by businesses and consumers around the world.

Characterizing privacy as a human right also increases the likelihood that such regulation will be upheld against challenges based on other rights offended by that regulation. And this approach decreases the room for compromise or accommodation when reconciling European law with that of other nations and trading partners.

The primacy of the right to privacy is reflected in the text of the directive itself, which permits member states to carve out exceptions "for the processing of personal data carried out solely for journalistic purposes or the purposes of artistic or literary expressions which prove necessary to reconcile the right to privacy with the rules governing freedom of expression," but only with regard to two of the directive's substantive provisions.[65] Member states may create exceptions to the prohibition on processing sensitive data[66] and the requirement that data subjects be notified of information processing activities.[67] By the omission of any reference to the other substantive rights from the article permitting exceptions for expressive undertakings, it is clear that the directive's drafters believe that the protection of privacy is paramount to freedom of expression and the activities of the press and other authors and artists.

The European Context

The breadth of the directive and the tone of the debate surrounding its adoption clearly reflect its European context. In large part, that is a historical context, as Commissioner Flaherty has written:

European data protection laws include the hidden agenda of discouraging a recurrence of the Nazi and Gestapo efforts to control the population, and so seek to prevent the reappearance of an oppressive bureaucracy that might use existing data for nefarious purposes. This concern is such a vital foundation of current legislation that it is rarely expressed in formal discussions. This helps to explain the general European preference for strict licensing systems of data protection. . . . Thus European legislators have reflected a real fear of Big Brother based on common experience with the potential destructiveness of surveillance through record-keeping. None wish to repeat the experiences endured under the Nazis during the second World War.[68]

It is ironic that the directive seeks to ensure the prevention of an authoritarian regime by creating government authorities with sweeping powers to oversee data-related activities. This approach is consistent with the distinctive societal context reflected in the laws and legal structures of most European nations. As civil law countries, most European nations have statutory codes that regulate behavior in detail. Moreover, many European governments provide, pay for, and heavily regulate essential services. Intensive government entanglement with daily life is accepted and often valued. Even in England, a common law country, the government often provides, or at least subsidizes, many essential services, including education, housing, and health care. Unlike in the United States—where the Constitution gives citizens rights against the government, but imposes few affirmative obligations on the government and provides no rights against private parties—European governments are often the guarantors of citizen rights and entitlements.

Moreover, the substantive legal rights surrounding privacy and information are often quite different from the U.S. counterparts. For example, no European nation affords its citizens a fundamental, constitutional guarantee of freedom of expression or freedom of the press. While the right to receive and impart information is protected in the European Convention for the Protection of Human Rights and Fundamental Freedoms[69] and in other multinational documents,[70] expression of all forms is subject to much greater governmental restraint and to considerably more administrative scrutiny in Europe than in the United States. In many European countries, the most powerful electronic media are just beginning to emerge from state ownership, and even private media face significant restrictions, even on political expression such as the coverage of trials, terrorist activities, government actions, and even political parties. Under another European directive, the *EC Council Directive Concerning the Pursuit of Television Broadcasting Activities*, adopted by the Council of Ministers on October 3, 1989, broadcasters face a panoply of regulations ranging from extensive rules restricting advertising and sponsorship to a broad prohibition against airing any harmful programming.[71] Under the most controversial provision, broadcasters must ensure that a majority of broadcast transmission time, excluding time occupied by news, sports, games, advertising and teletext, is reserved for "European works."[72] In France, the Conseil supérieur de l'audiovisuel announced in 1989 that it would fine television stations $10,000 for every hour of programming that exceeded French national broadcasting quotas, and promptly imposed a $6 million fine against the station, La Cinq, for failing to adhere to existing national quotas limiting non-French programming.[73]

The data protection directive thus reflects not only the civil law context of most European nations, but also an acceptance of considerable government involvement in communications and the flow of information, even to the extent of state-subsidized popular media.

Consensus on Privacy Principles

Finally, adoption of the data protection directive, while not without controversy, reflects a high degree of consensus within and among European nations as to the applicable principles of data protection. The existence of such consensus is itself noteworthy. But the breadth of those principles, as reflected in the text of the directive and national laws, is equally striking.

Paul Schwartz and Joel Reidenberg have identified four broad principles in their recent sweeping study, *Data Privacy Law*:

(a) the establishment of obligations and responsibilities for personal information; (b) the maintenance of transparent processing of personal information; (c) the creation of special protection for sensitive data; and (d) the establishment of enforcement rights and effective oversight of the treatment of personal information.[74]

OBLIGATIONS AND RESPONSIBILITIES. The creation of obligations and responsibilities for personal information includes at least five specific elements: that information be collected only for specific and specified purposes; such information may be used only in ways that are compatible with those purposes; information unnecessary to those purposes may not be collected; the information may be stored no longer than is necessary for those purposes; and individuals must have a right to access their personal information and to correct inaccurate information.[75]

TRANSPARENT PROCESSING. Guaranteeing transparent processing of personal data requires that processing activities "be structured in a manner that will be open and understandable."[76] At minimum, this requires that individuals be given notice whenever personal information about them is collected and that, at least in some cases, consent must be obtained for certain uses of personal information.

SPECIAL PROTECTION FOR SENSITIVE DATA. The principle that special protection be provided for sensitive data requires that there be special government scrutiny of data collection and processing activities of data identifying "racial or ethnic origin, political opinions, religious beliefs, philosophical or ethical persuasion . . . [or] concerning health or sexual life."[77] Under the directive, such data collection or processing is generally forbidden outright.

ENFORCEMENT RIGHTS AND EFFECTIVE OVERSIGHT. The fourth principle requires that individuals have legally enforceable rights against data collectors and processors who fail to adhere to the law. This principle requires that the government oversee the data processing activities of private parties and enforce the law when necessary. Under the directive, that oversight includes registration of all data processors and collection and processing activities. As a result, no person in Europe, other than an individual engaged in a "purely private and personal activity," may collect information that identifies specific individuals without the knowledge and permission of a national government.[78]

Implementation

To be certain, implementation of these principles of data protection will vary among European nations, as has implementation of prior multinational agreements. Existing national laws diverge widely, and even those national data protection authorities with the greatest responsibility and apparent authority, for example, the French CNIL, have lacked the focus and resources necessary to carry out the full data protection mandate of their national laws. It remains to be seen what effect the directive will have on these laws. Although the directive is designed to create a common floor of data protection across Europe, some countries, such as the United Kingdom, have already indicated that they intend to use a "minimalist approach" in implementing its terms. Other countries already have in place more rigorous protection than is required by the directive. And bilateral and multilateral negotiations are under way to resolve pressing diplomatic and business issues about enforcement of article 25's restrictions on transborder data transfers. The disparities among European nations with regard both to their present commitment to data protection and to their implementation of the directive highlight the number and variety of cultural and legal contexts present in the EU and accentuate the political accomplishment reflected in adoption of the directive.

Summary

Europe is the site of the first privacy legislation, the earliest national privacy statute, and now the most comprehensive protection for information privacy in the world. That protection reflects apparent consensus within Europe that privacy is a fundamental human right which few if any other rights equal. In the context of European history and civil law culture, that consensus makes possible extensive, detailed regulation of virtually all activities concerning "any information relating to an identified or identifiable natural person."[79] It is difficult to imagine a regulatory regime offering any greater protection to information privacy, or any greater contrast to U.S. law.

CHAPTER FIVE

Privacy Regulation in the United States: The Public Sector

The social, political, and legal contexts in which privacy issues are addressed in the United States differ significantly from those in Europe. Europe is experiencing greater centralization and coordination of government authority, even at the supranational level, as reflected in the move from the 1957 Treaty of Rome to the 1992 Treaty on European Union signed in Maastricht, and the more than 240 European Commission directives designed to harmonize law across Europe.[1] In the United States, however, legal regulation is characterized by its disparate sources. This variety is largely the result of three factors. First, the federal Constitution establishes a hierarchical division of power among federal, state, and local regulators. Second, the Constitution also creates a tripartite system of government—responsible for legislative, executive, and judicial functions—on the federal level, which is mirrored in most state governments. The legislative, executive, and judicial branches often conflict with one another in the performance of their separate functions. They often undertake to perform the same function—lawmaking—with frequently contradictory results. Finally, the U.S. common law system creates a body of often disparate case law, owing to conflicting interpretation and application of legal precedent and the considerable subjectivity inherent in this judicial process.

Moreover, while the United States has experienced a dramatic increase in regulation and government activism beginning with President Franklin D. Roosevelt's New Deal, widespread political pressure now exists for reduced government activity, particularly at the federal level. This trend was clearly evident in the 1980s during the Reagan Revolution and, more recently, in the Republican Contract with America and the deregulatory and states-rights activities of the Republican-controlled second session of the 104th Congress. This direction has paralleled and contributed to an undercurrent of anti-internationalism much in evidence during recent U.S. presidential elections. Although globalization may be uniting the world's markets, work forces, and communications, preoccupation with national interest characterizes U.S. relations with multinational bodies, such as the United Nations, and with other nations, especially when important economic, national security, or political interests are at stake.

Consequently, one might expect regulation in the United States of any subject to be complex, fundamentally nationalistic, and indicative of the little interest in codification at the national, much less the supranational, level. In the case of privacy regulation, such expectations are met.

The U.S. Constitution and Privacy Protection

Fundamental rights in the United States are generally articulated in the federal Constitution. Two features of those rights are central to understanding the legal protection of privacy in the United States. First, rights articulated in the Constitution generally are protected only against government actions. Only the Thirteenth Amendment, which prohibits slavery, applies directly to private parties.[2] All other constitutional rights—whether to speak freely, confront accusers, or be tried by a jury of one's peers—regulate the public, but not the private, sector. In the absence of state action, therefore, constitutional rights are not implicated in questions surrounding privacy regulation. Although state action is usually found when the state acts toward a private person, the Supreme Court has also found state action when the state affords a legal right to one private party that impinges on the constitutional rights of another,[3] in rare cases when a private party undertakes a traditionally public function,[4] or when the activities of the state and a private entity are sufficiently intertwined to render the private parties' activities public.[5]

The second significant characteristic of constitutional rights is that they are generally "negative"; they do not obligate the government to do anything but rather to refrain from taking certain actions.

These two features reflect a historical dichotomy between the government and the citizenry and a longstanding commitment to limited government power. The Constitution establishes the federal government and regulates its conduct in relation to the citizens. It does not grant rights to citizens, nor does it regulate citizens' interaction with one another. Instead, it limits the power of the government to act on citizens. The First Amendment's so-called right to free expression does not, in fact, create such a right in the citizenry. Rather, the amendment denies to the government in most circumstances the power to restrict the expression of its citizens, either directly, by restraining a given speaker or form of speech, or indirectly, by creating a legal right whereby one citizen may employ the power of the state to restrict the speech of another citizen. Although the government cannot abridge freedom of expression, it is under no obligation to provide the means to speak or to provide an equitable array of opportunities for expression.

An assessment of constitutional rights is essential to any discussion of privacy regulation in the United States precisely because the Constitution constrains the power of the government to act on the citizenry and to create and enforce laws regulating conduct among citizens. Federal and state governments exercise extensive power to pursue objectives not expressly articulated within the Constitution, but that power is always circumscribed by the limits that are articulated therein.

There is no explicit constitutional guarantee of a right to privacy. The Supreme Court, however, has interpreted many of the amendments constituting the Bill of Rights to provide some protection to a variety of elements of individual privacy against intrusive government activities. These include the First Amendment provisions for freedom of expression and association, the Third Amendment restriction on quartering soldiers in private homes, the Fourth Amendment prohibition on unreasonable searches and seizures, the due process clause and guarantee against self-incrimination in the Fifth Amendment, the Ninth and Tenth Amendment reservations of power in the people and the states, and the equal protection and due process clauses of the Fourteenth Amendment.

None of these provisions refers to privacy explicitly, and the circumstances in which privacy rights are implicated are as widely varied as the constitutional sources of those rights. As a result, the Supreme Court's interpretation of constitutional protection for individual privacy is confused, the scope of that protection is narrow, and the value of privacy interests is often limited when weighed against other, more explicit, constitutional rights. This is clearly the case even in the four areas—expression and association, searches and seizures, fundamental decision-making, and informational privacy—in which the Court has most often addressed constitutional privacy rights.

Expression, Association, and Religion

The Court has identified a number of privacy interests implicit in the First Amendment.[6] In *NAACP* v. *Alabama*,[7] the U.S. Supreme Court struck down an Alabama ordinance requiring the National Association for the Advancement of Colored People (NAACP) to disclose its membership lists, finding that such a requirement constituted an unconstitutional infringement on NAACP members' First Amendment right of association.[8] In *Breard* v. *City of Alexandria*,[9] the Court upheld an ordinance prohibiting solicitation of private residences without prior permission. The Court found in the First Amendment's free speech guarantee an implicit balance between "some householders' desire for privacy and the publisher's right to distribute publications in the precise way that those soliciting for him think brings the best results."[10] The Court has invoked this same implied balancing test in numerous other cases. In *Kovacs v. Cooper*,[11] the Court upheld a Trenton, New Jersey, ordinance prohibiting the use of sound trucks and loudspeakers:

> The unwilling listener is not like the passer-by who may be offered a pamphlet in the street but cannot be made to take it. In his home or on the street he is practically helpless to escape this interference with his privacy by loudspeakers except through the protection of the municipality.[12]

In *Rowan v. U.S. Post Office*, the Court upheld a federal statute which permitted homeowners to specify that the Post Office not deliver to their homes "erotically arousing" and "sexually provocative" mail.[13] In *Federal Communications Commission v. Pacifica Foundation*,[14] the Court allowed the Federal Communications Commission to sanction a radio station for broadcasting "indecent" programming, finding that "the individual's right to be left alone plainly outweighs the First Amendment rights of an intruder."[15] In *Frisby et al. v. Schultz et al.*,[16] the Court upheld a Brookfield, Wisconsin, statute that banned all residential picketing, writing that the home was "the one retreat to which men and women can repair to escape from the tribulations of their daily pursuits"[17] and "the last citadel of the tired, the weary, and the sick."[18] In *Carey v. Brown*,[19] the Court wrote that "the State's interest in protecting the well-being, tranquility, and privacy of the home is certainly of the highest order in a free and civilized society."[20]

Although the Court rarely specifies the source of these privacy rights, it treats them as values implicitly balanced with the First Amendment right to free expression. In *Stanley v. Georgia*,[21] however, the Court explicitly linked privacy and free expression by identifying the mutual interests they serve. The Court overturned a conviction under Georgia law for possessing obscene material in the home. While the "States retain broad power to regulate obscenity," Justice Marshall wrote for the unanimous Court, "that power simply does not extend to mere possession by the individual in the privacy of his own home."[22]

The Court based its decision squarely on the First Amendment, which the Court found included the "right to be free, except in very limited circumstances, from unwanted governmental intrusions into one's privacy."[23] The Court concluded, "If the First Amendment means anything, it means that a State has no business telling a man, sitting alone in his own house, what books he may read or what films he may watch. Our whole constitutional heritage rebels at the thought of giving government the power to control men's minds."[24]

In this sense, the First Amendment's protection for expression, as well as its prohibition on the government abridging the freedom of religion, may be seen as the ultimate privacy protection. At its core, Thomas Emerson has written, the First Amendment recognizes that "suppression of belief, opinion, or other expression is an affront to the dignity of man, a negation of man's essential nature."[25] The Supreme Court recognizes in the First Amendment an absolute prohibition on the state interfering with the thoughts and beliefs of the individual. This guarantees to every person an inner sanctum where the state may not intrude and marks the core of U.S. privacy protection. The state is simply denied the power to coerce individuals' minds. "If there is any fixed star in our constitutional constellation, it is that no official, high or petty, can prescribe what shall be orthodox in politics, nationalism, religion, or other matters of opinion, or force citizens to confess by word or act their faith therein."[26]

This is not a merely metaphysical aspiration, because the Court interprets the Constitution to recognize and protect the intrinsic link between thought and expression, between religious belief and religious practice. To be free from government restraint, thoughts and beliefs must be informed and conveyed by the expression of the individual's choosing. Rodney Smolla has written of the bond between speech and "man's capacity to think, imagine, and create." According to Smolla, "The linkage of speech to thought, to man's central capacity to reason and wonder, is what places speech above other forms of fulfillment, and beyond the routine jurisdiction of the state."[27] The Court has therefore found in the First Amendment a constitutional guarantee that individuals may not only believe what they wish, but also to a great extent that they may express their beliefs free from government interference.

However, the extraordinary power of this privacy protection also indicates its limits. Just as the First Amendment protects the privacy of every person to think and to express thoughts freely, it also fundamentally blocks the power of the government to restrict expression, even in order to protect the privacy of other individuals. As a result, the First Amendment—perhaps the most significant protection for privacy in the Constitution— restrains the power of the government to control expression or to facilitate its control by private parties in an effort to protect privacy. The First Amendment is therefore of little use as a basis for protecting information privacy; on the contrary, in most cases, it stands in opposition to such protection.

This tension between the First Amendment as protecting privacy and as prohibiting the government from restricting expression in order to protect privacy runs throughout First Amendment jurisprudence. Ken Gormley has written that over time, "The First Amendment came to be viewed as possessing two distinct hemispheres."[28] One was the traditional freedom to speak and associate without governmental interference. The other was "the less familiar freedom of the citizen to think and engage in private thoughts, free from the clutter and bombardment of outside speech."[29] Neither yields any significant protection for privacy, beyond that already implicit in the First Amendment's guarantees to speak, associate, and worship without governmental interference.

For example, the association and expression cases clearly suggest the recognition of a constitutional right of privacy—in the sense of solitude or seclusion from intrusion—based on the First Amendment. That right necessarily is limited, however, to restricting the conduct of government and the government's creation of legal rights that private parties might use to interfere with the privacy of others. Moreover, case law recognizing the right is relatively overshadowed by cases indicating that the right carries little weight when balanced against other, explicit constitutional rights, especially in situations involving activities outside of the private home. For example, the Court has accorded privacy rights little protection when confronted with freedom of association claims of groups such as the American Communist Party.[30] The Court often has overturned ordinances restricting door-to-door solicitation with little if any comment on the privacy interests of the occupants.[31]

Similarly, the Court often has demonstrated little concern for the privacy interests of unwilling viewers or listeners, rejecting claims against broadcasts of radio programs in Washington, D.C., streetcars,[32] R-rated movies at a drive-in theater in Jacksonville, Florida,[33] and a jacket bearing an "unseemly expletive" worn in the corridors of the Los Angeles County Courthouse.[34] And plaintiffs rarely win suits brought against the press for disclosing private information. When information is true and obtained lawfully, the Supreme Court repeatedly has held that the state may not restrict its publication without showing that the government's interest in doing so is "compelling" and that the restriction is no greater than is necessary to achieve that interest.[35] This is "strict scrutiny," the highest level of constitutional review available in the United States. Protection of privacy rarely constitutes a sufficiently compelling interest to survive strict scrutiny. Even if information published by the press is subsequently proved false, the Supreme Court has demonstrated extraordinary deference to the First Amendment expression rights of the press and little concern for the privacy interests involved.[36]

The practical impact of any First Amendment–based constitutional right of privacy, then, is uncertain, as well as limited to government activity. When the context is the privacy of the home and the invasion or intrusion is inescapable, such as amplified noise coming from a protester on the doorstep, the right is at its strongest. Outside of the context of the home, or when the intrusion is easier to avoid, whether by averting one's eyes or saying no to a door-to-door salesperson, the right appears weak, especially when balanced against other First Amendment rights. And when important public interests are at stake, such as the press reporting on matters of public interest, the right appears least forceful and wholly inadequate to satisfy strict scrutiny.

Searches and Seizures

Most of the Supreme Court's jurisprudence concerning a constitutional right to privacy has centered on the Fourth Amendment's prohibition on unreasonable searches and seizures.[37] This prohibition reflects two deeply rooted concerns: that citizens' property be protected from seizure by the government and that citizens' homes and persons be protected from warrantless or arbitrary searches. These concerns are reflected in the Declaration of Independence and many of the colonial debates and writings, as well as in the Constitution. In 1886 the Supreme Court first applied the term "priva[cy]" to the interests protected by the Fourth Amendment.[38] Four years later, Supreme Court Justice Louis Brandeis joined forces with Samuel Warren to articulate "The Right to Privacy" in the *Harvard Law Review*.[39] Justice Brandeis boldly stated his views on privacy in his 1928 dissent in *Olmstead* v. *United States*.[40] Five of the nine justices had found that wiretapping of telephone wires by federal officials did not constitute a search or seizure since there had been no physical trespass and nothing tangible had been taken. Justice Brandeis wrote:

> The protection guaranteed by the [Fourth and Fifth] Amendments is much broader in scope. The makers of our Constitution undertook to secure conditions favorable to the pursuit of happiness. They recognized the significance of man's spiritual nature, of his feelings and of his intellect. They knew that only a part of the pain, pleasure and satisfactions of life are to be found in material things. They sought to protect Americans in their beliefs, their thoughts, their emotions and their sensations. They conferred, as against the Government, the right to be let alone—the most comprehensive of rights and the right most valued by civilized men. To protect that right, every unjustifiable intrusion by the Government upon the privacy of the individual, whatever the means employed, must be deemed a violation of the Fourth Amendment. And the use, as evidence in a criminal proceeding, of facts ascertained by such intrusion must be deemed a violation of the Fifth.[41]

Almost forty years later, the Court adopted the reasoning of Justice Brandeis in *Katz* v. *United States*.[42] The case addressed the constitutionality of federal authorities' use of an electronic listening device attached to the outside of a telephone booth used by Charles Katz, whom the authorities suspected of violating gambling laws. The Court found that this method of gathering evidence infringed on his Fourth Amendment rights, even though his property had not been invaded. The Court found that the Constitution protects whatever one "seeks to preserve as private, even in an area accessible to the public."[43] In his concurrence, Justice Harlan introduced what was later to become the Court's test for what was "private" within the meaning of the Fourth Amendment.[44] Justice Harlan wrote that the protected zone of Fourth Amendment privacy was defined by the individual's "actual," subjective expectation of privacy, and the extent to which that expectation was "one that society [was] prepared to recognize as 'reasonable.'"[45] The Court adopted that test in 1968 and continues to apply it today, with somewhat uneven results.[46] The Court has found "reasonable" expectations of privacy in homes, businesses, sealed luggage and packages, and even drums of chemicals, but no "reasonable" expectations of privacy in bank records, voice or writing samples, phone numbers, conversations recorded by concealed microphones, and automobile passenger compartments, trunks, and glove boxes.[47]

Although the Fourth Amendment right of privacy is clearly established and routinely, if unevenly, applied, it is of limited value outside of the criminal defense context, for several reasons. First, like all constitutional rights, it applies only to government activities. Second, the Supreme Court has determined that it applies neither to readily discernible activities or objects[48] nor to objects controlled by a third person, such as bank records.[49] Paul M. Schwartz and Joel R. Reidenberg have noted the ironic juxtaposition between the Fourth Amendment's "little protection for personal data already controlled by third parties or the government itself" and the "precondition to modern life that increasing amounts of personal information be stored outside an individual's control."[50] Third, in measuring the right to privacy, the Court tends to focus on the tension between that right and some other societal interest, such as the prevention and detection of crime.

As a result, the "reasonableness" of a given expectation depends in part on the importance of the interest against which it is being measured. As Ken Gormley has observed, "Particularly where drug and alcohol crack-downs motivate the search, individual 'expectations' become quickly minimized in the name of society's massive stake in eradicating drug traffic and drunk driving."[51]

Fourth, the requirement that an expectation of privacy be "reasonable" fundamentally erodes the Fourth Amendment privacy right's usefulness as a way of protecting individuals against societal encroachment and diminishes its effectiveness in keeping pace with technological change. An expectation is "reasonable" only if already accepted and shared by society. Schwartz and Reidenberg have challenged this definition as being "tautological" and have observed aptly that "this amendment applies only when society already awaits it."[52] Moreover, what the public views as "reasonable" tends to evolve far more slowly than information technologies. As a result, the Court evaluates privacy issues presented in the context of new technologies against measures of reasonableness that were formed without regard for those technologies. By the time society incorporates into its view of "reasonableness" the benefits and risks of a new technology, the Court is likely to have already decided one or more cases determining the applicable expectation of privacy based on the inapplicable measure of reasonableness. Society's views have evolved, but the precedent established by those cases is not likely to change.

Finally, it is always difficult to have the Supreme Court attempt to discern what is reasonable for the population as a whole. The Court's small, nonrepresentational, and isolated nature makes it fundamentally ill-suited to know what modern society finds "reasonable." This is suggested by the Court's 1971 decision that the Fourth Amendment does not apply to wearing a hidden microphone because individuals do not, in the Court's opinion, reasonably expect that people with whom they speak will not be wired for sound,[53] or its 1995 ruling upholding mandatory drug testing on the grounds that student athletes' interest in not being observed while urinating is "negligible."[54]

Fundamental Decisionmaking

The U.S. Supreme Court's most controversial constitutional right to privacy ruling has developed within a series of cases involving decisionmaking about contraception, abortion, and other profoundly personal issues. In 1965 the Court decided in *Griswold* v. *Connecticut* that an eighty-year-old Connecticut law forbidding the use of contraceptives violated the constitutional right to "marital privacy."[55] Justice Douglas, writing for the Court, offered a variety of constitutional loci for this right:

> Various guarantees create zones of privacy. The right of association contained in the penumbra of the First Amendment is one. . . . The Third Amendment in its prohibition against the quartering of soldiers "in any house" in time of peace without the consent of the owner is another facet of that privacy. The Fourth Amendment explicitly affirms the "right of the people to be secure in their persons, houses, papers, and effects, against unreasonable searches and seizures." The Fifth Amendment in its Self-Incrimination Clause enables the citizen to create a zone of privacy which government may not force him to surrender to his detriment. The Ninth Amendment provides: "The enumeration in the Constitution, of certain rights, shall not be construed to deny or disparage others retained by the people."[56]

But the Court could not specifically identify a constitutional basis for the right to marital privacy. Instead, Justice Douglas wrote that the "specific guarantees in the Bill of Rights have penumbras, formed by emanations from those guarantees that help give them life and substance."[57] It was in these "penumbras, formed by emanations" that the Court grounded this new right.

Eight years later, the Court extended this privacy right in *Roe* v. *Wade* to encompass "a woman's decision whether or not to terminate her pregnancy."[58] Rather than base that right, directly or indirectly, on one or more of the specific guarantees of the Bill of Rights, the Court looked instead to "the Fourteenth Amendment's concept of personal liberty and restrictions upon state action."[59] Notwithstanding this broad foundation, however, the Court in *Roe* v. *Wade* found that the constitutional "guarantee of personal privacy" only includes "personal rights that can be deemed 'fundamental' or 'implicit in the concept of ordered liberty.'"[60] The Court specified that those fundamental rights include activities concerning marriage, procreation, contraception, family relationships, and child rearing and education.[61] Government regulation of those activities "may be justified only by a 'compelling state interest,'" and they must be "narrowly drawn to express only the legitimate state interests at stake."[62]

Although the Supreme Court indicated the government intrusion into inherently private areas of personal life would be subject to strict scrutiny, the Court has limited the scope of what it considers "private." In 1986 in *Bowers* v. *Hardwick*,[63] the Court declined to extend the right to privacy to the interests of homosexuals to engage in sodomy within their homes. In 1989, in *Webster* v. *Reproductive Health Services*,[64] the Court upheld a Missouri statute imposing significant limitations on performing abortions, including an outright ban on the use of public funds, employees, or facilities to perform abortions not necessary to save the mother's life or to counsel a woman to have such an abortion. Chief Justice Rehnquist, writing for a five- Justice plurality of the Court, argued that the privacy interest at issue was merely "a liberty interest protected by the Due Process Clause" and not a "fundamental" constitutional right.[65] As Laurence Tribe has written, the reasoning in *Webster* suggests that a woman's "right" to an abortion is "apparently no different from a 'right' to drive a car, say, or open a store, or work as a dentist."[66]

Bowers, *Webster*, and similar cases indicate that the "fundamental decisionmaking" concept of a constitutional right to privacy shares a number of limitations with the privacy right grounded in the Fourth Amendment. First, it applies only to government activities: the right says nothing about a private individual's interference with those activities associated with "fundamental" rights. Second, societal familiarity with and acceptance of the activity for which privacy is being sought bears heavily on the strength of that right. Defining a category of protected fundamental interests, as the Court did in *Roe* v. *Wade* and subsequent cases, necessarily contracts the range of privacy interests protected. Francis Chlapowski has written:

Constitutional liberty exists to prevent the government, and society, from encroaching on the individual. By limiting liberty to "traditionally protected" interests, however, the Constitution is rendered useless as a protective device, because it will be construed to apply only to those interests which are already protected by other traditional laws. In a democratic society, "traditionally protected" must mean, by definition, majoritarian. Therefore, this theory excludes individuals whose interests are different from those of the majority. By reflecting majoritarian values, this view allows the state to define constitutionally protected liberty.[67]

Correspondingly, this premise of a right to privacy shares with the Fourth Amendment–based right the difficulty of having the Supreme Court discern what is valued by the population as a whole.

Finally, while the right to make certain fundamental decisions, like the Fourth Amendment right, is protected by "strict scrutiny" of government incursions, there is little certainty or consistency about which activities the right encompasses. The Court has found that the right is put at risk by a state's efforts to prohibit access to contraceptives but not by efforts to ban sodomy. Whether the right extends to having an abortion continues to be questioned by the Court.

The contours and application of the fundamental decision-making privacy right are very important for information privacy protection in the United States, even though that right itself is inapplicable to most information processing activities by the government and all such activities by private parties. The Supreme Court has identified a constitutional interest in nondisclosure of certain information grounded in the same constitutional provisions as the fundamental decision-making right.

Nondisclosure

In 1977 the Supreme Court decided *Whalen* v. *Roe*,[68] a case involving a challenge to a New York statute requiring that copies of prescriptions for certain drugs be provided to the state, on the basis that the requirement would infringe patients' privacy rights. In his opinion for the unanimous Court, Justice Stevens wrote that the constitutionally protected "zone of privacy" included two separate interests: "the interest in independence in making certain kinds of important decisions" and "the individual interest in avoiding disclosure of personal matters."[69] The first interest is clearly grounded in *Roe* v. *Wade*, *Griswold*, and similar cases, to which Justice Stevens cited. The second interest appears to be a new creation of the Court in *Whalen*, although based on the "Fourteenth Amendment's concept of personal liberty" identified in *Roe* v. *Wade*.[70] Nevertheless, having found this new privacy interest in nondisclosure of personal information, the Court did not apply strict scrutiny, apparently because the interest was not a right involving a "fundamental" interest. Instead, the Court, applying a lower level of scrutiny, found that the statute did not infringe the individuals' interest in nondisclosure.[71]

Although the Supreme Court has never decided a case in which it found that a government regulation or action violated the constitutional privacy right created in *Whalen*, a number of federal appellate and district courts have done so. The U.S. Court of Appeals for the District of Columbia relied on *Whalen* to afford significant constitutional protection to information about both individuals and organizations. In *Tavoulareas* v. *Washington Post Company*,[72] the court addressed the constitutional protection for privacy in the context of confidential documents produced during discovery in civil litigation. The court noted that "recent Supreme Court decisions indicate that a litigant's interest in avoiding public disclosure of private information is grounded in the Constitution itself, in addition to federal statutes and the common law."[73] Moreover, the appellate court also found that even corporations possess constitutionally protected informational privacy rights: "A corporation's privacy interest in nondisclosure is essentially identical to that of an individual."[74] In order to resolve the conflict between privacy rights and the interests in public disclosure, the appellate court determined that the propriety of a governmental intrusion must be evaluated by

> balancing the need for the intrusion against its severity. . . . Indeed, when the intrusion is severe, a compelling interest is required to justify the intrusion. "Severe" intrusions include

public dissemination of confidential information as opposed to disclosure of such information only to the government or other litigants.[75]

Federal appellate courts in the Second, Third, Fifth, and Ninth Circuits have reached similar results, finding a constitutional right of privacy in individuals not being compelled by the government to disclose personal information, particularly medical records.[76] However, by extending the right of nondisclosure beyond fundamental rights, these courts have applied a lower standard of scrutiny than that applicable in cases involving marriage, procreation, contraception, family relationships, and child rearing and education. Instead of strict scrutiny, these courts used "intermediate" scrutiny:

> The government may seek and use information covered by the right to privacy only if it can show that its use of the information would advance a legitimate state interest and that its actions are narrowly tailored to meet the legitimate interest. . . . The more sensitive the information, the stronger the state's interest must be.[77]

Courts in the Fourth and Sixth Circuits, however, have severely limited the scope of the *Whalen* nondisclosure privacy right. In 1993 the Court of Appeals for the Fourth Circuit decided *Walls* v. *City of Petersburg*,[78] involving a city employee's claim that her dismissal for refusing to answer an official questionnaire violated her constitutional right to nondisclosure. The employee particularly objected to Question 40, which asked "Have you ever had sexual relations with a person of the same sex?"[79] The appellate court, while acknowledging that the "relevance of this question to Walls' employment is uncertain," nonetheless found that "Question 40 does not ask for information that Walls has a right to keep private."[80] The court reasoned that because the Supreme Court had found no fundamental right to *engage* in homosexual acts, there could be no constitutional right not to disclose such practices. The Court of Appeals for the Sixth Circuit has similarly restricted the right not to disclose personal information to information concerning fundamental rights.[81]

Summary

While there is no explicit constitutional guarantee of a right to privacy, the Supreme Court has found a number of privacy rights, primarily in four areas: First Amendment protection for expression, association, and religion; Fourth Amendment limits on searches and seizures; fundamental decisionmaking grounded in "penumbras" and "emanations" of the Bill of Rights; and Fourteenth Amendment guarantee of due process and protection for nondisclosure of personal information (also based on the Fourteenth Amendment).

Because constitutional rights protect only against state action, any constitutional concept of "privacy" would apply only against the government and would at most require that the government refrain from taking actions that impermissibly invade privacy. A constitutional privacy right would not require the government to take steps to affirmatively protect individual privacy. In the context of expression, association, and religion, the privacy right implicit in the First Amendment is balanced against other cherished First Amendment rights, and the result has been that the privacy right has little force outside of the context of the home, especially when an intrusion in a more public setting is easily avoided.

The Fourth Amendment right of privacy is better established and more routinely applied, but has little application outside of the context of the investigation and prosecution of criminal activity—"affirmative, unannounced, narrowly focused intrusions."[82] The right applies neither to readily discernible activities nor to objects controlled by a third person.

The fundamental decisionmaking concept of a constitutional right to privacy is limited to a handful of activities recognized by the Court as "fundamental." Like the Fourth Amendment right of privacy, its reach is defined by the Court according to the Court's perception of societal acceptance of the activities for which privacy is being sought. Neither of these rights is well-suited to keeping up with technological change or to protecting individuals who do not share majoritarian values.

Finally, after *Whalen*, it is clear that courts recognize a constitutional right, based on the due process and liberty guarantees of the Fourteenth Amendment, of individuals and organizations not to be compelled by the government to disclose certain personal information. As with other constitutional rights, this information privacy right applies only to government activities. This right protects only the interest of an individual in not disclosing, or not being forced to disclose, certain information. Some courts would limit this right to information concerning activities in areas in which the Court has recognized a fundamental right to make decisions. As those areas expand or contract, so too, presumably, would the right not to disclose related personal information. Other courts have found that the constitutional right not to disclose extends to areas beyond fundamental rights, but that broader right is reviewed under intermediate, not strict, scrutiny.

The U.S. Constitution, then, offers little support for information privacy—"the claim of individuals, groups, or institutions to determine for themselves when, how, and to what extent information about them is communicated to others."[83] The Supreme Court has crafted a limited framework for protecting individuals' right to privacy in the context of government activities concerning personal information and no support at all for privacy rights outside of the public sector.

State Constitutions

At least eight states have adopted explicit constitutional guarantees of personal privacy. As with federal constitutional protections, these rights virtually always impose restrictions only on governmental activities. Often these protections are vague and aspirational. Moreover, when state constitutional rights and federal law conflict, federal law prevails. Therefore, state constitutional privacy rights have thus far been of little significance in the day-to-day protection of personal privacy. Nonetheless, these provisions are significant to the extent that they restrict the activities of state governments, serve as a potential source of future restraints on government activities, and indicate a growing interest in privacy protection.

Some state constitutional privacy protections merely repeat federal constitutional provisions. For example, Minnesota includes in its constitution the text of the Fourth Amendment to the federal Constitution.[84] The Hawaii and Louisiana constitutions both include Fourth Amendment–like provisions, but they have been modified to explicitly prohibit "invasions of privacy."[85] Some state constitutional protections for privacy incorporate exceptions as broad as the protection they purport to afford privacy. Arizona's constitution provides that "no person shall be disturbed in his private affairs, or his home invaded, without authority of law."[86] Such a right presumably would exist even without this constitutional provision. In 1980 Florida amended its constitution to provide that "every natural person had the right to be let alone and free from government intrusion into his private life except as otherwise provided herein. This section shall not be construed to limit the public's right of access to public records and meetings as provided by law."[87]

Other states' provisions are less qualified or more specific. Alaska amended its constitution in 1972 to provide that "the right of the people to privacy is recognized and shall not be infringed."[88] In 1974 California added privacy to the "inalienable rights" protected under its constitution: "All people . . . have inalienable rights. Among these are . . . pursuing and obtaining . . . privacy."[89] This provision is particularly noteworthy, because in 1994 the California Supreme Court found that it is applicable to private, as well as governmental, actions.[90] The Illinois constitution provides that "the people shall have the right to be secure . . . against . . . invasions of privacy."[91] In 1978 Hawaii amended its constitution to add: "The right of the people to privacy is recognized and shall not be infringed without the showing of a compelling state interest."[92] This is the most specific and protective of any of the state constitutional provisions guarding privacy interests, in practice as well as on paper. At least partially based on this provision, a Hawaiian court ruled in December 1996 in favor of same-sex marriages.[93]

Even the most protective state constitutional provisions, however, have yielded little protection for information privacy. For example, even in the 1994 case in which the California Supreme Court extended the state constitutional right to privacy to private actions, the Court found that a mandatory drug-testing program for college athletes did not violate that right.[94] This is the same result reached by the U.S. Supreme Court the following year without the benefit of an explicit constitutional guarantee to privacy.[95] Moreover, in the context of global information networks and national and multinational information users, state protection is of limited significance.

Role of the First Amendment

The U.S. Constitution is the source not only of limited privacy rights but also of other significant rights against which all government efforts—treaty commitments, statutes, regulations, administrative and executive orders, and daily functions—must be measured. One of the most important of these rights, the one most often implicated by government efforts to protect privacy, and one of the most distinct products of U.S. history and culture, is the First Amendment restraint on government abridgement of freedom of expression or of the press. Any effort by the government to protect privacy, whether through direct regulation or the creation or enforcement of legal causes of action among private parties, must be consonant with the First Amendment if that protection is to survive constitutional review. To date, however, privacy rights have rarely prevailed in the Supreme Court when balanced against First Amendment rights.

The core of First Amendment protection, according to the Supreme Court, is in the arena of expression relating to self-governance.[96] Expression concerning the activities of the government and elected and appointed officials is critical, and protected by the First Amendment, because it is the information that the citizens of a democratic society must have to govern. This right expresses the most foundational of values in American society. As former Judge Robert Bork has written:

The First Amendment indicates that there is something special about speech. We would know that much even without a first amendment, for the entire structure of the Constitution creates a representative democracy, a form of government that would be meaningless without freedom to discuss government and its policies. Freedom for political speech could and should be inferred even if there were no First Amendment.[97]

Even though it defines self-governance expression very broadly, the Court has extended the First Amendment far beyond self-governance. The Court has often asserted that the First Amendment "was fashioned to assure the unfettered interchange of ideas for the bringing about of political and social changes desired by the people."[98] Under this concept of a speech "marketplace," the preferred "remedy" for dangerous expression is more and varied expression.[99] Expression may be regulated consistent with the marketplace metaphor only because of the tangible harm it causes and, even then, only with the greatest care and restraint. This is true even though the government or the society finds the expression offensive or contentious.[100] In *Terminiello* v. *Chicago*, Justice Douglas wrote for the Court that free speech "may indeed best serve its high purpose when it induces a condition of unrest, creates dissatisfaction with conditions as they are, or even stirs people to anger. It may strike at prejudices and preconceptions and have profound unsettling effects."[101] The Court recognized this in *Stanley*, when it wrote that the Constitution's protection of expression "is not confined to the expression of ideas that are conventional or shared by a majority."[102]

As discussed above, courts have also recognized the First Amendment importance of, and intrinsic link between, freedom of thought and self-expression. That expression may be offensive to others, but for the government to suppress it intrudes deeply on human identity and, in the words of David Richards, "the notion of self-respect that comes from a mature person's full and untrammeled exercise of capacities central to human rationality."[103]

The practical effect of a broad, powerful, and central First Amendment is that the Supreme Court interprets it to prevent the government from restricting expression prior to its utterance or publication or merely because the government disagrees with the sentiment expressed.[104] It also forbids the government from making impermissible distinctions based on content,[105] compelling speech, or granting access to the expressive capacity of another[106] without demonstrating that the government's action survives strict scrutiny, that is, that the abridgement is narrowly tailored to serve a compelling governmental interest. These First Amendment principles restrict not merely Congress but all federal and state governmental agencies.[107] They may also apply to expression that the Court has determined does not independently warrant protection (such as false or defamatory expression),[108] conduct that involves no speech (such as burning a flag or picketing),[109] and activities ancillary to expression (such as funding expression).[110]

When privacy rights conflict with free expression rights before the Court, the latter prevail, virtually without exception. When information is true and obtained lawfully, the Supreme Court has repeatedly held that the state may not restrict its publication without showing a very closely tailored, compelling governmental interest. Under this requirement, the Court has struck down laws restricting the publication of confidential government reports,[111] and of the names of judges under investigation,[112] juvenile suspects,[113] and rape victims.[114] The dominance of the free expression interests over the privacy interests is so great that Peter Edelman has written:

> The Court [has] virtually extinguished privacy plaintiffs'
> chances of recovery for injuries caused by truthful speech that
> violates their interest in nondisclosure. . . . If the right to pub-
> lish private information collides with an individual's right not to
> have that information published, the Court consistently subor-
> dinates the privacy interest to the free speech concerns.[115]

Moreover, there can be no recovery for defamation that is not false[116] and no recovery for invasion of privacy unless the information published is highly offensive to a reasonable person and either false[117] or not newsworthy.[118] The Court has permitted the publication of fabricated quotes.[119] And the Court has accorded a variety of procedural protections to all expression, whether true or false.[120]

The Supreme Court has been loathe to restrict the collection and dissemination of information on matters of public interest, particularly information concerning government officials and candidates. Even expression that is false, if it is on a matter of public interest, is protected unless the plaintiff can prove its falsity.[121] The Court has eliminated any recourse by public officials or public figures for the publication of true information, even if defamatory or highly personal.[122] Public plaintiffs may not recover for damage caused by false expression unless they can demonstrate with "convincing clarity" that the publisher knew of the falsity or was reckless concerning it.[123]

These strictures apply irrespective of whether the speaker is an individual or an institution. Even wholly commercial expression is protected by the First Amendment. The Court has found that such expression, if about lawful activity and not misleading, is protected from government intrusion unless the government can demonstrate a "substantial" public interest and that the intrusion "directly advances" that interest and is "narrowly tailored to achieve the desired objective."[124] The Court does not characterize expression as "commercial"—and therefore subject to government regulations concerning it to this "intermediate scrutiny"—just because it occurs in a commercial context. The speech of corporations is routinely accorded the highest First Amendment protection—"strict scrutiny" review—unless the Court finds that the purpose of the expression is to propose a commercial transaction[125] or that the expression occurs in the context of a regulated industry or market (such as the securities exchanges) and concerns activities that are, if fact, being regulated (the sale of securities).[126]

Any government effort to protect privacy, either directly or through the passage or enforcement of laws permitting suits by private parties, faces significant First Amendment obstacles. This is particularly true when the privacy protection would apply to information concerning government activities and the qualifications and behavior of government officials or would restrict access on the basis of the content of the material to be protected.

Role of the Fifth Amendment

The Fifth Amendment to the U.S. Constitution prohibits the government from taking private property for public use without both due process of law and just compensation.[127] Historically, the Supreme Court has applied the "takings clause" to require compensation when the government physically appropriated real property, even if only a tiny portion of the property at issue was occupied[128] or if that occupation was only temporary.[129] Beginning in 1922, however, the Court has found a compensable taking even when the government does not engage in physical occupation[130] and when the property involved is not land or even tangible, corporeal property, but rather a legal entitlement,[131] government benefit,[132] or interest in continued employment.[133] In 1984 the Court decided *Ruckelshaus* v. *Monsanto Co.*, in which it extended the Fifth Amendment's takings clause to protect stored data.[134]

The Supreme Court's recognition of these "regulatory takings"—including takings of stored data—suggests that privacy regulations that substantially interfere with a private party's use of data that have been collected or processed, may require compensation under the Fifth Amendment. In *Ruckelshaus*, the Supreme Court found that the Environmental Protection Agency's use of Monsanto's proprietary research data constituted a compensable taking. The Court in *Ruckelshaus*, as in all regulatory takings cases, faced two fundamental questions: whether there was "property" and, if so, whether it was "taken" by the government's action. The first question presented little difficulty, because state law recognizes a property right in "trade secrets" and other confidential business information, and the possessors of such data have long been accorded property-like rights to control access to, and the use of, business information. To answer the second question, the Court focused on Monsanto's "reasonable investment-backed expectations" with respect to its control over the use and dissemination of the data, finding that Monsanto had invested substantial resources in creating the data and reasonably believed that they would not be disclosed by the EPA.[135]

To be certain, not all regulations of private property constitute takings. Although the Court has put forward a number of tests for determining when a regulatory taking occurs, the common element in them all is that a taking occurs when the government's regulation "denies an owner economically viable use" of his property.[136] In the classic formulation of property rights as a bundle of sticks, a taking *may* exist where the government eliminates any one of those sticks, but a taking *is certain to* exist when the government effectively seizes the entire bundle by eliminating all of the sticks.

Even when a government regulation deprives a property owner of all use of his property, the Supreme Court has historically declined to find a taking and therefore not required compensation when the regulation merely abated a "noxious use" or "nuisance-like" conduct. Such a regulation does not constitute a taking of private property, because one never has a property right to harm others.[137] In 1992, however, the Supreme Court backed away from this "prevention of harmful use" exception, recognizing that the government could virtually always claim that it was regulating to prevent a harmful use.[138] Instead, the Court now requires that when a government regulation deprives property "of all economically beneficial use," the government must show that the power to promulgate the regulation inhered in the "background principles of the State's law of property and nuisance."[139] In other words, the Court seems to be asking if the property owner's expectations were reasonable in light of the government's recognized power and past practice.

Data protection regulation may legitimately prompt takings claims. If the government prohibits the processing of personal data, it could deny the owner all or most of the "economically viable use" of that data. Moreover, if Congress were to enact privacy protection along the lines of the EU Directive, that legislation might very well restrict all use of that data and thereby constitute a complete taking.[140] At first glance this may seem an odd result, since the data collected or processed, in order to be subject to privacy regulation in the first place, must be about another person. How can one person have a constitutional property right to hold and use data about another? However, this result is not that surprising in light of current law in the United States, which rarely accords individuals ownership interests in key information about themselves. As Anne Wells Branscomb has amply demonstrated in her powerful study *Who Owns Information?*, in the United States, telephone numbers, addresses, social security numbers, medical history, and similar personal identifying data are almost always owned by someone else—the Post Office, the government, or a physician or hospital.[141] Moreover, individuals exercise few rights in data about themselves that are readily perceptible, such as gender, age, or skin color. A photographer who takes a picture on a public street has the legal right to use that picture for a wide variety of noncommercial and even commercial uses without the permission of the individuals depicted. In fact, those individuals, without the photographer's permission, have no legal right to market or even copy or publicly display the photograph that includes their images.[142]

A data processor exercises property rights in his data because of his investment in collecting and aggregating them with other useful data. It is the often substantial investment that is necessary to make data accessible and useful, as well as the data's content, that the law protects. In the current regulatory environment in the United States, it is reasonable for an information processor to believe and to invest resources in the belief that she will be able, within some limits, to use the data she collects and processes. In fact, as Arthur Miller has argued, the "expand[ing] protection for commercial information reflects a growing awareness that the legal system's recognition of the property status of such information promotes socially useful behavior" and therefore encourages reliance by data processors.[143] A legislative, regulatory, or even judicial[144] determination that denies processors the right to use their data could very likely constitute a taking and require compensation. Data processors who acquire or process data after enactment of new privacy standards would be on notice and therefore less likely to succeed in claiming takings. But for the billions of data files currently possessed and used by U.S. individuals and institutions, a dramatic alteration in user rights makes a compelling case for the existence of a taking.

The determination of whether a government action constitutes a taking, of course, turns on the details of the specific action and property involved. It is sufficient to note that the personal information held by others is probably the subject of property and related rights. Those rights are in almost every case possessed by the data processor, not the persons to whom the data pertain. And because these data are accorded property-like protection, they are subject to being taken by government regulation, thereby triggering an obligation to compensate the data owner.

These conclusions highlight the intrinsic link between privacy and property. As the Supreme Court has noted in the context of challenges to government searches and seizures, expectations of privacy "must have a source outside of the Fourth Amendment," and the likely location for that source is "by reference to concepts of real or personal property law."[145] The legal recognition of property rights not only makes possible the physical separation and isolation that contribute to privacy but also empowers the state to help protect those rights. As Jeanne Schroeder has written, "Clearly, the Framers of the U.S. Constitution thought that private property was essential to human liberty, or they would not have given it such extraordinary protection."[146] "The great and chief end therefore, of Men uniting into Commonwealths, and putting themselves under Government," John Locke wrote, "is the Preservation of their Property."[147] Government is supposed to assure the people "secure Enjoyment of their Properties, and a greater Security against any that are not of it."[148] Property therefore not only "guards the troubled boundary between individual man and the state," as Charles Reich has argued, but also the boundary between fellow citizens.[149] The laws that attend private property are what empower one person to exclude another from her land and home and papers and possessions, and to call upon the state to protect those objects from physical intrusion and interference. At the same time, those same laws accord significant rights to individuals who acquire and use data. In some situations, interference with those rights constitutes a taking and requires compensation. But even shy of a compensable taking, the constitutional centrality of property cautions against unduly interfering with those rights.

Statutes

The statutory and regulatory control of government information practices is critical to any discussion of U.S. privacy regulation, because, as the U.S. Office of Management and Budget has observed, "The federal government is the largest single producer, consumer, and disseminator of information in the United States."[150] British Columbia's Data Protection Commissioner David Flaherty has suggested that "it would probably be fair to extend this characterization to the U.S. Government's ranking in the entire world."[151] The government uses the world's largest collections of computers and, as of 1992, was spending more than $17 billion annually on information technology.[152] From the citizens' perspective, controlling the government's use of personal information is an essential step to protecting privacy. Moreover, as Lillian BeVier has aptly noted, the government does not participate in a private sector competitive market where, "because businesses can gain by satisfying their customers' preferences for privacy, and thus have incentives to do so, markets can develop to measure both the demand for privacy on the one hand, and the value of data sharing on the other."[153] On the contrary, "When information is in the government's hands, no such incentives exist because government officials cannot internalize the gains from satisfying citizens' demands for privacy."[154] Legal controls are therefore more significant.

This section surveys the major controls on the government's collection and use of data, outside of the criminal investigation and prosecution context. The goal is not to provide specific details as to the operation of the laws discussed but rather to identify the general scope of those controls. A key feature is the emphasis, carried over from First Amendment jurisprudence, on ensuring widespread access to data to support democratic self-governance. The privacy safeguards contained in the laws discussed below are in constant tension with that core value.

Freedom of Information Act

Much of the privacy legislation applicable to federal and state governments comes in the form of exemptions to laws requiring disclosure of information by the government. For example, the federal Freedom of Information Act (FOIA) permits "any person" to obtain access to all federal "agency records," subject to nine enumerated exemptions.[155] Two of the nine exemptions are designed to protect privacy: exemption 6 precludes disclosure of "personnel and medical files and similar files the disclosure of which would constitute a clearly unwarranted invasion of privacy," and exemption 7(C) bans release of "records or information compiled for law enforcement purposes [which] . . . could reasonably be expected to constitute an unwarranted invasion of privacy."[156] In 1989 the Supreme Court lent additional force to these privacy rights when it ruled unanimously, in applying the section 7(C) exemption, that determinations of what constituted an invasion of privacy should reflect the FOIA's purpose "to open *agency* action to the light of public scrutiny."[157] The Court wrote that the Act "indeed focuses on the citizens' right to be informed about 'what their government is up to.' . . . FOIA's central purpose is to ensure that the *Government's* activities be opened to the sharp eye of public scrutiny."[158] In other words, in considering whether information in law enforcement records "could reasonably be expected to constitute an unwarranted invasion of privacy," agencies and courts should consider the extent to which that information yields insight into government, as opposed to private, activities. Many states have government disclosure statutes with privacy-based exemptions similar to those provided in the Freedom of Information Act.

Privacy Act

Congress has also enacted a federal Privacy Act, which obligates agencies to (1) store only relevant and necessary personal information; (2) collect information to the extent possible for the data subject; (3) maintain records with accuracy and completeness; and (4) establish administrative and technical safeguards to protect the security of records.[159] The Privacy Act also limits disclosure of individuals' records.[160]

The power of the interest in expression and dissemination is evident, however, in the act's provision explicitly restricting it from prohibiting the release of any material for which disclosure is required under the FOIA.[161] In other words, any information to which the FOIA applies and which is not within one of the FOIA's nine enumerated exemptions, must be disclosed irrespective of the Privacy Act. The Privacy Act also provides twelve exemptions that permit disclosure of information to other government agencies.[162] For example, the act does not apply to Congress. It does not restrict disclosures to law enforcement agencies. Under the broadest exemption, the act does not apply to data requested by another government agency for "routine use." Commissioner David Flaherty has called the routine-use exemption "a huge loophole."[163] Schwartz and Reidenberg have observed that agencies have used that exemption to justify almost "any use" of data.[164]

Other Protections

Many other statutes and regulations protect the privacy of citizen information from government intrusion or misuse. Often, these protections are procedural rather than substantive. For example, the Computer Matching and Privacy Protection Act, with which Congress amended the Privacy Act in 1988, establishes procedural guidelines for agencies to follow before and after matching electronic records.[165] Such procedural protections are frequently the unanticipated result of laws and regulations designed to reduce government paperwork and improve efficiency.

There are many agency- or topic-specific restrictions on government disclosure of data, although these generally apply only to disclosure and often include significant loopholes even to that protection. For example, federal law prohibits the Department of Health and Human Services from disclosing social security records but permits all disclosures "otherwise provided by Federal law" or regulation.[166] Similarly, federal law prohibits the Internal Revenue Service from disclosing information on income tax returns[167] and the Census Bureau from disclosing certain categories of census data.[168] Many states have adopted laws and regulations that mirror their federal counterparts.

One of the most recent privacy-related actions in Congress concerning data held by the government was the Driver's Privacy Protection Act of 1994.[169] The law was enacted as part of a package of anticrime legislation in response to the 1989 murder of actress Rebecca Schaeffer, who was killed by an obsessed fan who reportedly obtained her address, through a private investigator, from her California Department of Motor Vehicles (DMV) record.[170] The law prohibits state DMVs and their employees from releasing "personal information" from any person's driver's record unless the request fits within any of fourteen exemptions.[171] The exemptions, as with much of federal privacy law, nearly swallow the rule. They include, for example, use by any government agency,[172] insurance company,[173] or licensed private investigator (the category of user who supplied the information to Schaeffer's murderer);[174] any use related to vehicle safety, emissions, or research;[175] and any use at all if the relevant DMV has provided drivers with the opportunity to waive their statutory rights in nondisclosure.[176]

Privacy-based controls on the government's collection and use of data, outside of the criminal investigation and prosecution context, are very limited. Those controls often apply to limited categories of information or to specified agencies. They often restrict only the government's dissemination, rather than collection, use, or storage, of personal information, and they frequently create procedural, rather than substantive, obligations. Even when they do apply, privacy controls applicable to the public sector are characterized by sweeping exemptions and a general preference, clearly reflected in the FOIA, for disclosure as the norm. Enforcement of privacy protections usually requires recourse to the courts and is expensive, time consuming, and, in many cases, ineffective, because of the absence of firm substantive rights. Privacy advocates have widely criticized the present approach to privacy protection from government intrusion as inadequate.

CHAPTER SIX

Privacy Regulation in the United States: The Private Sector

Although the U.S. government may deal with more personal information than any other single entity, its information-related activities pale when compared with the combined activities of nongovernmental organizations. This chapter surveys briefly the statutory and common law protections for personal privacy applicable to the private sector. As with the discussion of statutes and regulations applicable to the public sector in the previous chapter, this survey is intended only to outline the contours, not to examine the details, of private sector protection for information privacy. It is divided into federal and state statutory provisions and common law torts.

Federal Statutes

The laws and regulations governing the use of personal information in the private sector are many and varied, but as a rule they each address a specific industry or economic sector and often only specific issues. This "targeted approach" results in a patchwork of uneven, inconsistent, and often irrational privacy protec-

80

tion.[1] For example, information about a person's video rentals receives considerable statutory protection; information about medical condition and treatment does not. Even when legal protection is at its height—for information involving financial transactions, telecommunications and video services, the workplace, and educational records—it is still often limited to certain activities, such as disclosure of personal data, and qualified by exemptions.[2]

Financial Transactions

Congress has enacted a variety of laws addressing the protection of personal information in the context of financial transactions, such as those involved in banking, consumer credit, and mortgage financing. The first of those laws, the Fair Credit Reporting Act of 1970,[3] "sets forth rights for individuals and responsibilities for consumer credit reporting agencies in connection with the preparation and dissemination of personal information in a consumer report bearing on the individual's creditworthiness, credit standing, credit capacity, character, general reputation, personal characteristics or mode of living."[4] The act requires that credit reporting agencies follow "reasonable procedures to assure maximum possible accuracy" of the information in their credit reports[5] and implement a dispute resolution process to investigate and correct errors.[6] Agencies must also inform consumers about whom adverse decisions on credit, employment, or insurance are made, based on a consumer report, of the use and source of the report. The agencies must provide consumers with a copy of their reports upon request.[7]

Before being amended at the end of 1996, the act's protections were weakened by a series of broad loopholes. For example, the act did not require credit reporting agencies to notify individuals of their right to be informed of the data concerning them maintained by the credit reporting agency and of the names of recipients of that information.[8] Moreover, medical information was specifically exempted: agencies did not have to disclose to consumers the medical information about them contained in agencies' credit files. The act permits disclosure of credit information only for statutorily specified purposes, but one of those purposes, prior to the act's revision, included any purpose related to a "legitimate business need" of the requester.[9] Similarly, the act prohibits the dissemination of certain types of obsolete information, such as bankruptcy adjudications more than ten years prior to the report, suits and judgments older than seven years, paid tax liens older than seven years, record of arrests and convictions older than seven years, and any other adverse information older than seven years.[10] However, the act contained an exception that permits even obsolete information to be disseminated if requested in connection with an employment application for a position with a salary over $20,000, a credit transaction over $50,000, or the underwriting of life insurance over $50,000.[11] Although these dollar thresholds were set in 1970, they had not been increased in twenty-five years to keep pace with inflation.[12]

On September 30, 1996, Congress passed the Consumer Credit Reporting Reform Act,[13] which closed many of these loopholes and strengthened significantly the protection for information privacy provided by the Fair Credit Reporting Act. For example, the Reform Act narrowed the broad "legitimate business need" purpose for which credit reports could be disseminated to permit the distribution of credit reports only for a "legitimate business need" in connection with a "business transaction that is initiated by the consumer" or "to review an account to determine whether the consumer continues to meet the terms of the account."[14] Consumer credit reports may now be furnished for employment purposes only if the employer certifies that the employee has consented in writing.[15] Medical information may no longer be included in a credit report furnished in connection with employment, credit, insurance, or direct marketing, without the consent of the consumer.[16] If a credit reporting agency furnishes consumer credit information to be used for marketing credit or insurance opportunities to consumers, the agency must establish and publish a toll-free telephone number that consumers can call to have their names removed from lists provided for such direct marketing purposes.[17] Persons who acquire such information from credit reporting agencies for marketing credit and insurance services must inform consumers that credit information was used, identify the credit agency from which the data were obtained, and provide information about consumers' legal rights.[18]

The new amendments permit the dissemination of obsolete information only in connection with an employment application for a position with a salary over $75,000, a credit transaction over $150,000, or the underwriting of life insurance over $150,000, thus substantially raising these thresholds from their 1970 levels.[19] The revised act specifies a number of situations in which credit agencies and, in some cases, the persons to whom they supply information, must provide information to consumers, including a general requirement that agencies inform consumers of their legal rights under the Fair Credit Reporting Act.[20] In a dramatic extension of the law, the Reform Act provides that credit reporting agencies must delete any disputed data that they cannot verify within thirty days, as well as comply with a variety of new procedural requirements concerning correcting data and notifying recipients of credit reports of disputed or inaccurate data.[21] No longer must the consumer prove information false to have it excluded. In a second significant development, the act now requires anyone who furnishes data to a credit reporting agency to correct inaccurate data, to notify any agency to which it has reported data if it determines that those data are inaccurate, and to disclose to any agency to which it is reporting data if the accuracy of those data is disputed.[22] Finally, the Reform Act directed the Federal Reserve Board to make recommendations to Congress within six months concerning the data processing activities of organizations not covered by the Fair Credit Reporting Act and the extent to which those activities "create undue potential for fraud and risk of loss to insured depository institutions."[23]

After passage of the Reform Act's amendments, the Fair Credit Reporting Act significantly restricts the content, disclosure, and use of credit information. Although the act does not address the collection of personal information generally,[24] it otherwise signals the move, at least when financial information is involved, toward a stronger regulatory approach to protecting privacy in the United States.

The second significant federal statute concerning personal information involved in financial transactions is the Electronic

Funds Transfer Act of 1978,[25] which "establishes mandatory guidelines for the relationship between consumers and financial institutions in connection with electronic fund transactions."[26] While the act does require the routine disclosure to the customer of specified information concerning that customer's account,[27] and does specify dispute resolution mechanisms,[28] it does not restrict the use or disclosure to third parties of information about customer transactions. Nor does it restrict the gathering of personal information or limit the duration of storage of transaction records.[29]

Other statutes provide a modicum of protection for certain specific privacy-related interests. For example, the Fair Credit Billing Act of 1974[30] requires that creditors furnish consumers with copies of their credit transaction records and provide consumers with an opportunity to dispute errors, during which time creditors are restricted from disclosing information about delinquent payments.[31] The Fair Debt Collection Practices Act of 1977[32] limits debt collectors' disclosures to some third parties (but not credit reporting agencies) of a debtor's financial situation.

Telecommunications and Video Services

The Electronic Communications Privacy Act of 1986[33] prohibits the interception or disclosure of the contents of any electronic communication, such as telephone conversations or e-mail, or even of any conversation in which the participants exhibit "an expectation that such communication is not subject to interception under circumstances justifying such an expectation."[34] This apparently broad privacy right is riddled with exceptions, the most significant of which is that the prohibition does not apply if any *one* party to the communication consents to disclosure.[35] The prohibition also does not apply to switchboard operators, employees of telecommunications service providers, employees of the Federal Communications Commission, or anyone assisting the holder of a warrant, provided they are acting within the scope of their duties.[36] The prohibition also does not apply if the communication intercepted was "made through an electronic communication system that is configured so that such electronic communication is readily accessible to the general public," including any marine or aeronautical system, amateur and citizens band radio, or "general mobile radio services."[37]

Before 1996, there was no statutory protection for information *about* telecommunications transactions, such as telephone numbers or time, place, and duration of call.[38] The Electronic Communications Privacy Act did not apply to "transactional" information, so service providers faced no legal limits on collecting, storing, or disclosing such data. In fact, the statute explicitly authorizes the use of "a pen register or a trap and trace device" to record information about other individuals' conversations or transmissions.[39] On February 1, 1996, however, Congress passed the Telecommunications Act of 1996, including provisions protecting the privacy of "Customer Proprietary Network Information" (CPNI).[40] The act defines CPNI as "information that relates to the quantity, technical configuration, type, destination, and amount of use of a telecommunications service subscribed to by any customer of a telecommunications carrier, and that is made available to the carrier by the customer solely by virtue of the carrier-customer relationship."[41] Under the act, service providers may "use, disclose, or permit access to individually identifiable" CPNI only as necessary to provide the telecommunications service from which the information is derived or services necessary to that telecommunications service.[42] Service providers are free to use CPNI as necessary to protect their own business interests.[43] Although the act only restricts the disclosure of information, and the exemption for related services such as telephone directories is considerable, the new provision reflects growing attention by Congress to privacy concerns.

The Cable Communications Policy Act of 1984 provides extensive privacy-related regulation of cable television service providers.[44] The act restricts the collection, storage, and disclosure of "personally identifiable information" without the subscriber's consent and requires that service providers provide their subscribers with access to information collected about them. The act also requires that the cable service provider inform the customer at least once a year of the information it collects, the "nature, frequency, and purpose of any disclosure" of that information, the duration of its storage, the times and places at which a customer may have access to that information, and the terms of the statute.[45] The act provides for statutory damages against cable operators who violate their customers' rights under the act.[46] The act includes some exemptions, particularly for disclosures of information "necessary to render, or conduct a legitimate business activity related to," the provision of cable service, but it nonetheless constitutes the broadest set of privacy rights in any federal statute.[47]

Federal law also protects against the disclosure of video tape rental and sale records. The Video Privacy Protection Act of 1988,[48] adopted in response to congressional outrage over the disclosure of the list of videos rented by Judge Robert Bork during his ill-fated Supreme Court nomination confirmation hearings, prohibits the disclosure of titles of particular films rented by identifiable customers. The statute also requires the destruction of personally identifiable information not later than one year after the information if no longer necessary for the purpose for which it was collected.[49] There are significant exemptions, for example, "if the disclosure is incident [sic] to the ordinary course of business of the video tape service provider."[50] And data about user viewing habits may be disclosed for marketing purposes if the user has been given an opportunity to "opt out" of such disclosure.[51] As a result, lists are widely available containing information on user viewing habits and other demographic information, such as median age and income.

The Workplace

Given the breadth of regulation of the workplace generally, there is surprisingly little protection for privacy in relation to employment. The Equal Employment Opportunity Act prohibits discrimination in hiring, firing, or the terms of employment on the basis of an individual's "race, color, religion, sex, or national origin" but does not prohibit the collection, storage, or dissemination of such information.[52] Similarly, the Fair Housing Act prohibits discrimination in the sale or lease of housing on the basis of "race, color, religion, sex, familial status, or national origin"

but is silent on all aspects of data processing.[53] The Employee
Polygraph Protection Act of 1988 prohibits an employer's use of
lie detectors and the results of lie detector tests.[54] Although this
law may protect information privacy by restricting the collection
of information by one particular technique and the use of information gathered by that technique in one setting, the law does
not regulate the collection, storage, or dissemination of personal
information.

Educational Records

The Family Education Rights and Privacy Act of 1974 provides a fairly extensive array of information privacy rights to
students who attend educational institutions that receive public
funds and these students' parents.[55] Such institutions must accord parents the "right to inspect and review the education records of their children."[56] Students eighteen or older, or in college,
are also entitled to view such records. The educational institution
must accord parents (or students) a hearing to challenge the
contents of student records that they claim are "inaccurate, misleading, or otherwise in violation of the privacy or other rights of
students," and the opportunity to correct or delete such information or to include in the records a written explanation of their
content.[57] Educational institutions are prohibited from disclosing
student records to third parties without written consent, and
they must include in the records the identities of all third parties
who have requested or obtained access to student educational
records.[58] The act further requires that third parties receiving
such information not disseminate it further.[59] Educational institutions must inform students and their parents of their rights
under this law.[60] The law even goes so far as to protect the
confidentiality of parents' financial records from access by their
student children and to restrict the terms under which a student
may waive her right of access to confidential letters of recommendation.[61] The act excludes "directory information" such as name,
address, telephone listing, date and place of birth, and so on, but
provides that parents or students may designate specifically that
such information not be released without prior consent.[62] The

statute does not restrict the types or sources of information that schools may gather, nor does it limit the duration of storage of personal information contained in student files. The penalty for failing to comply with the act is termination of federal funds; there is no private right of action.[63]

State Statutes

This volume is concerned primarily with national and multi-national protections for information privacy. However, there is some legislative protection for privacy at the state level. State constitutional provisions have been outlined already.[64] At least thirteen states have general privacy statutes applicable to government activities. Some states also have statutory privacy rights that apply to the private sector. Reidenberg has identified three approaches to these state statutory provisions.[65]

At least two states—Massachusetts and Wisconsin—have adopted general rights of privacy, although these statutes largely restate the common law privacy torts discussed below. For example, Massachusetts provides that "a person shall have a right against unreasonable, substantial or serious interference with his privacy,"[66] but state courts largely limit this right to the "public disclosure of private facts" tort discussed below.[67] Similarly, Wisconsin's facially broad privacy statute–"The right of privacy is recognized in this state"–is restricted to the torts of intrusion, public disclosure of private facts, and misappropriation.[68] Even in those limited contexts, the statute specifically exempts from any prior restraint designed to protect privacy "constitutionally protected communication privately and through the public media."[69]

A number of states have eschewed the appearance of broad privacy protection and instead have codified one or more of the common law privacy torts, discussed below.[70] Finally, many states have enacted industry-specific privacy legislation in areas similar to federal private sector statutes.[71] Like their federal counterparts, "each state law generally seeks to resolve a narrow problem within a given industry and does not systematically address all the privacy concerns relating to the acquisition, storage, transmission, use and disclosure of personal information."[72]

Tort Law

"The Right to Privacy" by Samuel Warren and Louis Brandeis was published in the *Harvard Law Review* in 1890. Seventy years passed before William Prosser proposed a structure for the common law privacy rights that Warren and Brandeis advocated.[73] Prosser analyzed the numerous state court opinions recognizing various forms of a "right to privacy" and then categorized that right into four distinct torts: physical intrusion, misappropriation, false light, and publication of private facts.[74] This structure, included in the *Restatement (Second) of Torts* (for which Prosser served as reporter), replaced the single privacy right found in the first *Restatement of Torts*. The second *Restatement* provides:

> Section 652A. General Principle
> (1) One who invades the right of privacy of another is subject to liability for the resulting harm to the interests of the other.
> (2) The right of privacy is invaded by (a) unreasonable intrusion upon the seclusion of another, as stated in § 652B; or (b) appropriation of the other's name or likeness, as stated in § 652C; or (c) unreasonable publicity given to the other's private life, as stated in § 652D; or (d) publicity that unreasonably places the other in a false light before the public, as stated in § 652E.[75]

The tort of unreasonable intrusion lends little support to information privacy, other than as a potential restriction on the means of gathering information. Like the other three privacy torts, this one requires that the intrusion involve "solitude or seclusion of another or his private affairs or concerns" and that it be "highly offensive to a reasonable person."[76] This tort is recognized in all but six states.

The tort of appropriation only applies to the "name or likeness" of an individual, and therefore is of limited value as a protection for information privacy.[77] Only about two-thirds of the states recognize this tort, and most of them require that the appropriation be for "commercial gain," such as advertising.

The tort of "unreasonable publicity given to the other's private life" applies only when there is a disclosure to a large audience of private information that would be "highly offensive to a reasonable person" and is not of "legitimate public concern to the public."[78] Besides these limits, the U.S. Supreme Court has ruled that lawfully obtained, truthful information on a matter of public significance can never be the subject of legal liability, at least not without satisfying the requirements of strict scrutiny.[79] In *Philadelphia Newspaper, Inc.* v. *Hepps*, the Court reaffirmed that punishing true speech was "antithetical to the First Amendment's protection."[80] Susan M. Gilles has noted that "if the constitutional requirement of proof of falsity articulated in libel cases is extended to privacy cases, then the private-facts tort is unconstitutional."[81] This tort is recognized in all but six states, but the number of successful public disclosure actions has been insignificant.

The final privacy tort is "publicity that unreasonably places the other in a false light before the public." To be actionable under the false light tort, the publication must be both false and highly offensive to a reasonable person.[82] In 1967 in *Time, Inc.* v. *Hill*,[83] the Supreme Court extended the First Amendment privileges previously recognized in the context of defamation to actions for false-light privacy. The Court thus required plaintiffs to show that the defendant knew the publication was false or recklessly disregarded its truth or falsity. Fewer than two-thirds of the states recognize this tort.

These state tort actions are the principal source today of adjudicated legal rights concerning privacy. However, they offer little protection for information privacy. Even in their limited areas, only one award to a privacy tort plaintiff has ever survived the Supreme Court's First Amendment scrutiny.[84]

U.S. Privacy Concepts and Principles

The administration of President Bill Clinton has focused considerable attention on the value of a national and, more recently, global information infrastructure. As candidates in 1992, Clinton and Al Gore campaigned on a promise to create a network that would "link every home, business, lab, classroom and library by the year 2015."[85] Once in office, the president and vice president created the Information Infrastructure Task Force, chaired by the late Secretary of Commerce Ronald H. Brown. The task force, which includes representatives from most cabinet departments, is charged with articulating the administration's vision for the National and Global Information Infrastructures (NII and GII, respectively), and identifying and eliminating obstacles to their deployment. The task force is divided into three committees and subcommittees, one of which—the Privacy Working Group of the Information Policy Committee—is responsible for addressing the privacy issues posed by the proliferation of electronic information networks.[86]

The ITF Working Group Principles

The Privacy Working Group issued the final version of its *Principles for Providing and Using Personal Information* in June 1995.[87] The principles are important for a number of reasons. They are the product of a committee and process that is broadly representative of executive branch agencies. They are broad based and apply across industry lines. They are the most recent statement from the federal government on the subject of privacy since the 1977 final report of the Privacy Protection Study Commission created by the Privacy Act of 1974.[88] They directly address the issue of information privacy. They were debated and adopted contemporaneously with the final discussion of the EU data protection directive and, while not carrying the force of law, may therefore form the basis for a useful comparison with European privacy principles.

The principles are divided into three categories: general principles for all NII participants, principles for users of personal information, and principles for individuals who provide personal information. In the first category, the working group identified three principles:

—Information privacy principle. Personal information should be acquired,disclosed, and used only in ways that respect an individual's privacy. . . .
—Information integrity principle. Personal information should not be improperly altered or destroyed. . . .
—Information quality principle. Personal information should be accurate, timely, complete, and relevant for the purpose for which it is provided and used.[89]

In its commentary on these principles, the working group appeared to adopt the Fourth Amendment "reasonableness" test to determine whether an expectation of privacy was "subjectively held by the individual and deemed objectively reasonable by society."[90] But the report went on to specify that a reasonable expectation of privacy under the principles may exceed what is reasonable under the Fourth Amendment. The commentary also indicated the working group's support for contractual protections for privacy but cautioned that "society should ensure privacy at some basic level" to address those situations in which unequal bargaining power or other conditions impede "mutually agreeable" privacy protections.

In the second category—principles for information users—the working group identified five principles. The first four appear to create substantive limits on users' information-related activities:

—Acquisition principles. Information users should: 1. Assess the impact on privacy in deciding whether to acquire, disclose, or use personal information. 2. Acquire and keep only information reasonably expected to support current or planned activities. . . .
—Notice principle. Information users who collect personal information directly from the individual should provide adequate, relevant information about: 1. Why they are collecting the information; 2. What the information is expected to be used for; 3. What steps will be taken to protect its confidentiality, integrity, and quality; 4. The consequences of providing or withholding information; and 5. Any rights of redress. . . .
—Protection principle. Information users should use appropriate technical and managerial controls to protect the confidentiality and integrity of personal information. . . .
—Fairness principle. Information users should not use personal information in ways that are incompatible with the individual's

understanding of how it will be used, unless there is a compelling public interest for such use.[91]

These principles address the complete range of information processing activities—data collection, storage, use, and dissemination—as well as establishing what is often considered the foundation of any form of information privacy protection: notice. Moreover, the commentary makes clear that the principles are intended to apply broadly, for example, to all of the parties who collect information in a transaction, not just the party dealing directly with the consumer. Despite the breadth of these four principles, however, the working group makes only one recommendation for the creation of "some basic level of privacy protection," presumably through federal legislation. That recommendation concerns restricting the collection of personal information when individuals either have no choice about whether or not to disclose it or when the failure to disclosure the information will result in the denial of a "benefit that individuals need to participate fully in society."[92] Moreover, in the commentary the working group explicitly leaves a number of specific issues to the discretion of information users, such as whether explicit consent from the persons from whom the data are to be collected is necessary (the "opt in" alternative) or whether they should only be given an opportunity to "opt out."[93] Finally, the working group noted the existence of situations in which no formal notice is necessary. Notice may not be required because the intended use is clear from the context in which the data are being provided—for example, giving an address to an airline to mail a ticket need not be predicated on notice that the airline intends to use the information to mail the ticket. Also, a use that is incompatible with the reasons for which the information was first provided may be permitted without notice when the benefit to the society is sufficiently great or the effect on the individual's information privacy interest is sufficiently trivial.[94]

The fifth principle applicable to information users is the education principle: "Information users should educate themselves and the public about how information privacy can be maintained."[95] In this principle, the working group recognizes the limit of legal protections for information privacy:

There are many uses of the NII for which individuals cannot rely completely on governmental or other organizational controls to protect their privacy. Although individuals often rely on such legal and institutional controls to protect their privacy, many people will engage in activities outside of these controls, especially as they engage in the informal exchange of information on the NII. Thus, individuals must be aware of the hazards of providing personal information, and must make judgments about whether providing personal information is to their benefit.[96]

In an unusual development for privacy protection, the working group included a third category of principles, applicable to individuals who provide information. Included in this category are three principles, the first of which restates the notice principle as an obligation on data suppliers:

—Awareness principle. Individuals should obtain adequate, relevant information about: 1. Why the information is being collected; 2. What the information is expected to be used for; 3. What steps will be taken to protect its confidentiality, integrity, and quality; 4. The consequences of providing or withholding information; and 5. Any rights of redress.[97]

The second principle applicable to information suppliers provides:

—Empowerment principles. Individuals should be able to safeguard their own privacy by having: 1. A means to obtain their personal information; 2. A means to correct their personal information that lacks sufficient quality to ensure fairness in its use; 3. The opportunity to use appropriate technical controls, such as encryption, to protect the confidentiality and integrity of communications and transactions; and 4. The opportunity to remain anonymous when appropriate.[98]

This principle purports to recommend the creation of substantive rights, but the commentary clarifies that the extent to which those rights are actually provided "depends on various factors, including the seriousness of the consequences to the individual of using the personal information and any First Amendment rights held by the information user."[99] The commentary also highlights the importance of self-help measures, such as encryption and anonymity, while not resolving the extent to which the law should protect an individual's right to avail himself of those means.[100]

The final principle, the redress principle, provides that "individuals should, as appropriate, have a means of redress if harmed by an improper disclosure or use of personal information."[101] The working group would extend the right of redress to include decisionmaking based on "personal information of inadequate quality—information that is not accurate, timely, complete, or relevant for the purpose for which it is provided and used."[102] According to the commentary, redress may take a wide variety of forms, including government enforcement, civil litigation, and extrajudicial means such as informal complaint resolution, mediation, and arbitration.[103]

The protection for information privacy envisioned by the working group in the *Principles for Providing and Using Personal Information* is best characterized by contextuality and lack of reliance on specific legal measures. The contextuality is evident in the frequent discussion of the extent to which a given principle must be balanced against other competing interests, such as society's need for the information and society's interest in free expression. Rather than resolve any of the wide range of issues involved in information privacy, the principles articulate the need for balance and for personal privacy to be part of that balance. The principles recognize, however, that the outcome of the balance will depend upon the nature of the information involved, what the public regards as "reasonable" practice, and even the industrial or governmental sector in which the information collection or use takes place. It is impossible to predict, based on the principles, how any balance will come out or when or how much any specific information will be protected.

The principles also evince little reliance on specific legal measures, reflecting the paucity and inconsistency of existing legal protection for privacy in the United States. The working group recommends that "society should ensure privacy at some basic level" in only two instances: when unequal bargaining power or other conditions impede "mutually agreeable" privacy protections, and when individuals either have no choice as to whether or not to disclose personal information or when the failure to disclose the information will result in the denial of an important benefit. The principles, however, reflect no effort to define key concepts such as "unequal bargaining power" or "important benefit," and therefore offer little meaningful guidance as to when the working group believes specific legal measures to protect privacy are appropriate. The principles set forth important considerations and goals, but, with the two exceptions when "society should ensure privacy at some basic level," the balancing of those factors with other important issues is committed to the discretion of individual information suppliers and users. The working group explicitly sets forth examples of nonregulatory measures for protecting privacy, such as contracts, education, negotiation, and mediation.

This understanding of the principles is borne out by the one instance in which the U.S. government has attempted to put them into practice. In October 1995, just four months after their publication, the National Telecommunications and Information Administration released its report *Privacy and the NII: Safeguarding Telecommunications-Related Personal Information*.[104] In the report, the NTIA, the president's principal adviser on telecommunications policy issues, addressed the privacy issues related to individuals' use of telecommunications and video services, such as telephone and cable television. The NTIA proposed "a modified contractual model that allows businesses and consumers to reach agreements concerning the collection, use, and dissemination of TRPI [telecommunications-related personal information—personal information that is created in the course of an individual's subscription to a telecommunications or information service or, as a result of his or her uses of that service], subject to two fundamental requirements–provider notice and customer consent."[105] Service providers must tell their customers what information they intend to collect, for what uses, and how it will be protected; they must obtain their customers' explicit consent before making ancillary uses of "sensitive" data; and they must provide an opportunity for customers to "opt out" of ancillary uses of nonsensitive data.[106] Other than those requirements, the NTIA's report—like that of the U.S. Privacy Working Group of the Information Policy Committee—focuses on service providers and customers reaching mutual agreement on the protection of personal privacy and on "enhanced consumer education."[107]

Comparison with European Privacy Law

Despite the notable differences between European and U.S. social, political, and legal contexts in which privacy issues are addressed, the legal systems still reflect many shared principles of information privacy, although they protect those principles in very different ways and to widely divergent degrees. For example, both the European data protection directive and the U.S. *Principles for Providing and Using Personal Information* create obligations and responsibilities for personal information users. Those obligations and responsibilities include collecting information only for specific and specified purposes; using information only in ways that are compatible with those purposes; not collecting information unnecessary to those purposes; and not storing that information longer than is necessary for those purposes. Both frameworks recognize the importance of correcting inaccurate information, although the U.S. principles would not guarantee individuals a right to access their personal information and would require correction only when the inaccuracy was so great as to compromise the fairness of the use of the data.

Both the European directive and the U.S. principles require that individuals be given notice whenever personal information is collected about them and an opportunity to consent or withhold consent for certain uses of personal information. The two regimes diverge on the protection for sensitive data. The data protection directive generally prohibits the collection or use of data identifying "racial or ethnic origin, political opinions, religious beliefs, philosophical or ethical persuasion . . . [or] concerning health or sexual life," and requires special government scrutiny of any data collection and processing activities applicable to such information.[108] The principles make no such provision and provide for no government supervisory authority or data protection register. Nonetheless, U.S. law generally affords greater protection to sensitive data by weighing the privacy interests at stake when information concerning "fundamental rights" is involved more heavily.

Europe and the United State also diverge on the issue of enforcement. In Europe, a key principle of information privacy is government oversight of the data processing activities of private parties and enforcement of the law when necessary. Under the directive, that oversight includes registration of all data processors and collection and processing activities. The U.S. privacy principles are silent on the enforcement of privacy rights against data collectors and processors, and the constitutional commitment to a government of limited powers, particularly when expression is involved, poses a substantial obstacle to the creation of a government privacy authority.

Clearly, Europe and the United States share many, but not all, principles of information privacy. To be sure, the respective legal systems reflect those principles differently. The differences may at present seem to outweigh the similarities, but the importance of the existence of some shared core values should not be underestimated. As concern about privacy continues to rise in Europe and the United States in the face of proliferating information technologies and services, further legal protection for information privacy seems certain. Though the legal cultures concerning privacy are unlikely ever to converge completely, they are likely to grow closer together to the extent they share common values.

Summary

The protection for information privacy in the United States is disjointed, inconsistent, and limited by conflicting interests. There is no explicit constitutional guarantee of a right to privacy in the United States. Although the Supreme Court has fashioned a variety of privacy rights out of the Bill of Rights and the Fourteenth Amendment, "information privacy" has received little protection, primarily based on the Fourth and Fourteenth Amendments. In the Fourth Amendment arena, the Court has found constitutional violations when the police have searched for or seized records without a warrant or meeting one of the exceptions to the warrant requirement. The Court, however, has written that the Fourth Amendment privacy right has little application outside of the context of the investigation and prosecution of criminal activity. Moreover, this protection against such searches does not extend to information controlled by a third person. Under the Fourteenth Amendment, the Court has recognized a constitutional right restricting the government from compelling individuals to disclose certain personal information. This right protects only the interest of an individual in not disclosing certain information, and that right is evaluated under intermediate scrutiny, as opposed to the strict scrutiny required when fundamental rights are at stake.

As with all constitutional rights, these apply only against the government, not private actors. The requirement for state action and the "negative" nature of constitutional rights require only that the government refrain from taking actions that impermissibly invaded individuals' information privacy rights, not that the government take steps to affirmatively protect those rights. The Constitution also requires, however, that the government avoid actions that infringe other rights enumerated therein, such as the protection for expression in the First Amendment. When privacy and free expression rights collide, the latter have virtually always prevailed. Similarly, under the Fifth Amendment, the government cannot take private property, whether by physical occupation or extensive regulation, without according due process and paying just compensation to the owner.

Outside of the constitutional arena, protection for information privacy relies on hundreds of federal and state laws and regulations, each of which applies only to a specific category of information user (such as the government or retailers of videotapes), context (applying for credit or subscribing to cable television), type of information (criminal records or financial information), or use for that information (computer matching or impermissible discrimination). Privacy laws in the United States most often prohibit certain disclosures, rather than collection, use, or storage, of personal information. When those protections extend to the use of personal information, it is often as a byproduct of legislative commitment to another goal, such as eliminating discrimination. And the role provided for the government in most U.S. privacy laws is often limited to providing a judicial form for resolving disputes.

Passage of the privacy provisions in the Cable Communications Policy Act, and recent passage of the Consumer Credit Reporting Reform Act and the CPNI provision of the Telecommunications Act, demonstrate that Congress can enact serious privacy protection, even if limited to narrow sectoral environments. The latter two acts and the expanding debate in Washington over privacy evince the growing attention to the development of laws and regulations to protect privacy.

However, as the limits and exceptions within existing privacy laws indicate, privacy protection in the United States is fundamentally in tension with other cherished values. The legal regulation of privacy is significantly influenced by the importance placed by society on the prevention of crime and prosecution of criminals, free expression and an investigatory press, the acquisition and use of property, and a limited role for government involvement in daily life. A comparison of the legal regimes of the EU and the United States suggests that in Europe privacy is more valued and less in conflict with other widely shared values.

CHAPTER SEVEN

Electronic Privacy in the Twenty-First Century

Privacy is a necessary element of quality life in modern society. Some protection for identifiable personal information about individuals and institutions is an essential part of privacy, as both European and U.S. law recognize. As information technologies spread and reliance on them increases, as the volume of data generated and recorded skyrockets, and as the cost of processing those data declines, the perceived need to protect information privacy is growing. This is particularly true as an increasing number of significant activities, such as banking, filing tax returns, and obtaining medical information, are shifted from the physical world to the virtual world. The proliferation of electronic information, and data about our use of these electronic services, seems certain to raise the stakes that society places on protecting information privacy.

The Privacy Balance

As important as the values served by information privacy are today, and are likely to be in the future, none is absolute. Privacy values vary dramatically and often conflict with one another. More important, privacy is only one of the elements essential to modern life. Privacy is necessary and useful, but it is not sufficient. It is therefore only one tool, which must be used in coordination with other tools, to achieve the ends we desire, such as self-fulfillment and self-determination, societal productivity, and higher quality of life. As a result, individuals and institutions as a whole share an interest in identifying and facilitating those means—including privacy—that are necessary to achieve desired ends. What is needed is a balance, of which privacy is a part.

An important part of that balance is recognizing that protecting privacy imposes real costs. It facilitates the dissemination of false and misleading information, increases the cost of providing products and services, and interferes with meaningful evaluation of students and employees. Privacy conflicts with other important values within the society, such as society's interest in free expression, preventing and punishing crime, protection of private property, and the efficient operation of government. Privacy even conflicts with what may seem to be more mundane interests such as the desire for instant credit, better targeted mass mailings, lower insurance rates, faster service when ordering merchandise by telephone, qualified employees, or special recognition for frequent travelers. All of these and countless other benefits come at the expense of some privacy. The same features of information technologies and markets that raise the stakes of not protecting personal privacy, raise the risks of overprotecting it.

Privacy values are therefore constantly in tension with themselves and with other values. That tension is inescapable. Balancing those diverse, competing values is inherently contextual and, within each specific context, that balance will reflect a weighing of competing interests, such as cost, convenience, and quality and variety of services. Another important part of the context in which information privacy issues must be addressed are the other concerns raised by digital information, including enforcing intellectual property rights, protecting free expression, facilitating the economic stability of information networks, harmonizing divergent regulatory schemes, resolving the role of on-line anonymity, and ensuring the security of electronic transactions. No protection for information privacy is workable or desirable if it fails to take into account the variety and importance of contextual factors and the existence of competing values and concerns.

Principles for Privacy Protection

The contextuality of information privacy does not mean that it is impossible to identify fundamental principles of privacy protection. On the contrary, the importance of context and the competition of values heightens the importance of articulating basic principles to help guide the resolution of privacy issues. At the same time, these features mandate that those principles, and the ways in which they are implemented, clearly take into account the contextual issues affecting privacy's protection. This volume proposes four sets of principles, drawn from the European and U.S. experience.

Primacy of Individual Responsibility and Nongovernmental Action

The most important protection for information privacy is individual responsibility and action. This can take many forms. It certainly requires an awareness of the privacy implications of individual activities, particularly on the Internet or other networks. For many novice computer users, or people unacquainted with privacy issues, developing this awareness may require education. One must learn about the often invisible actions of software and hardware by reading instruction manuals and help screens, finding resources about privacy in print or on the Internet, and perusing the fine print in credit and other consumer transactions. A consortium of privacy advocates and software companies has announced the development of a service to make privacy self-help easier on the Internet. It is launching eTRUST, a program that will rate Internet sites according to how well they protect individual privacy. Internet sites that provide sufficient protection for individual privacy—including not collecting personal information, not disseminating information to third parties, and not using information for secondary purposes—will earn the right to display the eTRUST logo.[1]

Individual privacy action often requires the use of a technological or other forms of self-help, such as an anonymous remailer or encryption software. Protecting passwords for computer accounts and restricting access to equipment are often necessary steps to take to ensure privacy protection. Other steps include refusing to provide unnecessary personal information to product and service suppliers, one of the most effective means of protecting one's privacy. Individuals may need to restructure an activity to enhance privacy protection, perhaps by changing companies or paying with cash rather than check or credit card.

Individual responsibility always requires ascertaining why data are being collected and how the collector intends to control the use, dissemination, and retention of personal information. This knowledge is exceptionally important in the context of commercial services, as many companies now promote their privacy policies for competitive purposes. If one credit card company, for example, does not offer adequate protection for personal information, others almost certainly will. If enough consumers demand better privacy protection and back up that demand, if necessary, by withdrawing their patronage, companies are certain to respond. In fact, when competitive markets exist, consumer inquiries about, and response to, corporate privacy policies are an excellent measure of how much that society really values privacy.

Public protest also has proved an effective restraint on planned corporate data processing activities. In 1991 Lotus Development Corporation and Equifax abandoned plans to sell Households, a CD-ROM database containing names, addresses, and marketing information on 120 million consumers, after they received 30,000 calls and letters from individuals asking to be removed from the database.[2] Ironically, cancellation of Households led Lotus to abandon Lotus Marketplace, a similar CD-ROM database with information on 7 million U.S. businesses.[3] Eight months later, Equifax, one of the largest credit bureaus in the United States, decided to stop selling consumer names and addresses to direct marketing firms altogether, a business that had earned the company $11 million the previous year.[4]

More recently, Lexis-Nexis, operator of one of the largest legal and general information databases in the world, has revamped plans for P-Track, a service that provides personal information, including maiden names and aliases about "virtually every individual in America," to anyone willing to pay a search fee of eighty-five to one hundred dollars.[5] In response to a storm of protest, Lexis-Nexis has decided against providing social security numbers and is honoring the requests of anyone who wishes to be deleted from the database. The situation highlights not only the effectiveness of protests but also the potential for the very technologies that facilitate the collection and disclosure of personal information to be used to protect privacy. Word about the planned service was widely circulated by e-mail on the Internet, and many of the protests to the company have been delivered the same way.[6] Moreover, the public outcry over the planned activities by Lotus and Lexis-Nexis demonstrate the significant role of the media in informing consumers and facilitating a popular response.

Direct contact with companies may not only alert them to the value of privacy to their customers but also achieve direct, immediate results, as happens, for example, when the company receives a letter from a consumer who demands to be removed from a mailing list. Industry organizations, such as the Direct Marketing Association, also provide important rights that help to address information privacy issues more broadly. For example, the DMA operates the Mail Preference Service and the Telephone Preference Service. With a single request to each it is possible to be removed from most DMA-member company mailing and telephone solicitation lists. However, although the Mail Preference Service has been available since 1971, the DMA reports that the service is used by approximately 2 percent of the U.S. adult population.[7] This number suggests that concern over direct mail solicitations is not that great or that the public is unaware of, or not taking the initiative to use, this free service. A proposed use of data can hardly be considered unfairly invasive of personal privacy if the user gives data subjects a meaningful opportunity to object to the use. One has little ground for complaint if one fails to take advantage of those opportunities.

Individuals, rather than waiting for the government to take action, must accept the responsibility to know and insist on legal rights. For example, in the United States, any citizen may demand from the government a copy of all information, other than that within one of the Freedom of Information Act's nine enumerated exemptions, that the government possesses about her.[8] Taking advantage of this right is an effective step toward discovering and correcting inaccurate or misleading information. Similarly, every person has a legal right to the information about her held by a credit reporting agency.[9] If she has been denied credit or other benefits on the basis of a credit report, there is no charge for the access.[10] Taking advantage of that opportunity, reviewing the data carefully, and disputing incorrect or outdated information are vital ways to protect one's information privacy.

Some privacy rights exist in private agreements. The Bankcard Holders of America Association urges consumers to "just say no" to allowing merchants to record information such as a driver's license or telephone number on credit card slips.[11] Merchants are prohibited from requiring this information by their agreement with Visa and Mastercard. Similarly, some merchants require credit card information as a way of guaranteeing a check, but Visa and Mastercard prohibit this practice too.[12] These restrictions help protect individuals' privacy, and they highlight the importance of learning about, and insisting upon, consumers' rights wherever found. And there are situations, discussed below, in which recourse to a government agency or to the courts is appropriate.[13]

Individual responsibility, of course, applies to information users as well as to those wishing to protect their privacy. Individuals and institutions collecting, storing, using, and disseminating identifiable personal information should recognize the competitive potential of rational, articulated policies to protect personal privacy. Besides the potential for attracting customers, such policies may also serve as effective housecleaning tools, reducing information that is inaccurate or out-of-date. Such information has little value and may diminish the value of other information held by the user. Information privacy policies that include limits on data collection and retention, and procedures of updating information, serve the interests of data users as well as data subjects. Those policies and practices may also forestall government regulation and avoid costly litigation.

Often, industry associations, such as the Information Industry Association and the Interactive Services Association, have adopted guidelines and principles that may serve as models for individual policies or standards against which those policies may be judged.[14] The Direct Marketing Association offers an interactive tool for developing effective notices to consumers about the collection and use of data. These documents establish important norms of data protection of which both data subjects and users should be aware, and which may serve as a basis for negotiations between consumers and service providers. Corporate compliance with these standards and other privacy standards may constitute an important accolade in competitive markets, much like the Good Housekeeping Seal of Approval, while inattention to them might be a source of public embarrassment and competitive disadvantage in the eyes of consumers who are concerned about protecting their privacy. Moreover, industry associations can often be approached to help persuade member organizations to adopt and adhere to industry norms for privacy protection. The DMA, for example, has begun issuing quarterly reports on members who are being disciplined for violating DMA codes of conduct.

Steven Bibas, Scott Shorr, and others have written about a contractual approach to information privacy, in which privacy would be protected according to an explicit agreement between the data subject and the data user.[15] This is the practical outgrowth of both information supplier and user exercising individual responsibility for information privacy. Information contracts allow targeted privacy protection for those consumers who are concerned about it. They are especially effective in the absence of consensus about privacy, and they may be preferable to uniform privacy protection because they are more sensitive to the specific context and to individual preferences. Like price mechanisms in general, this approach to privacy "takes into account individual values, needs, and tradeoffs, allocating resources to their most-valued uses. . . . A contractual approach, by pricing information, would thus more efficiently allocate data than would a centrally planned solution."[16] Privacy protection based on mutual consent is not possible in all situations, for example, when the data subject and the data processor have no direct contact, but when applicable, this approach is an excellent example of the benefits of individual action to protect privacy.

Individual responsibility is not a panacea. Commissioner David Flaherty, Paul M. Schwartz and Joel R. Reidenberg, Colin Bennett, and many other privacy scholars have noted flaws in the U.S. self-regulation, self-help model of privacy protection. Many of the criticisms center on what is perceived as the intrinsic conflict that occurs when data users promulgate their own data protection codes of conduct; the lack of public disclosure of, and scrutiny over, corporate privacy policies; the unwillingness of companies and industry organizations to take privacy protection seriously; and the failure of many of these groups to act consistently with their public pronouncements on privacy or to live up to the promises they make.[17] These observations are pertinent to the direct marketing industry in the United States, while they are less relevant, and becoming even less so, in industries such as consumer banking and credit, which have increasingly adopted and publicized their privacy policies as a competitive strategy.

Some of the critiques are misplaced, because they judge self-help efforts against normative standards that are found nowhere else in U.S. legal or commercial culture. As desirable as some privacy advocates believe European standards of data protection to be, they are not the appropriate tests of U.S. organizational behavior. And many of the criticisms fail to reflect significant recent successes of the self-regulatory, self-help model. Nonetheless, the failures of the past highlight the importance of making individual responsibility work better by ensuring that consumers become more aware of their own privacy and the options they have for protecting it. They signal the significance of new technological and market developments that increase the potential for exercising individual responsibility for privacy. Past shortcomings also focus attention on the importance on collective action by data subjects, rather than just by data users. And they suggest the contours of legal rights necessary to help facilitate and supplement individual measures to protect personal privacy.

The Role of National Law

Individual and collective nongovernmental action is critical to protecting information privacy; there can be no effective protection of information privacy without it. However, private action alone is likely to be insufficient to protect information privacy adequately. Particularly when the absence of competition interferes with the development of market mechanisms for protecting privacy, citizens will need to have recourse to legal protection for certain basic privacy rights. This will help guarantee the availability of sufficient, reliable information on the proposed use of the data to make individual action meaningful, and protect privacy in situations in which consent and other forms of self-help are unworkable or inapplicable.

The specific content of privacy laws is a matter of considerable disagreement among nations, information users and subjects, and privacy scholars. My recommendations for the essential components of privacy protection are set forth below.[18] As important as the specific rights protected by those laws are, however, the clarity, consistency, precision, and intelligibility of that protection and the laws that afford it are equally significant. The interests of information suppliers and users are best served by laws that are consistent, deliberate, and specific. This can be accomplished through a single, omnibus privacy law, supplemented as necessary by specific legal measures, or through a series of sectoral privacy statutes, each of which addresses an industrial sector or specific type of information. In either case, the laws that protect privacy should result in consistent protection for similar privacy interests in similar situations.

In the United States, existing privacy protection is a cacophony of constitutional rights, narrow sectoral statutes, state legislation, federal regulations, and common law torts. This undesirable situation results in ineffective, incomplete, inconsistent, and inefficient privacy protection. In its report on telecommunications-related personal information, the National Telecommunications and Information Administration stressed the inconsistency of current legal protections:

> Like services do not have like privacy protection. With respect to telephony services, for example, Federal regulations grant individuals the right to ask for confidential treatment of CPNI [Customer Proprietary Network Information] but only from certain telephone companies—the Bell companies and GTE.

Similarly, the notice requirements that apply to the Bell companies and GTE differ depending on the type of customer. Multi-
line customers are given notice about their privacy rights; sin-
gle-line customers are not. To complicate matters further, a few
states provide privacy protection for intrastate service regardless of which telephone company is involved.

There is also a lack of intraservice uniformity for video car-
riage. The privacy provisions of the Cable Act do not apply to
DBS [direct broadcast satellite] and wireless cable operations. . . .

In addition, there is lack of *inter*service uniformity because
like-types of information are not treated in like-ways, across
different communications services.[19]

The inconsistency in protection for CPNI and other information largely results from two factors: the absence of uniform,
rational principles undergirding information privacy protection
in the United States, and the diversity of laws, agencies, industries, and issues involved in information privacy. Much statutory
privacy protection in the United States is a by-product of some
other legislative effort, most often regulating an industry such as
telephone service, banking, or cable television. Privacy protection
is an afterthought or a secondary purpose. A statutory approach
that provides a basic level of privacy protection, either across the
board or at least across a given industry or type of information,
would yield more rational and consistent protection.

The need for consistency also argues for increased federal
attention to privacy and a corresponding preemption of some
state activity in the area. Although some privacy rights are ame-
nable to local regulation, information privacy, especially when it
involves information technologies—telephone service, broadcast
and cable television, and the Internet—and institutions with
geographically far-flung activities—national banking, insurance,
and credit reporting companies—ought to be the subject of national, or even multinational, attention. This is one of the great
strengths of the European Union data protection directive: it
establishes detailed, across-the-board privacy protection applicable throughout the fifteen European member states.[20] Individual
nations may adopt additional protections or may implement the

directive in various ways consistent with its terms, but the directive establishes a uniform base of protection.

Clarity is also an essential feature of effective privacy protection. Clarity requires specificity as well as care in the drafting of statutes. Privacy legislation may do more harm than good if its rights and obligations cannot be readily understood by information users and suppliers. Moreover, to the extent that measures designed to protect information privacy run the risk of conflicting with other legally protected rights, precise drafting may help avoid constitutional infirmity.

What to protect and how much to protect it are at the heart of the current debate over information privacy. The EU directive provides very high protection, with a necessarily high degree of resulting intrusion into the activities and expression of individuals and institutions. That level of protection is unworkable and undesirable in the U.S. context. However, U.S. citizens and institutions would benefit from a more definitive set of information privacy protections. Dozens of organizations and scholars have recommended what components should constitute basic privacy protection. Many of those recommendations embrace the breadth of the EU directive, while shying away from its legal force. The effect is often to propose very little concrete protection for a wide variety of rights. Other proposals have sought to replicate the directive in U.S. law, resulting in recommendations that are unlikely to pass constitutional scrutiny, contrary to many other widely shared values in American society, and politically unworkable.

The specific content of privacy laws is no more important than the consistency, rationality, and accessibility of those laws. Moreover, the concept of privacy and the principles undergirding a democratic political system and a market economy focus on the importance of individual choice. It is therefore important that privacy laws provide only the protection necessary to facilitate nongovernmental action and fill the gaps left by such arrangements, and that those laws extend protection consonant with other legally protected, popularly shared values. With those goals in mind, statutory privacy protection should include three elements. These elements would overlay existing privacy protection, such as that provided by the Fourth Amendment, which applies outside of the information privacy context.

NOTICE. The law should require any person collecting identifiable information about any other natural person to disclose the reason for which he is collecting the information, the extent to which he may put it to other uses, whether he will disseminate it to others, how long he will store it or on what basis he will make the determination to retain the information, whether the information must be provided, and, if so, under what compulsion. This notice requirement guarantees that the necessary information is available so that one may determine whether or not to furnish the requested data.

This notice requirement would apply only to identifiable information—information on the physical, physiological, mental, economic, cultural, political, or social identity of a living individual which directly or indirectly identifies that person. This information would include all information about living people, except for aggregate data that could not be interpreted as referring to a specific person. Such data reveal nothing about an individual and therefore pose no risk to a person's privacy. The notice requirement would be triggered only when the person identified by the information is an individual, as opposed to a company, institution, or association. Although organizations, as well as individuals, benefit from privacy, their disclosures are governed in the United States by other laws relating to publicly traded securities, corporate organization and governance, trade secrets, misappropriation, unfair competition, employment, disabilities, and many other subjects.[21] The restriction of the notice requirement to information about living people reflects the maxim in U.S. law that interests in privacy, like those in reputation, are personal and do not survive the individual.[22]

Notice should be required only to the person supplying the data (the data supplier), who may or may not be the person whom the information is about (the data subject). As a practical matter, identifiable personal information may be transferred from the data subject to the ultimate users of that information in one of two ways: the data subject may *deliberately disclose* it, either voluntarily or under some compulsion, or the activities of the data subject may *generate* personal information, of which the data subject may not even be aware. This is true irrespective of the technological context. A consumer who makes a purchase in a book store may deliberately disclose data, such as his credit card number or the address printed on his check. His participation in that transaction may also, unbeknownst to him, generate personal data if, for instance, the clerk writes down his name and the name of the book purchased or a bystander photographs the consumer entering or leaving the store. Similarly, a consumer who purchases a book by Internet is certain to disclose information knowingly, most likely by providing a credit card number and mailing address, and to generate additional information by logging onto the Internet and accessing the bookseller's site. In the same way, if the consumer orders the book by telephone, he deliberately discloses information (the contents of the telephone call), while the act of placing the call generates additional data (the information necessary for the telephone company to place his call and bill him for the service).

The information user may obtain the deliberately disclosed information directly from the data subject or from some intermediary, such as someone who sells customer lists. The generated information cannot be obtained directly from the data subject because he usually is not even aware of creating the data, but it can be observed directly by the user or acquired from some intermediary who observed the data. The source of the data—the data supplier—may be the data subject, the data user, or one of many intermediaries.

Notice should be required when an information user is obtaining identifiable personal information from another party—a data subject or an intermediary—but only upon the request of the data supplier. In some situations, the data supplier may not request the notice because the information it would provide is already known from the specific context of the request. For example, if one invites a friend to dinner and the friend asks the host to supply his address, the host is unlikely to seek notice. In other situations, the data supplier may not request the notice because he intends to provide the requested information irrespective of the content of the notice. In most situations, notice would be sought as a protection against future, unanticipated uses of the data. Congress or an administrative agency could modify or eliminate the requirement in situations in which the information is not necessary or in which the duty to provide the notice conflicts directly with other fundamental rights, such as the ability of the press to gather information. When applicable, however, the notice must be available prior to the information being provided the first time and, in appropriate situations (such as continuing credit transactions), at regular intervals thereafter.

Clearly, the notice is important if the information is being knowingly provided by the data subject. But what if the data are being observed or provided by an intermediary? Notice should be required, if requested, to the supplier of the information even if he is not the subject of the information. This allows the data supplier to evaluate better whether to provide the requested information, and it facilitates his explaining his own data protection standards to data subjects or other intermediary data suppliers. It also helps the data supplier to adhere to agreements concerning personal information he may have entered into with data subjects or suppliers.

Requiring notice when data may be observed, rather than solicited, is more complicated. If the data are observed in a traditionally public setting, no notice should be necessary. Our book purchaser may be photographed entering the store without his consent. This comports with widely shared U.S. societal values, reflected in U.S. constitutional, statutory, and decisional law, that one has no legal right to hide activities that take place in public. To restrict the collection and dissemination of information observed in public settings would run afoul of the First Amendment and be nonsensical. Under current law, one may restrain certain highly offensive or misleading commercial uses of publicly observed information (such as using a photograph of a celebrity to endorse a product without her consent). But there is and should be no legal power to interfere otherwise with the collection and use of those data.

If the information user is gathering the data itself from observations not generally available to the public, such as through the provision of telephone, cable, or Internet service, then notice should be required. This is especially true when the ability to collect the information results from a relationship between the information supplier and user. When a relationship exists, such as a patient visiting a physician or a customer subscribing to Internet service, notice is particularly useful and can be provided at relatively low cost. For example, notice can be given when the patient or customer first arranges for service, and, if he chooses, the patient or customer can act on that notice and seek service elsewhere, from someone who better protects privacy. If the information user is gathering data generated by the data subject's actions in a private setting in which the user has no legal authority to be, then his actions already are likely to violate existing European and U.S. laws prohibiting wiretapping, eavesdropping, theft, and trespass. Because these activities are already against the law, the question of notice is moot, although notice might still be required as a further disincentive to those activities.

In sum, notice should therefore be required, upon request, if the information user is asking the data subject or any other data supplier to disclose identifiable personal information. Notice should also be required when the data user is observing data being generated by the data subject, and the data user is in the position to make those observations because of some existing relationship with the data subject. Notice is not required to collect information being generated by the data subject when the activities generating those data take place in a traditionally public setting. "Traditionally public setting" is defined as a physical or virtual space in which an information user may observe the activities of a data subject not because of any special relationship or service being provided to the data subject, but rather on an equal basis with any other member of the public. Activities which occur in a physical or virtual space that can be accessed only through permission of the data subject, or a physical invasion or theft of property, are never public.

An Internet service provider, through which subscribers obtain access to the Internet, would be required to meet the notice requirement, upon request, regarding its treatment and use of identifiable personal subscriber data. However, an Internet user who collects data on the electronic addresses of other Internet users who access specific World Wide Web pages would have no obligation to disclose his activities to those users.

As a practical matter, the notice requirement will be carried out by most companies through routine disclosures, printed on the back of application forms or account statements or included on World Wide Web pages. The burden of notice is therefore presumed to be light, although it may nonetheless discourage the gathering of gratuitous data. The requirement will facilitate more informed decisionmaking by consumers, as well as attention to data processing activities by data users. It also creates a chain of custody and knowledge. A data supplier seeking to comply with its own privacy policies or with legal constraints such as the EU directive's prohibition on transferring data to countries lacking an "adequate level of protection," would have ready access to information about how its data will be used and what protections will guard against its misuse.[23]

CONSENT. The law should provide an opportunity for data suppliers to consent to, or withhold consent for, the information processing activities outlined in the notice. Historically, the requirement for obtaining consent can take many forms and have many ramifications. As a general matter, unless an information collector wishes to provide opportunities for a more detailed response, the law would merely require that the data supplier be given an a opportunity to give (to "opt in") or deny (to "opt out") consent to all of the data processing activities proposed by a single user. In a situation in which notice was not required, neither would the opportunity to consent be necessary.

The failure to consent can result in the denial of service. Although this may have the immediate effect of denying access to a product or service, in the longer term it is likely to compel data processors to conform their activities to widely accepted norms to avoid decreasing their potential market. Individuals seeking greater protection than that provided by the norm may seek to obtain it through the self-help measures outlined above, but they cannot impose the additional protection, and the cost associated with it, on society as a whole.

There is no requirement that consent be explicit: information users may, after providing the required notice, specify that a failure to object (opt out) within a reasonable period of time will constitute consent. This provision should be clear and specific, but it is adequate in all contexts except those in which registering an objection is impossible, impractical, or unduly expensive or burdensome in relation to the transaction generating the data. In those limited situations, affirmative consent (opting in) may be necessary. For example, if notice was not provided to the data supplier, or if it failed to contain an address or other way of contacting the party to whom the objection must be given, or if it specified only a telephone number that was always busy, opting out would not be a viable option. The data supplier would therefore have to obtain explicit consent for subsequent use of the data. Similarly, even a procedure for opting out that required the data supplier to bear the cost of calling a long-distance telephone might be unduly burdensome if the data resulted from a routine, face-to-face transaction. As these examples suggest, the effect of these provisions is to encourage data users to provide clear, straightforward notice, with a meaningful, convenient opportunity to object, so that a court does not subsequently find that the notice was inadequate or the opportunity to object impractical or unduly burdensome, and therefore prohibit the use of the data without first obtaining explicit consent. In addition, new consent would always be necessary whenever a change in conditions rendered the notice under which consent was obtained inaccurate.

Many commentators have forcefully suggested that subsequent disclosure or use of "sensitive" information such as medical information should require explicit consent. I do not agree. There is no consensus as to what constitutes "sensitive" information, and the definition appears to depend on personal preferences. For many individuals, information in their medical files is no more sensitive than their financial information, unlisted telephone numbers, or college transcripts. There should be no special requirement of explicit consent for the use of such an ill-defined category of data. Moreover, the EU directive defines "sensitive" information to include data on "racial or ethnic origin, political opinions, religious beliefs, [and] philosophical or ethical persuasion,"[24] despite the fact that much of this type of data is either readily observable or known only if disclosed by the data subject. Why should the law accord special protection to information that can be observed by any passerby or that is voluntarily disclosed by the data subject?

The same features that may make information sensitive may also heighten the importance of its availability. For example, a criminal record may be sensitive information, but it is precisely the type of information one would want to know before hiring a house cleaner or security guard.[25] Many people may be loathe to accurately report medical information to a new employer, but the cost of failing to report or reporting inaccurately a preexisting medical condition may be very high and is ultimately borne by the employer and its other employees. The EU directive specifically includes within its definition of "sensitive" information data on "sexual life." Yet knowledge about sexually transmitted diseases is exactly what a potential sexual partner, health care provider, or anyone who will come into intimate contact with the data subject needs to have. The law should facilitate the disclosure and verification of such data.

In the regulatory framework I am proposing, a different consent requirement for sensitive information than for other information would make little sense in any event, because consent is provided by the data supplier, who in many cases will not be the data subject. Information that may be sensitive to the data subject is not likely to be viewed differently from other information by subsequent data suppliers. Requiring the explicit consent of data suppliers for the use of information that may or may not have been sensitive to the data subject merely imposes a greater burden and higher cost on the data user with no discernible benefit. Most important, however, the whole thrust of the notice and consent requirements specified above is that notice be clear and intelligible and the opportunity to withhold consent for the data processing activities covered by the notice convenient and accessible. In the light of these requirements, the distinction between "opting in" and "opting out" is simply not that significant vis-à-vis the data subject. However, allowing individuals to opt out avoids the high costs that an opt-in system would impose on data users. Such a price for so little resulting benefit is not worth paying.

ACCOUNTABILITY. The law should hold information users accountable for the claims they make in their notices to data suppliers. Users should be liable if their representations are not substantially accurate as to why information is being collected, how it will be used, whether it will be disseminated to others, how long it will be stored and how that decision will be made, whether the information must be provided, and, if so, upon what compulsion. Liability would also exist when a data user failed to respect withholding of consent by a data supplier. Liability would attach only with respect to information that is linked to a specific living individual, as opposed to aggregate data or information about an organization or deceased person.

Liability may be established in many ways and take many forms. For reasons already outlined and further discussed below, I do not believe that government enforcement of rules concerning information is generally appropriate. The preferred remedy is civil liability, established by an aggrieved data supplier or data subject bringing a claim in federal court. The penalty could take the form of actual or statutory damages, or an injunction, and should be calculated to provide a disincentive for providing inaccurate information or failing to adhere to promises made to data suppliers. There may be specific contexts, such as violations by an industry regulated by a federal agency, in which administrative review and a government-imposed fine or other sanction would be appropriate. Those situations could be identified in sectoral statutes or administrative regulations. In any case, the standard of liability should be that the information user knew or had reason to know that its notice was substantially false or misleading or that it knew or should have known that a subsequent activity exceeded the scope of the notice or the consent obtained.

These three concepts—notice, consent, and accountability— should form the basis of protection for information privacy. That protection may be implemented in many ways. In Europe, these rights—and many others—are provided in an omnibus directive that applies across the continent. Although each nation has adopted its own legal protections consistent with the data protection directive, thereby creating the potential for some variation in implementation, even at the national level the approach is broad-based protection. The United States might choose to adopt an omnibus information privacy law providing the basic protections outlined above, or it could deploy those same protections through well-targeted sectoral statutes. In either case, protection must extend nationally, and therefore the statute(s) should be enacted by Congress. Moreover, the focus of these legal rights is to ensure adequate notice and a meaningful opportunity to grant or deny consent only in those situations in which nongovernmental action is unlikely to supply adequate protection for information privacy. Those rights are intended to maximize individual choice, not supplant it.

The advantages of a single law are that it facilitates more uniform protection; it avoids definitional problems in crafting sectoral statutes; it eliminates the potential for conflicting interpretations of overlapping laws; and it emerges from a process that is likely to facilitate more thoughtful and comprehensive debate. On the other hand, an omnibus law runs the risk of imposing a one-size-fits-all legislative solution on diverse issues that occur in a wide variety of distinct contexts, thereby creating too little or too much protection in specific situations. A single law may need to be supplemented with other laws designed to address specific situations or types of information or may require separate administrative agencies to craft divergent regulations for implementing that law in the sectors they regulate. The result could easily be as much inconsistency as would result from sectoral protection from the outset. Finally, broad-ranging laws are often politically controversial and difficult to move through Congress because of the many interests affected. This is why Congress only infrequently rewrites comprehensive laws, such as the Copyright Act (completely revised in 1909 and again in 1976), preferring instead to rely on specific amendments, even those that fundamentally alter the underlying law.

Sectoral privacy protection presents parallel opportunities and risks. Such laws may be crafted with the input of more of the affected parties and respond more sensitively to the needs of a particular sector. However, separate laws run the risk of conflict and overlap, or Congress may simply tire of the process of adopting such laws, resulting in long delays in obtaining broad protection or possibly never obtaining such protection at all. In the current legal environment in the United States, in which all statutory privacy protection (except that applicable to the federal government itself) is sectoral, sectoral protection is most likely. But in the long term, a single basic law, even if supplemented when necessary by specific laws, may be preferable, provided that it facilitates, rather than interferes with, the development of private mechanisms for protecting privacy and the exercise of individual choice.

The Role of Government

Governments can play numerous roles in protecting information privacy, including articulating principles, enacting and enforcing laws, administering data protection systems, registering data collection and use activities and the persons who engage in them, negotiating multinational agreements, and adjudicating disputes. Some legal cultures, particularly in Europe, assign to their governments some or all of those roles. In fact, the EU directive and European national privacy laws provide for the creation of supervisory authorities, whose responsibilities include monitoring the implementation of data protection laws, registering persons who wish to collect, process, use, store, and disseminate personal information, registering those activities themselves, enforcing privacy laws, and acting as an ombudsman for individuals who desire access to records about themselves or who believe their privacy rights have been violated.

In the United States, the role of the government in privacy matters is much more limited, because of constitutional constraints, different weighing of competing values, and the existence of less legal protection for privacy. Already, however, the government has participated in articulating principles for information privacy and enacting laws that protect privacy. The courts adjudicate disputes in those few situations in which privacy protections create enforceable rights. In the future, as more legal constraints on information-related activities are adopted, the courts, properly, are likely to play a greater role.

There are two potential roles that the government should not play and two that it should pursue more aggressively.

ENFORCEMENT OF PRIVACY RIGHTS. To date, government authorities in the United States have played little role in enforcing privacy rights, other than by adjudicating disputes concerning those rights. The government rarely investigates violations of privacy statutes; in the unusual instances in which such investigations do take place, they most often are the result of an investigation into another matter. For example, an investigation into possible employment or housing discrimination may also generate information about impermissible uses of data describing individuals' race or gender.

This lack of government enforcement is characteristic of many legally protected rights. The government does not usually initiate enforcement of First Amendment or Fourth Amendment rights, for example. An individual who believes that the government has abridged his right to free expression or searched his house without a warrant may sue the government, but the government does not enforce those rights. Outside of regulated industries and offenses for which criminal penalties are provided, the government plays little role in enforcing its laws. Even when criminal penalties are available, such as for violation of the copyright law, the government rarely initiates litigation. Certainly for tortious activities, including those covered by the privacy torts, the government wholly defers to the individuals allegedly harmed to pursue their own judicial remedy. Litigation, instigated by private parties who believe their legally protected rights have been infringed, is the principal means by which civil laws are enforced in the United States today.

The enforcement of privacy laws should be no different, particularly in light of constitutional values—including freedom from government invasions of privacy—that government-enforced privacy rights offend. The public seems to share this view of government involvement in protecting privacy. In the 1996 Equifax/Harris Consumer Privacy Survey, 65 percent of U.S. individuals polled agreed that "protecting the privacy of consumer information" is very important to them.[26] Forty-four percent reported that they believe "consumer privacy protection" will get worse by the year 2000.[27] Yet only 28 percent favored creation of a government privacy commission.[28] Even those who reported that they had been the victim of a privacy invasion or were pessimistic about the future of privacy protection overwhelmingly opposed creation of a government data protection authority.[29] According to the survey: "Although the public does express concern about how businesses handle personal information, consumers appear more concerned about the actions of government and would prefer to let businesses adopt *voluntary* policies rather than have the government step in—except where voluntary policies have been seen to fail."[30]

Jane Kirtley, executive director of the Reporters Committee for Freedom of the Press, characterizes the U.S. public's view toward the role of the government as one of "distrust":

> Privacy advocates urge the adoption of the European model for data protection in the name of protecting individual civil liberties. But in so doing, they ignore, or repudiate, an important aspect of the American democratic tradition: distrust of powerful central government. . . . When it comes to privacy, Americans generally do not assume that the government necessarily has citizens' best interests at heart. . . . The European paradigm assumes a much higher comfort level with a far more authoritarian government.[31]

The present system of enforcement is not perfect. It is expensive and time consuming and thus often discriminates against parties with limited resources. However, treating enforcement of privacy rights differently from the enforcement of other highly valued rights is impossible to justify. Authorizing the government to engage in the independent, self-initiated investigation and enforcement of privacy rights is constitutionally problematic and unlikely to yield less litigation, as the targets of government-imposed penalties seek review in the courts. The result of government enforcement is potentially less enforcement, as the government shrinks from investing the resources necessary to investigate and prosecute information users' privacy practices. In addition, to the extent that government enforcement substitutes for individual recourse to the courts, it would diminish the power of individuals to protect their own privacy rights.

An obvious exception exists when the government is the party accused of violating the law. Then, as is the case with other legally protected interests, the government has a duty to investigate and take action against the responsible officials. Even in that case, however, if the aggrieved individual is not satisfied with the resolution, his only legal recourse should be to the courts, not to another government authority to bring suit against the offending agency.

REGISTRATION OF DATA PROCESSING AND DATA PROCESSORS. The EU directive requires persons who wish to collect, process, use, store, and disseminate personal information to register with their national data protection supervisory authority. This scheme is anathema to the U.S. constitutional system, which so highly values freedom of expression and of the press, freedom from government intrusion, and protection of private property. As we have already seen, the public seems highly skeptical of government involvement in protecting privacy. Moreover, in an expansive information economy, it cannot provide meaningful privacy protection. The delay associated with mandatory registration and the cost to the government and to private parties of participating in such a system are likely to result in decisions not to provide certain services that would require registration, efforts to avoid registration through noncompliance and legal maneuvers, and poor enforcement by the government. The ultimate result would probably be to undermine the effectiveness and the value of the privacy protection obtained from a registration system.

The centralization of data and knowledge about data processing activities in the hands of a single government agency is also
likely to be a greater threat to personal privacy than the diverse
activities being registered. Lillian R. BeVier writes: "In a way,
the proposal for a Privacy Protection Board seems a little like
recommending that the fox, albeit dressed up as a benign and
friendly farmer, guard the chickens."[32] Even in the limited context of personal information held by the government, BeVier
concludes: "It may well be that the very diffusion of data and data
banks within the government, the diversity and decentralization
of data collection and data protection practices within the myriad
federal agencies are not the problem, but the solution."[33] This is
all the more true when applied to disparate data processing
activities in the private sector: government control is not the
answer. European and U.S. systems diverge more widely on this
point than on any other.

DISCUSSION, EDUCATION, AND INDUSTRY PRACTICE. The government already fills important and less dangerous roles in securing
protection for personal information. These roles should be expanded in the future. One such role is facilitating the expanding
debate about privacy protection. Many useful ends are served by
this function. A structured, informed discussion can help inform
lawmakers and regulators in their efforts to craft appropriate
legal protections for privacy. It can educate information users
and suppliers about the privacy implications of their activities,
ways of protecting their privacy, and ways of improving their
information practices so to avoid unnecessarily invading personal
privacy. Finally, the government's activities can support and
encourage voluntary activity by specific information users and
industry associations, particularly in the case of regulated industries.

The federal government certainly has been active already in
this area, particularly through the Information Infrastructure
Task Force, the National Telecommunications and Information
Administration, and the Federal Trade Commission. But other
agencies could play a greater role in focusing attention on these

issues, providing forums for their discussions and highlighting exemplary practices.

MULTINATIONAL NEGOTIATION. Finally, the government must be more concerned with privacy protection across national boundaries and the consistency of national laws. Privacy interests do not end at national borders. The technologies of the Internet and other digital networks and the growth of multinational business activities necessitate greater attention to the interaction of national privacy protections.

The EU directive highlights this issue. Article 25 requires member states to enact laws prohibiting the transfer of personal data to nonmember states that fail to ensure an "adequate level of protection."[34] The directive provides that the adequacy of the protection offered by the transferee country "shall be assessed in the light of all circumstances surrounding a data transfer," including the nature of the data, the purpose and duration of the proposed processing, the "legislative provisions, both general and sectoral" in the transferee country, and the "professional rules which are complied with" in that country.[35] The directive, therefore, reflects a pan-European extension of privacy laws beyond the territories of the nations enacting those laws.

This effort is understandable, particularly in light of the European understanding of privacy as a human right, and necessary if the privacy of European nationals is to be protected effectively in a global information economy. Article 25 is justifiably criticized, however, as an effort to establish European protection for information privacy as a global standard. Because of the difficulty of separating data collected within Europe from data collected elsewhere, the directive effectively requires multinational businesses to conform all of their data processing activities to EU law. Even businesses that do not operate in Europe may run afoul of the directive if they collect, process, or disseminate personal data via multinational networks. The restriction on transborder data flow is also criticized as a potentially protectionist measure, to the extent it creates an incentive for multinational businesses to move their data processing operations into Europe to avoid having to satisfy the "adequate level of protection" standard. This conclusion is strengthened by the directive's provision forbidding member states from restricting the flow of personal data among themselves because of data protection or privacy concerns.[36]

As a result, American businesses with interests in personal data collected, stored, or processed in Europe, and particularly American businesses with operations in Europe, fear that they will be unable to move those data legally—even if they "own" them—to the United States. Commissioner Flaherty writes:

> The European data protectors view the current situation as an excellent opportunity to put pressure on Canada and the United States for improved data protection. They anticipate blocking the movement of personal data from European branches of multinationals to Canadian or American branches, because equivalent data protection does not exist. For various reasons, including nationalistic ones, they are very serious about this. . . .
>
> The American private sector, accustomed as it is to no government regulation for data protection, is especially exercised about the potential impact of the [then-]draft Directive on the data handling activities of American-controlled multinationals and has made predictable approaches for protection to the Department of State and the Office of the International Trade Representative.[37]

The concerns of non-European information users are not misplaced. Although the directive does not take effect until 1998, the British Data Protection Registrar has forbidden, under British law, a proposed sale of a British mailing list to a U.S. direct mail organization.[38] France, acting under French domestic law, has prohibited the French subsidiary of an Italian parent company from transferring data to Italy because Italy did not have an omnibus data protection law.[39] The French Commission nationale de l'informatique et des libertés has required that identifying information be removed from patient records before they could be transferred to Belgium, Switzerland, and the United States.[40]

Discussion is ongoing within Europe and between Europe and the United States about how articles 25 and 26 will be interpreted and enforced. The directive includes reference to "professional rules," and there is current debate over whether a data exporter could meet the "adequate level of protection" standard by contracting with the non-European data importer to comply with standards consonant with European law. Some major multinational companies are involved in negotiations with national data protection authorities over policies and other arrangements for satisfying the requirements of article 25, in the absence of legal requirements in the non-European countries in which those companies also operate to provide an "adequate level of protection."

Many are optimistic that current attempts to satisfy article 25 will not lead to a trade dispute between the EU and the United States. There may still be reason for concern, however, as Sprios Simitis has observed. Because privacy is a fundamental right in European legal culture, data protection "is not a subject you can bargain about."[41] As the effective date of the directive draws near, more effort is necessary to avoid that dispute to ensure meaningful protection for personal information and to guarantee that other important interests are not compromised by the extraterritorial application of European law.

The Role of Multinational Standards

The debate between Europe and the United States over application of the directive suggests that the ultimate goal should be the creation of multinational standards for information privacy. Information today is fundamentally global. The technologies that carry it ignore national borders. Multinational corporations and consortiums of organizations that share data dot the globe. In the case of the Internet, multinational banking networks such as CHIPS and SWIFT, credit and financial services networks such as Visa International, MasterCard International, and American Express, and stock and commodities networks like the Global Futures Exchange and Aurora, it is virtually meaningless to talk of national privacy law. What consumers and service providers alike need are common standards applicable throughout the world. Commonality does not require identical laws but rather legal regimes that, while still reflecting national contexts, are based on shared principles. In the field of copyright, the century-old Berne Convention for the Protection of Literary and Artistic Works establishes the basic principles governing copyright law.[42] The national laws of the 111 countries that adhere to the Berne Convention are consistent, though not identical, on major points. It is illustrative that the United States only acceded to the Berne Convention in 1988, when the pressure to secure broader multinational protection for U.S. works and to use the consensus and moral force reflected in Berne to combat piracy of the U.S. works, compelled the U.S. Congress to amend national copyright law as necessary to adhere to Berne.[43] It is time for a Berne Convention for privacy.

The failure to reach international consensus on basic privacy protections imposes similarly real and increasing costs. The lack of common principles burdens information users, compromises privacy protections for individuals, requires greater national bureaucracies to administer national laws in multinational contexts, and threatens the deployment of new and valued services. For U.S. companies such as Citicorp, the nation's largest bank and operator of the Citicorp Global Information Network in 93 countries, the variety of legal standards with which the network must comply threatens the existence of the network and its ability to offer services such as automated currency conversion.[44] A uniform, multinational standard would be of obvious value; the absence of such a standard will stymie innovative activities by multinational companies. The government, multinational businesses, and privacy scholars should prioritize the development of multinational standards for information privacy.

Conclusion

The proliferation of computers, networks, electronic information services, and digital data has increased concern about privacy in Europe, in the United States, and around the world. How those concerns have been and should be addressed depends on many factors: how privacy is defined; what values privacy is perceived to serve; what values conflict or are affected by the protection of privacy; the societal, legal, and cultural setting in which the issues are raised; and the services, products, and benefits associated with the activities that impinge on personal privacy. In short, while privacy may be characterized as a fundamental human right in Europe and as an amorphous, shifting constitutional right in the United States, the protection of information privacy is always balanced with competing rights and the contours of that protection are shaped by context. As U.S. Supreme Court Justice John Harlan wrote almost thirty years ago: "Our expectations [of privacy], and the risks we assume, are in large part reflections of laws that translate into rules the customs and values of the past and present."[45]

Despite the considerable differences in their legal rights to privacy, Europe and the United State share many, but not all, basic principles undergirding information privacy. For example, both the European data protection directive and the U.S. *Privacy and the National Information Infrastructure: Principles for Providing and Using Personal Information* recognize similar obligations and responsibilities for personal information users.[46] Both the EU directive and the U.S. principles require that individuals be given notice whenever personal information about them is collected and an opportunity to grant or withhold consent for certain uses of personal information. Both extend greater protection to sensitive data. Europe and the United States diverge most sharply on the role of the government in protecting privacy. In Europe, an important principle of information privacy is that the government oversee the data processing activities of private parties and enforce the law when necessary. The United States does not generally recognize this principle, and the nation's constitutional commitment to a government of limited powers, particularly when expression is involved, poses a substantial obstacle to the creation of a government privacy authority. This suggests the most fundamental difference between European and U.S. privacy protection: the extent to which other values restrict the government's role in protecting information privacy. European laws suggest that European citizens fear the invasive activities of private parties more than the involvement of the government; in the United States, the opposite is true.

Meaningful privacy protection in the context of the explosion in digital data and the globalization of networks, markets, and institutions, requires not only national legal protections but also nongovernmental action, such as individual self-help and market-based solutions and intergovernmental action to create a multinational framework to protect information privacy.

In the U.S. context, information subjects and users must continue to develop their own privacy protection through their separate activities, mutual agreements, market-based accommodations, group action, and adherence to voluntary codes of practice. Individual responsibility, not regulation, is the principal and most effective form of privacy protection in most settings.

The law should serve as a gap-filler, facilitating individual action in those situations in which the lack of competition has interfered with private privacy protection. In those situations, the law should only provide limited, basic privacy rights, including requiring notice of why information is being collected, the extent to which it may be put to other uses, whether it will be disseminated to others, how long it will be stored, whether the information must be provided, and, if so, under what authority; providing an opportunity to data suppliers to grant or withhold consent for the information processing activities outlined in the notice; and holding information users accountable for the claims they make in their notices and for the extent to which they respect the consent, or lack of consent, by information suppliers. The purpose of these rights is to facilitate—not interfere with—the development of private mechanisms and individual choice as a means of valuing and protecting privacy.

These rights could be contained in a single law or in a series of sectoral laws, provided that the protection afforded is consistent, deliberate, and specific. This is a particular challenge in light of the current frenzy of attention, although little action, in Washington about privacy. During its two years of work, the 104th Congress faced 980 bills—more than 12 percent of all bills introduced—that included provisions on a wide range of privacy issues. The pressure to "do something" often interferes with the research and thoughtful deliberation necessary to develop effective laws that are consistent with one another and with other important values.

The government should play a circumscribed role, limited primarily to articulating principles for information privacy, enacting laws when necessary to protect the rights outlined above, adjudicating disputes concerning such rights, facilitating discussion, education, and cooperation, and leading multinational negotiations to resolve conflicts among competing national privacy laws. The long-term goal is the promulgation of basic multinational principles on privacy protection to facilitate the activities of information users and the valuable services and products they offer, ensure consistent international privacy protection for personal information, and reduce the cost of administering and complying with inconsistent national legal regimes.

The European Union Directive

DIRECTIVE 95/46/EC OF THE EUROPEAN PARLIAMENT AND OF THE COUNCIL

of 24 October 1995

on the protection of individuals with regard to the processing of personal data and on the free movement of such data

THE EUROPEAN PARLIAMENT AND THE COUNCIL OF THE EUROPEAN UNION

Having regard to the Treaty establishing the European Community, and in particular Article 100a thereof,

Having regard to the proposal from the Commission,[1]

Having regard to the opinion of the Economic and Social Committee,[2]

---

1. OJ *[Official Journal of the European Communities]* No C 277, 5.11.1990, p. 3 and OJ No C 311, 27.11.1992, p. 30.
2. OJ No C 159, 17.6.1991, p 38.

Acting in accordance with the procedure referred to in Article 189b of the Treaty,[3]

(1) Whereas the objectives of the Community, as laid down in the Treaty, as amended by the Treaty on European Union, include creating an ever closer union among the peoples of Europe, fostering closer relations between the States belonging to the Community, ensuring economic and social progress by common action to eliminate the barriers which divide Europe, encouraging the constant improvement of the living conditions of its peoples, preserving and strengthening peace and liberty and promoting democracy on the basis of the fundamental rights recognized in the constitution and laws of the Member States and in the European Convention for the Protection of Human Rights and Fundamental Freedoms;

(2) Whereas data-processing systems are designed to serve man; whereas they must, whatever the nationality or residence of natural persons, respect their fundamental rights and freedoms, notably the right to privacy, and contribute to economic and social progress, trade expansion and the well-being of individuals;

(3) Whereas the establishment and functioning of an internal market in which, in accordance with Article 7a of the Treaty, the free movement of goods, persons, services and capital is ensured require not only that personal data should be able to flow freely from one Member State to another, but also that the fundamental rights of individuals should be safeguarded;

(4) Whereas increasingly frequent recourse is being had in the Community to the processing of personal data in the various spheres of economic and social activity; whereas the progress made in information technology is making the processing and exchange of such data considerably easier;

---

3. Opinion of the European Parliament of 11 March 1992 (OJ No C 94, 13.4.1992, p. 198), confirmed on 2 December 1993 (OJ No C 342, 20.12.1993, p. 30); Council common position of 20 February 1995 (OJ No C 93, 13.4.1995, p. 1) and Decision of the European Parliament of 15 June 1995 (OJ No C 166, 3.7.1995).

(5) Whereas the economic and social integration resulting from the establishment and functioning of the internal market within the meaning of Article 7a of the Treaty will necessarily lead to a substantial increase in cross-border flows of personal data between all those involved in a private or public capacity in economic and social activity in the Member States; whereas the exchange of personal data between undertakings in different Member States is set to increase; whereas the national authorities in the various Member States are being called upon by virtue of Community law to collaborate and exchange personal data so as to be able to perform their duties or carry out tasks on behalf of an authority in another Member State within the context of the area without internal frontiers as constituted by the internal market;

(6) Whereas, furthermore, the increase in scientific and technical cooperation and the coordinated introduction of new telecommunications networks in the Community necessitate and facilitate cross-border flows of personal data;

(7) Whereas the difference in levels of protection of the rights and freedoms of individuals, notably the right to privacy, with regard to the processing of personal data afforded in the Member States may prevent the transmission of such data from the territory of one Member State to that of another Member State; whereas this difference may therefore constitute an obstacle to the pursuit of a number of economic activities at Community level, distort competition and impede authorities in the discharge of their responsibilities under Community law; whereas this difference in levels of protection is due to the existence of a wide variety of national laws, regulations and administrative provisions;

(8) Whereas, in order to remove the obstacles to flows of personal data, the level of protection of the rights and freedoms of individuals with regard to the processing of such data must be equivalent in all Member States; whereas this objective is vital to the internal market but cannot be achieved by the Member States alone, especially in view of the scale of the divergences

which currently exist between the relevant laws in the Member States and the need to coordinate the laws of the Member States so as to ensure that the cross-border flow of personal data is regulated in a consistent manner that is in keeping with the objective of the internal market as provided for in Article 7a of the Treaty; whereas Community action to approximate those laws is therefore needed;

(9) Whereas, given the equivalent protection resulting from the approximation of national laws, the Member States will no longer be able to inhibit the free movement between them of personal data on grounds relating to protection of the rights and freedoms of individuals, and in particular the right to privacy; whereas Member States will be left a margin for manoeuvre, which may, in the context of implementation of the Directive, also be exercised by the business and social partners; whereas Member States will therefore be able to specify in their national law the general conditions governing the lawfulness of data processing; whereas in doing so the Member States shall strive to improve the protection currently provided by their legislation; whereas, within the limits of this margin for manoeuvre and in accordance with Community law, disparities could arise in the implementation of the Directive, and this could have an effect on the movement of data within a Member State as well as within the Community;

(10) Whereas the object of the national laws on the processing of personal data is to protect fundamental rights and freedoms, notably the right to privacy, which is recognized both in Article 8 of the European Convention for the Protection of Human Rights and Fundamental Freedoms and in the general principles of Community law; whereas, for that reason, the approximation of those laws must not result in any lessening of the protection they afford but must, on the contrary, seek to ensure a high level of protection in the Community;

(11) Whereas the principles of the protection of the rights and freedoms of individuals, notably the right to privacy, which are contained in this Directive, give substance to and amplify those

contained in the Council of Europe Convention of 28 January 1981 for the Protection of Individuals with regard to Automatic Processing of Personal Data;

(12) Whereas the protection principles must apply to all processing of personal data by any person whose activities are governed by Community law; whereas there should be excluded the processing of data carried out by a natural person in the exercise of activities which are exclusively personal or domestic, such as correspondence and the holding of records of addresses;

(13) Whereas the activities referred to in Titles V and VI of the Treaty on European Union regarding public safety, defence, State security or the activities of the State in the area of criminal laws fall outside the scope of Community law, without prejudice to the obligations incumbent upon Member States under Article 56(2), Article 57 or Article 100a of the Treaty establishing the European Community; whereas the processing of personal data that is necessary to safeguard the economic well-being of the State does not fall within the scope of this Directive where such processing relates to State security matters;

(14) Whereas, given the importance of the developments under way, in the framework of the information society, of the techniques used to capture, transmit, manipulate, record, store or communicate sound and image data relating to natural persons, this Directive should be applicable to processing involving such data;

(15) Whereas the processing of such data is covered by this Directive only if it is automated or if the data processed are contained or are intended to be contained in a filing system structured according to specific criteria relating to individuals, so as to permit easy access to the personal data in question;

(16) Whereas the processing of sound and image data, such as in cases of video surveillance, does not come within the scope of this Directive if it is carried out for the purposes of public security, defence, national security or in the course of State activities

relating to the area of criminal law or of other activities which do not come within the scope of Community law;

(17) Whereas, as far as the processing of sound and image data carried out for purposes of journalism or the purposes of literary or artistic expression is concerned, in particular in the audiovisual field, the principles of the Directive are to apply in a restricted manner according to the provisions laid down in Article 9;

(18) Whereas, in order to ensure that individuals are not deprived of the protection to which they are entitled under this Directive, any processing of personal data in the Community must be carried out in accordance with the law of one of the Member States; whereas, in this connection, processing carried out under the responsibility of a controller who is established in a Member State should be governed by the law of that State;

(19) Whereas establishment on the territory of a Member State implies the effective and real exercise of activity through stable arrangements; whereas the legal form of such an establishment, whether simply a branch or a subsidiary with a legal personality, is not the determining factor in this respect; whereas, when a single controller is established on the territory of several Member States, particularly by means of subsidiaries, he must ensure, in order to avoid any circumvention of national rules, that each of the establishments fulfils the obligations imposed by the national law applicable to its activities;

(20) Whereas the fact that the processing of data is carried out by a person established in a third country must not stand in the way of the protection of individuals provided for in this Directive; whereas in these cases, the processing should be governed by the law of the Member State in which the means used are located, and there should be guarantees to ensure that the rights and obligations provided for in this Directive are respected in practice;

(21) Whereas this Directive is without prejudice to the rules of territoriality applicable in criminal matters;

(22) Whereas Member States shall more precisely define in the laws they enact or when bringing into force the measures taken under this Directive the general circumstances in which processing is lawful; whereas in particular Article 5, in conjunction with Articles 7 and 8, allows Member States, independently of general rules, to provide for special processing conditions for specific sectors and for the various categories of data covered by Article 8;

(23) Whereas Member States are empowered to ensure the implementation of the protection of individuals both by means of a general law on the protection of individuals as regards the processing of personal data and by sectorial laws such as those relating, for example, to statistical institutes;

(24) Whereas the legislation concerning the protection of legal persons with regard to the processing data which concerns them is not affected by this Directive;

(25) Whereas the principles of protection must be reflected, on the one hand, in the obligations imposed on persons, public authorities, enterprises, agencies or other bodies responsible for processing, in particular regarding data quality, technical security, notification to the supervisory authority, and the circumstances under which processing can be carried out, and, on the other hand, in the right conferred on individuals, the data on whom are the subject of processing, to be informed that processing is taking place, to consult the data, to request corrections and even to object to processing in certain circumstances;

(26) Whereas the principles of protection must apply to any information concerning an identified or identifiable person; whereas, to determine whether a person is identifiable, account should be taken of all the means likely reasonably to be used either by the controller or by any other person to identify the said person; whereas the principles of protection shall not apply to data rendered anonymous in such a way that the data subject is no longer identifiable; whereas codes of conduct within the meaning of Article 27 may be a useful instrument for providing guidance as to the ways in which data may be rendered anonymous

and retained in a form in which identification of the data subject is no longer possible;

(27) Whereas the protection of individuals must apply as much to automatic processing of data as to manual processing; whereas the scope of this protection must not in effect depend on the techniques used, otherwise this would create a serious risk of circumvention; whereas, nonetheless, as regards manual processing, this Directive covers only filing systems, not unstructured files; whereas, in particular, the content of a filing system must be structured according to specific criteria relating to individuals allowing easy access to the personal data; whereas, in line with the definition in Article 2(c), the different criteria for determining the constituents of a structured set of personal data, and the different criteria governing access to such a set, may be laid down by each Member State; whereas files or sets of files as well as their cover pages, which are not structured according to specific criteria, shall under no circumstances fall within the scope of this Directive;

(28) Whereas any processing of personal data must be lawful and fair to the individuals concerned; whereas, in particular, the data must be adequate, relevant and not excessive in relation to the purposes for which they are processed; whereas such purposes must be explicit and legitimate and must be determined at the time of collection of the data; whereas the purposes of processing further to collection shall not be incompatible with the purposes as they were originally specified;

(29) Whereas the further processing of personal data for historical, statistical or scientific purposes is not generally to be considered incompatible with the purposes for which the data have previously been collected provided that Member States furnish suitable safeguards; whereas these safeguards must in particular rule out the use of the data in support of measures or decisions regarding any particular individual;

(30) Whereas, in order to be lawful, the processing of personal data must in addition be carried out with the consent of the data subject or be necessary for the conclusion or performance of a

contract binding on the data subject, or as a legal requirement, or for the performance of a task carried out in the public interest or in the exercise of official authority, or in the legitimate interests of a natural or legal person, provided that the interests or the rights and freedoms of the data subject are not overriding; whereas, in particular, in order to maintain a balance between the interests involved while guaranteeing effective competition, Member States may determine the circumstances in which personal data may be used or disclosed to a third party in the context of the legitimate ordinary business activities of companies and other bodies; whereas Member States may similarly specify the conditions under which personal data may be disclosed to a third party for the purposes of marketing whether carried out commercially or by a charitable organization or by any other association or foundation, of a political nature for example, subject to the provisions allowing a data subject to object to the processing of data regarding him, at no cost and without having to state his reasons;

(31) Whereas the processing of personal data must equally be regarded as lawful where it is carried out in order to protect an interest which is essential for the data subject's life;

(32) Whereas it is for national legislation to determine whether the controller performing a task carried out in the public interest or in the exercise of official authority should be a public administration or another natural or legal person governed by public law, or by private law such as a professional association;

(33) Whereas data which are capable by their nature of infringing fundamental freedoms or privacy should not be processed unless the data subject gives his explicit consent; whereas, however, derogations from this prohibition must be explicitly provided for in respect of specific needs, in particular where the processing of these data is carried out for certain health-related purposes by persons subject to a legal obligation of professional secrecy or in the course of legitimate activities by certain associations or foundations the purpose of which is to permit the exercise of fundamental freedoms;

(34) Whereas Member States must also be authorized, when justified by grounds of important public interest, to derogate from the prohibition on processing sensitive categories of data where important reasons of public interest so justify in areas such as public health and social protection—especially in order to ensure the quality and cost-effectiveness of the procedures used for settling claims for benefits and services in the health insurance system—scientific research and government statistics; whereas it is incumbent on them, however, to provide specific and suitable safeguards so as to protect the fundamental rights and the privacy of individuals;

(35) Whereas, moreover, the processing of personal data by official authorities for achieving aims, laid down in constitutional law or international public law, of officially recognized religious associations is carried out on important grounds of public interest;

(36) Whereas where, in the course of electoral activities, the operation of the democratic system requires in certain Member States that political parties compile data on people's political opinion, the processing of such data may be permitted for reasons of important public interest, provided that appropriate safeguards are established;

(37) Whereas the processing of personal data for purposes of journalism or for purposes of literary or artistic expression, in particular in the audiovisual field, should qualify for exemption from the requirements of certain provisions of this Directive in so far as this is necessary to reconcile the fundamental rights of individuals with freedom of information and notably the right to receive and impart information, as guaranteed in particular in Article 10 of the European Convention for the Protection of Human Rights and Fundamental Freedoms; whereas Member States should therefore lay down exemptions and derogations necessary for the purpose of balance between fundamental rights as regards general measures on the legitimacy of data processing, measures on the transfer of data to third countries and the power of the supervisory authority; whereas this should not, however,

lead Member States to lay down exemptions from the measures to ensure security of processing; whereas at least the supervisory authority responsible for this sector should also be provided with certain ex-post powers, e.g. to publish a regular report or to refer matters to the judicial authorities;

(38) Whereas, if the processing of data is to be fair, the data subject must be in a position to learn of the existence of a processing operation and, where data are collected from him, must be given accurate and full information, bearing in mind the circumstances of the collection;

(39) Whereas certain processing operations involve data which the controller has not collected directly from the data subject; whereas, furthermore, data can be legitimately disclosed to a third party, even if the disclosure was not anticipated at the time the data were collected from the data subject; whereas, in all these cases, the data subject should be informed when the data are recorded or at the latest when the data are first disclosed to a third party;

(40) Whereas, however, it is not necessary to impose this obligation if the data subject already has the information; whereas, moreover, there will be no such obligation if the recording or disclosure are expressly provided for by law or if the provision of information to the data subject proves impossible or would involve disproportionate efforts, which could be the case where processing is for historical, statistical or scientific purposes; whereas, in this regard, the number of data subjects, the age of the data, and any compensatory measures adopted may be taken into consideration;

(41) Whereas any person must be able to exercise the right of access to data relating to him which are being processed, in order to verify in particular the accuracy of the data and the lawfulness of the processing; whereas, for the same reasons, every data subject must also have the right to know the logic involved in the automatic processing of data concerning him, at least in the case of the automated decisions referred to in Article 15(1); whereas this right must not adversely affect trade secrets or intellectual

property and in particular the copyright protecting the software; whereas these considerations must not, however, result in the data subject being refused all information;

(42) Whereas Member States may, in the interest of the data subject or so as to protect the rights and freedoms of others, restrict rights of access and information; whereas they may, for example, specify that access to medical data may be obtained only through a health professional;

(43) Whereas restrictions on the rights of access and information and on certain obligations of the controller may similarly be imposed by Member States in so far as they are necessary to safeguard, for example, national security, defence, public safety, or important economic or financial interests of a Member State or the Union, as well as criminal investigations and prosecutions and action in respect of breaches of ethics in the regulated professions; whereas the list of exceptions and limitations should include the tasks of monitoring, inspection or regulation necessary in the three last-mentioned areas concerning public security, economic or financial interests and crime prevention; whereas the listing of tasks in these three areas does not affect the legitimacy of exceptions or restrictions for reasons of State security or defence;

(44) Whereas Member States may also be led, by virtue of the provisions of Community law, to derogate from the provisions of this Directive concerning the right of access, the obligation to inform individuals, and the quality of data, in order to secure certain of the purposes referred to above;

(45) Whereas, in cases where data might lawfully be processed on grounds of public interest, official authority or the legitimate interests of a natural or legal person, any data subject should nevertheless be entitled, on legitimate and compelling grounds relating to his particular situation, to object to the processing of any data relating to himself; whereas Member States may nevertheless lay down national provisions to the contrary;

(46) Whereas the protection of the rights and freedoms of data subjects with regard to the processing of personal data requires that appropriate technical and organizational measures be taken, both at the time of the design of the processing system and at the time of the processing itself, particularly in order to maintain security and thereby to prevent any unauthorized processing; whereas it is incumbent on the Member States to ensure that controllers comply with these measures; whereas these measures must ensure an appropriate level of security, taking into account the state of the art and the costs of their implementation in relation to the risks inherent in the processing and the nature of the data to be protected;

(47) Whereas where a message containing personal data is transmitted by means of a telecommunications or electronic mail service, the sole purpose of which is the transmission of such messages, the controller in respect of the personal data contained in the message will normally be considered to be the person from whom the message originates, rather than the person offering the transmission services; whereas, nevertheless, those offering such services will normally be considered controllers in respect of the processing of the additional personal data necessary for the operation of the service;

(48) Whereas the procedures for notifying the supervisory authority are designed to ensure disclosure of the purposes and main features of any processing operation for the purpose of verification that the operation is in accordance with the national measures taken under this Directive;

(49) Whereas, in order to avoid unsuitable administrative formalities, exemptions from the obligation to notify and simplification of the notification required may be provided for by Member States in cases where processing is unlikely adversely to affect the rights and freedoms of data subjects, provided that it is in accordance with a measure taken by a Member State specifying its limits; whereas exemption or simplification may similarly be provided for by Member States where a person appointed by

the controller ensures that the processing carried out is not likely adversely to affect the rights and freedoms of data subjects; whereas such a data protection official, whether or not an employee of the controller, must be in a position to exercise his functions in complete independence;

(50) Whereas exemption or simplification could be provided for in cases of processing operations whose sole purpose is the keeping of a register intended, according to national law, to provide information to the public and open to consultation by the public or by any person demonstrating a legitimate interest;

(51) Whereas, nevertheless, simplification or exemption from the obligation to notify shall not release the controller from any of the other obligations resulting from this Directive;

(52) Whereas, in this context, ex post facto verification by the competent authorities must in general be considered a sufficient measure;

(53) Whereas, however, certain processing operations are likely to pose specific risks to the rights and freedoms of data subjects by virtue of their nature, their scope or their purposes, such as that of excluding individuals from a right, benefit or a contract, or by virtue of the specific use of new technologies; whereas it is for Member States, if they so wish, to specify such risks in their legislation;

(54) Whereas with regard to all the processing undertaken in society, the amount posing such specific risks should be very limited; whereas Member States must provide that the supervisory authority, or the data protection official in cooperation with the authority, check such processing prior to it being carried out; whereas following this prior check, the supervisory authority may, according to its national law, give an opinion or an authorization regarding the processing; whereas such checking may equally take place in the course of the preparation either of a measure of the national parliament or of a measure based on such a legislative measure, which defines the nature of the processing and lays down appropriate safeguards;

(55) Whereas, if the controller fails to respect the rights of data subjects, national legislation must provide for a judicial remedy; whereas any damage which a person may suffer as a result of unlawful processing must be compensated for by the controller, who may be exempted from liability if he proves that he is not responsible for the damage, in particular in cases where he establishes fault on the part of the data subject or in case of force majeure; whereas sanctions must be imposed on any person, whether governed by private of public law, who fails to comply with the national measures taken under this Directive;

(56) Whereas cross-border flows of personal data are necessary to the expansion of international trade; whereas the protection of individuals, guaranteed in the Community by this Directive does not stand in the way of transfers of personal data to third countries which ensure an adequate level of protection; whereas the adequacy of the level of protection afforded by a third country must be assessed in the light of all the circumstances surrounding the transfer operation or set of transfer operations;

(57) Whereas, on the other hand, the transfer of personal data to a third country which does not ensure an adequate level of protection must be prohibited;

(58) Whereas provisions should be made for exemptions from this prohibition in certain circumstances where the data subject has given his consent, where the transfer is necessary in relation to a contract or a legal claim, where protection of an important public interest so requires, for example in cases of international transfers of data between tax or customs administrations or between services competent for social security matters, or where the transfer is made from a register established by law and intended for consultation by the public or persons having a legitimate interest; whereas in this case such a transfer should not involve the entirety of the data or entire categories of the data contained in the register and, when the register is intended for consultation by persons having a legitimate interest, the transfer should be made only at the request of those persons or if they are to be the recipients;

(59) Whereas particular measures may be taken to compensate for the lack of protection in a third country in cases where the controller offers appropriate safeguards; whereas, moreover, provision must be made for procedures for negotiations between the Community and such third countries;

(60) Whereas, in any event, transfers to third countries may be effected only in full compliance with the provisions adopted by the Member States pursuant to this Directive, and in particular Article 8 thereof;

(61) Whereas Member States and the Commission, in their respective spheres of competence, must encourage the trade associations and other representative organizations concerned to draw up codes of conduct so as to facilitate the application of this Directive, taking account of the specific characteristics of the processing carried out in certain sectors, and respecting the national provisions adopted for its implementation;

(62) Whereas the establishment in Member States of supervisory authorities, exercising their functions with complete independence, is an essential component of the protection of individuals with regard to the processing of personal data;

(63) Whereas such authorities must have the necessary means to perform their duties, including powers of investigation and intervention, particularly in cases of complaints from individuals, and powers to engage in legal proceedings; whereas such authorities must help to ensure transparency of processing in the Member States within whose jurisdiction they fall;

(64) Whereas the authorities in the different Member States will need to assist one another in performing their duties so as to ensure that the rules of protection are properly respected throughout the European Union;

(65) Whereas, at Community level, a Working Party on the Protection of Individuals with regard to the Processing of Personal Data must be set up and be completely independent in the performance of its functions; whereas, having regard to its specific nature, it must advise the Commission and, in particular,

contribute to the uniform application of the national rules adopted pursuant to this Directive;

(66) Whereas, with regard to the transfer of data to third countries, the application of this Directive calls for the conferment of powers of implementation on the Commission and the establishment of a procedure as laid down in Council Decision 87/373/EEC;[4]

(67) Whereas an agreement on a modus vivendi between the European Parliament, the Council and the Commission concerning the implementing measures for acts adopted in accordance with the procedure laid down in Article 189b of the EC Treaty was reached on 20 December 1994;

(68) Whereas the principles set out in this Directive regarding the protection of the rights and freedoms of individuals, notably their right to privacy, with regard to the processing of personal data may be supplemented or clarified, in particular as far as certain sectors are concerned, by specific rules based on those principles;

(69) Whereas Member States should be allowed a period of not more than three years from the entry into force of the national measures transposing this Directive in which to apply such new national rules progressively to all processing operations already under way; whereas, in order to facilitate their cost-effective implementation, a further period expiring 12 years after the date on which this Directive is adopted will be allowed to Member States to ensure the conformity of existing manual filing systems with certain of the Directive's provisions; whereas, where data contained in such filing systems are manually processed during this extended transition period, those systems must be brought into conformity with these provisions at the time of such processing;

(70) Whereas it is not necessary for the data subject to give his consent again so as to allow the controller to continue to

---

4. OJ No L 197, 18. 7. 1987, p. 33.

process, after the national provisions taken pursuant to this Directive enter into force, any sensitive data necessary for the performance of a contract concluded on the basis of free and informed consent before the entry into force of these provisions;

(71) Whereas this Directive does not stand in the way of a Member State's regulating marketing activities aimed at consumers residing in territory in so far as such regulation does not concern the protection of individuals with regard to the processing of personal data;

(72) Whereas this Directive allows the principle of public access to official documents to be taken into account when implementing the principles set out in this Directive,

HAVE ADOPTED THIS DIRECTIVE:

CHAPTER I
GENERAL PROVISIONS

Article 1—Object of the Directive

1. In accordance with this Directive, Member States shall protect the fundamental rights and freedoms of natural persons, and in particular their right to privacy with respect to the processing of personal data.

2. Member States shall neither restrict nor prohibit the free flow of personal data between Member States for reasons connected with the protection afforded under paragraph 1.

Article 2—Definitions

For the purposes of this Directive:

(a) "personal data" shall mean any information relating to an identified or identifiable natural person ("data subject"); an identifiable person is one who can be identified, directly or indirectly, in particular by reference to an identification number or to one or more factors specific to his physical, physiological, mental, economic, cultural or social identity;

(b) "processing of personal data" ("processing") shall mean any operation or set of operations which is performed upon personal data, whether or not by automatic means, such as collection, recording, organization, storage, adaptation or alteration, retrieval, consultation, use, disclosure by transmission, dissemination or otherwise making available, alignment or combination, blocking, erasure or destruction;

(c) "personal data filing system" ("filing system") shall mean any structured set of personal data which are accessible according to specific criteria, whether centralized, decentralized or dispersed on a functional or geographical basis;

(d) "controller" shall mean the natural or legal person, public authority, agency or any other body which alone or jointly with others determines the purposes and means of the processing of personal data; where the purposes and means of processing are determined by national or Community laws or regulations, the controller or the specific criteria for his nomination may be designated by national or Community law;

(e) "processor" shall mean a natural or legal person, public authority, agency or any other body which processes personal data on behalf of the controller;

(f) "third party" shall mean any natural or legal person, public authority, agency or any other body other than the data subject, the controller, the processor and the persons who, under the direct authority of the controller or the processor, are authorized to process the data;

(g) "recipient" shall mean a natural or legal person, public authority, agency or any other body to whom data are disclosed, whether a third party or not; however, authorities which may receive data in the framework of a particular inquiry shall not be regarded as recipients;

(h) "the data subject's consent" shall mean any freely given specific and informed indication of his wishes by which the data subject signifies his agreement to personal data relating to him being processed.

Article 3—Scope

1. This Directive shall apply to the processing of personal data wholly or partly by automatic means, and to the processing otherwise than by automatic means of personal data which form part of a filing system or are intended to form part of a filing system.

2. This Directive shall not apply to the processing of personal data:

• in the course of an activity which falls outside the scope of Community law, such as those provided for by Titles V and VI of the Treaty on European Union and in any case to processing operations concerning public security, defence, State security (including the economic well-being of the State when the processing operation relates to State security matters) and the activities of the State in areas of criminal law,

• by a natural person in the course of a purely personal or household activity.

Article 4—National law applicable

1. Each Member State shall apply the national provisions it adopts pursuant to this Directive to the processing of personal data where:

(a) the processing is carried out in the context of the activities of an establishment of the controller on the territory of the Member State; when the same controller is established on the territory of several Member States, he must take the necessary measures to ensure that each of these establishments complies with the obligations laid down by the national law applicable;

(b) the controller is not established on the Member State's territory, but in a place where its national law applies by virtue of international public law;

(c) the controller is not established on Community territory and, for purposes of processing personal data, makes use of equipment, automated or otherwise, situated on the territory of the said Member State, unless such equipment is used only for purposes of transit through the territory of the Community.

2. In the circumstances referred to in paragraph 1(c), the controller must designate a representative established in the territory of that Member State, without prejudice to legal actions which could be initiated against the controller himself.

CHAPTER II
GENERAL RULES ON THE LAWFULNESS OF THE PROCESSING OF PERSONAL DATA

Article 5

Member States shall, within the limits of the provisions of this Chapter, determine more precisely the conditions under which the processing of personal data is lawful.

SECTION I
PRINCIPLES RELATING TO DATA QUALITY

Article 6

1. Member States shall provide that personal data must be:

(a) processed fairly and lawfully;

(b) collected for specified, explicit and legitimate purposes and not further processed in a way incompatible with those purposes. Further processing of data for historical, statistical or scientific purposes shall not be considered as incompatible provided that Member States provide appropriate safeguards;

(c) adequate, relevant and not excessive in relation to the purposes for which they are collected and/or further processed;

(d) accurate and, where necessary, kept up to date; every reasonable step must be taken to ensure that data which are inaccurate or incomplete, having regard to the purposes for which they were collected or for which they are further processed, are erased or rectified;

(e) kept in a form which permits identification of data subjects for no longer than is necessary for the purposes for which the data were collected or for which they are further processed. Member States shall lay down appropriate safeguards for personal data stored for longer periods for historical, statistical or scientific use.

2. It shall be for the controller to ensure that paragraph 1 is complied with.

SECTION II
CRITERIA FOR MAKING DATA PROCESSING LEGITIMATE

Article 7

Member States shall provide that personal data may be processed only if:

(a) the data subject has unambiguously given his consent; or

(b) processing is necessary for the performance of a contract to which the data subject is party or in order to take steps at the request of the data subject prior to entering into a contract; or

(c) processing is necessary for compliance with a legal obligation to which the controller is subject; or

(d) processing is necessary in order to protect the vital interests of the data subject; or

(e) processing is necessary for the performance of a task carried out in the public interest or in the exercise of official authority vested in the controller or in a third party to whom the data are disclosed; or

(f) processing is necessary for the purposes of the legitimate interests pursued by the controller or by the third party or parties to whom the data are disclosed, except where such interests are overridden by the interests for fundamental rights and freedoms of the data subject which require protection under Article 1(1).

SECTION III
SPECIAL CATEGORIES OF PROCESSING

Article 8—The processing of special categories of data

1. Member States shall prohibit the processing of personal data revealing racial or ethnic origin, political opinions, religious or philosophical beliefs, trade-union membership, and the processing of data concerning health or sex life.

2. Paragraph 1 shall not apply where:

(a) the data subject has given his explicit consent to the processing of those data, except where the laws of the Member State provide that the prohibition referred to in paragraph 1 may not be lifted by the data subject's giving his consent; or

(b) processing is necessary for the purposes of carrying out the obligations and specific rights of the controller in the field of employment law in so far as it is authorized by national law providing for adequate safeguards; or

(c) processing is necessary to protect the vital interests of the data subject or of another person where the data subject is physically or legally incapable of giving his consent; or

(d) processing is carried out in the course of its legitimate activities with appropriate guarantees by a foundation, association or any other non-profit-seeking body with a political, philosophical, religious or trade-union aim and on condition that the processing relates solely to the members of the body or to persons who have regular contact with it in connection with its purposes and that the data are not disclosed to a third party without the consent of the data subjects; or

(e) the processing relates to data which are manifestly made public by the data subject or is necessary for the establishment, exercise or defence of legal claims.

3. Paragraph 1 shall not apply where processing of the data is required for the purposes of preventive medicine, medical diagnosis, the provision of care or treatment or the management of

health-care services, and where those data are processed by a health professional subject under national law or rules established by national competent bodies to the obligation of professional secrecy or by another person also subject to an equivalent obligation of secrecy.

4. Subject to the provision of suitable safeguards, Member States may, for reasons of substantial public interest, lay down exemptions in addition to those laid down in paragraph 2 either by national law or by decision of the supervisory authority.

5. Processing of data relating to offences, criminal convictions or security measures may be carried out only under the control of official authority, or if suitable specific safeguards are provided under national law, subject to derogations which may be granted by the Member State under national provisions providing suitable specific safeguards. However, a complete register of criminal convictions may be kept only under the control of official authority.

Member States may provide that data relating to administrative sanctions or judgements in civil cases shall also be processed under the control of official authority.

6. Derogations from paragraph 1 provided for in paragraphs 4 and 5 shall be notified to the Commission.

7. Member States shall determine the conditions under which a national identification number or any other identifier of general application may be processed.

Article 9—Processing of personal data and freedom of expression

Member States shall provide for exemptions or derogations from the provisions of this Chapter, Chapter IV and Chapter VI for the processing of personal data carried out solely for journalistic purposes or the purpose of artistic or literary expression only if they are necessary to reconcile the right to privacy with the rules governing freedom of expression.

SECTION IV
INFORMATION TO BE GIVEN TO THE DATA SUBJECT

Article 10—Information in cases of collection of data from the data subject

Member States shall provide that the controller or his representative must provide a data subject from whom data relating to himself are collected with at least the following information, except where he already has it:

(a) the identity of the controller and of his representative, if any;

(b) the purposes of the processing for which the data are intended;

(c) any further information such as

- the recipients or categories of recipients of the data,
- whether replies to the questions are obligatory or voluntary, as well as the possible consequences of failure to reply,
- the existence of the right of access to and the right to rectify the data concerning him

in so far as such further information is necessary, having regard to the specific circumstances in which the data are collected, to guarantee fair processing in respect of the data subject.

Article 11—Information where the data have not been obtained from the data subject

1. Where the data have not been obtained from the data subject, Member States shall provide that the controller or his representative must at the time of undertaking the recording of personal data or if a disclosure to a third party is envisaged, no later than the time when the data are first disclosed provide the data subject with at least the following information, except where he already has it:

(a) the identity of the controller and of his representative, if any;

(b) the purposes of the processing;

(c) any further information such as

• the categories of data concerned,
• the recipients or categories of recipients,
• the existence of the right of access to and the right to rectify the data concerning him

in so far as such further information is necessary, having regard to the specific circumstances in which the data are processed, to guarantee fair processing in respect of the data subject.

2. Paragraph 1 shall not apply where, in particular for processing for statistical purposes or for the purposes of historical or scientific research, the provision of such information proves impossible or would involve a disproportionate effort or if recording or disclosure is expressly laid down by law. In these cases Member States shall provide appropriate safeguards.

SECTION V
THE DATA SUBJECT'S RIGHT OF ACCESS TO DATA

Article 12—Right of access

Member States shall guarantee every data right to obtain from the controller:

(a) without constraint at reasonable intervals and without excessive delay or expense:

• confirmation as to whether or not data relating to him are being processed and information at least as to the purposes of the processing, the categories of data concerned, and the recipients or categories of recipients to whom the data are disclosed,
• communication to him in an intelligible form of the data undergoing processing and of any available information as to their source,
• knowledge of the logic involved in any automatic processing of data concerning him at least in the case of the automated decisions referred to in Article 15(1);

(b) as appropriate the rectification, erasure or blocking of data the processing of which does not comply with the provisions of this Directive, in particular because of the incomplete or inaccurate nature of the data;

(c) notification to third parties to whom the data have been disclosed of any rectification, erasure or blocking carried out in compliance with (b), unless this proves impossible or involves a disproportionate effort.

SECTION VI
EXEMPTIONS AND RESTRICTIONS

Article 13

1. Member States may adopt legislative measures to restrict the scope of the obligations and rights provided for in Articles 6(1), 10, 11(1), 12 and 21 when such a restriction constitutes necessary measures to safeguard:

(a) national security;

(b) defence;

(c) public security;

(d) the prevention, investigation, detection and prosecution of criminal offences, or of breaches of ethics for regulated professions;

(e) an important economic or financial interest of a Member State or of the European Union, including monetary, budgetary and taxation matters;

(f) a monitoring, inspection or regulatory function connected, even occasionally, with the exercise of official authority in cases referred to in (c), (d) and (e);

(g) the protection of the data subject or of the rights and freedoms of others.

2. Subject to adequate legal safeguards, in particular that the data are not used for taking measures or decisions regarding any

particular individual, Member States may, where there is clearly no risk of breaching the privacy of the data subject, restrict by a legislative measure the rights provided for in Article 12 when data are processed solely for purposes of scientific research or are kept in personal form for a period which does not exceed the period necessary for the sole purpose of creating statistics.

SECTION VII
THE DATA SUBJECT'S RIGHT TO OBJECT

Article 14—The data subject's right to object

Member States shall grant the data subject the right:

(a) at least in the cases referred to in Article 7(e) and (f), to object at any time on compelling legitimate grounds relating to his particular situation to the processing of data relating to him, save where otherwise provided by national legislation. Where there is a justified objection, the processing instigated by the controller may no longer involve those data;

(b) to object, on request and free of charge, to the processing of personal data relating to him which the controller anticipates being processed for the purposes of direct marketing, or to be informed before personal data are disclosed for the first time to third parties or used on their behalf for the purposes of direct marketing, and to be expressly offered the right to object free of charge to such disclosures or uses.

Member States shall take the necessary measures to ensure that data subjects are aware of the existence of the right referred to in the first subparagraph of (b).

Article 15—Automated individual decisions

1. Member States shall grant the right to every person not to be subject to a decision which produces legal effects concerning him or significantly affects him and which is based solely on automated processing of data intended to evaluate certain per-

sonal aspects relating to him, such as his performance at work, creditworthiness, reliability, conduct, etc.

2. Subject to the other Articles of this Directive, Member States shall provide that a person may be subjected to a decision of the kind referred to in paragraph 1 if that decision:

(a) is taken in the course of the entering into or performance of a contract, provided the request for the entering into or the performance of the contract, lodged by the data subject, has been satisfied or that there are suitable measures to safeguard his legitimate interests, such as arrangements allowing him to put his point of view; or

(b) is authorized by a law which also lays down measures to safeguard the data subject's legitimate interests.

SECTION VIII
CONFIDENTIALITY AND SECURITY OF PROCESSING

Article 16—Confidentiality of processing

Any person acting under the authority of the controller or of the processor, including the processor himself, who has access to personal data must not process them except on instructions from the controller, unless he is required to do so by law.

Article 17—Security of processing

1. Member States shall provide that the controller must implement appropriate technical and organizational measures to protect personal data against accidental or unlawful destruction or accidental loss, alteration, unauthorized disclosure or access, in particular where the processing involves the transmission of data over a network, and against all other unlawful forms of processing.

Having regard to the state of the art and the cost of their implementation, such measures shall ensure a level of security appropriate to the risks represented by the processing and the nature of the data to be protected.

2. The Member States shall provide that the controller must, where processing is carried out on his behalf, choose a processor providing sufficient guarantees in respect of the technical security measures and organizational measures governing the processing to be carried out, and must ensure compliance with those measures.

3. The carrying out of processing by way of a processor must be governed by a contract or legal act binding the processor to the controller and stipulating in particular that:

• the processor shall act only on instructions from the controller,

• the obligations set out in paragraph 1, as defined by the law of the Member State in which the processor is established, shall also be incumbent on the processor.

4. For the purposes of keeping proof, the parts of the contract or the legal act relating to data protection and the requirements relating to the measures referred to in paragraph 1 shall be in writing or in another equivalent form.

SECTION IX
NOTIFICATION

Article 18—Obligation to notify the supervisory authority

1. Member States shall provide that the controller or his representative, if any, must notify the supervisory authority referred to in Article 28 before carrying out any wholly or partly automatic processing operation or set of such operations intended to serve a single purpose or several related purposes.

2. Member States may provide for the simplification of or exemption from notification only in the following cases and under the following conditions:

• where, for categories of processing operations which are unlikely, taking account of the data to be processed, to affect adversely the rights and freedoms of data subjects, they specify the purposes of the processing, the data or categories of data undergoing processing, the category or categories of data subject, the recipients or categories of recipient to whom the data are to be disclosed and the length of time the data are to be stored, and/or

• where the controller, in compliance with the national law which governs him, appoints a personal data protection official, responsible in particular:

• for ensuring in an independent manner the internal application of the national provisions taken pursuant to this Directive

• for keeping the register of processing operations carried out by the controller, containing the items of information referred to in Article 21(2),

thereby ensuring that the rights and freedoms of the data subjects are unlikely to be adversely affected by the processing operations.

3. Member States may provide that paragraph 1 does not apply to processing whose sole purpose is the keeping of a register which according to laws or regulations is intended to provide information to the public and which is open to consultation either by the public in general or by any person demonstrating a legitimate interest.

4. Member States may provide for an exemption from the obligation to notify or a simplification of the notification in the case of processing operations referred to in Article 8(2)(d).

5. Member States may stipulate that certain or all non-automatic processing operations involving personal data shall be notified, or provide for these processing operations to be subject to simplified notification.

Article 19—Contents of notification

1. Member States shall specify the information to be given in the notification. It shall include at least:

(a) the name and address of the controller and of his representative, if any;

(b) the purpose or purposes of the processing;

(c) a description of the category or categories of data subject and of the data or categories of data relating to them;

(d) the recipients or categories of recipient to whom the data might be disclosed;

(e) proposed transfers of data to third countries;

(f) a general description allowing a preliminary assessment to be made of the appropriateness of the measures taken pursuant to Article 17 to ensure security of processing.

2. Member States shall specify the procedures under which any change affecting the information referred to in paragraph 1 must be notified to the supervisory authority.

Article 20—Prior checking

1. Member States shall determine the processing operations likely to present specific risks to the rights and freedoms of data subjects and shall check that these processing operations are examined prior to the start thereof.

2. Such prior checks shall be carried out by the supervisory authority following receipt of a notification from the controller or by the data protection official, who, in cases of doubt, must consult the supervisory authority.

3. Member States may also carry out such checks in the context of preparation either of a measure of the national parliament or of a measure based on such a legislative measure, which define the nature of the processing and lay down appropriate safeguards.

Article 21—Publicizing of processing operations

1. Member States shall take measures to ensure that processing operations are publicized.

2. Member States shall provide that a register of processing operations notified in accordance with Article 18 shall be kept by the supervisory authority.

The register shall contain at least the information listed in Article 19(1)(a) to (e).

The register may be inspected by any person.

3. Member States shall provide, in relation to processing operations not subject to notification, that controllers or another body appointed by the Member States make available at least the information referred to in Article 19(1)(a) to (e) in an appropriate form to any person on request.

Member States may provide that this provision does not apply to processing whose sole purpose is the keeping of a register which according to laws or regulations is intended to provide information to the public and which is open to consultation either by the public in general or by any person who can provide proof of a legitimate interest.

CHAPTER III
JUDICIAL REMEDIES, LIABILITY AND SANCTIONS

Article 22—Remedies

Without prejudice to any administrative remedy for which provision may be made, inter alia before the supervisory authority referred to in Article 28, prior to referral to the judicial authority, Member States shall provide for the right of every person to a judicial remedy for any breach of the rights guaranteed him by the national law applicable to the processing in question.

Article 23—Liability

1. Member States shall provide that any person who has suffered damage as a result of an unlawful processing operation or of any act incompatible with the national provisions adopted pursuant to this Directive is entitled to receive compensation from the controller for the damage suffered.

2. The controller may be exempted from this liability, in whole or in part, if he proves that he is not responsible for the event giving rise to the damage.

Article 24—Sanctions

The Member States shall adopt suitable measures to ensure the full implementation of the provisions of this Directive and shall in particular lay down the sanctions to be imposed in case of infringement of the provisions adopted pursuant to this Directive.

CHAPTER IV
TRANSFER OF PERSONAL DATA TO THIRD COUNTRIES

Article 25—Principles

1. The Member States shall provide that the transfer to a third country of personal data which are undergoing processing or are intended for processing after transfer may take place only if, without prejudice to compliance with the national provisions adopted pursuant to the other provisions of this Directive, the third country in question ensures an adequate level of protection.

2. The adequacy of the level of protection afforded by a third country shall be assessed in the light of all the circumstances surrounding a data transfer operation or set of data transfer operations; particular consideration shall be given to the nature of the data, the purpose and duration of the proposed processing operation or operations, the country of origin and country of final destination, the rules of law, both general and sectoral, in force in the third country in question and the professional rules and security measures which are complied with in that country.

3. The Member States and the Commission shall inform each other of cases where they consider that a third country does not ensure an adequate level of protection within the meaning of paragraph 2.

4. Where the Commission finds, under the procedure provided for in Article 31(2), that a third country does not ensure an adequate level of protection within the meaning of paragraph 2 of this Article, Member States shall take the measures necessary to prevent any transfer of data of the same type to the third country in question.

5. At the appropriate time, the Commission shall enter into negotiations with a view to remedying the situation resulting from the finding made pursuant to paragraph 4.

6. The Commission may find, in accordance with the procedure referred to in Article 31(2), that a third country ensures an adequate level of protection within the meaning of paragraph 2 of this Article, by reason of its domestic law or of the international commitments it has entered into, particularly upon conclusion of the negotiations referred to in paragraph 5, for the protection of the private lives and basic freedoms and rights of individuals.

Member States shall take the measures necessary to comply with the Commission's decision.

Article 26—Derogations

1. By way of derogation from Article 25 and save where otherwise provided by domestic law governing particular cases, Member States shall provide that a transfer or a set of transfers of personal data to a third country which does not ensure an adequate level of protection within the meaning of Article 25(2) may take place on condition that:

(a) the data subject has given his consent unambiguously to the proposed transfer; or

(b) the transfer is necessary for the performance of a contract between the data subject and the controller or the implementation of precontractual measures taken in response to the data subject's request; or

(c) the transfer is necessary for the conclusion or performance of a contract concluded in the interest of the data subject between the controller and a third party; or

(d) the transfer is necessary or legally required on important public interest grounds, or for the establishment, exercise or defence of legal claims; or

(e) the transfer is necessary in order to protect the vital interests of the data subject; or

(f) the transfer is made from a register which according to laws or regulations is intended to provide information to the public and which is open to consultation either by the public in general or by any person who can demonstrate legitimate interest, to the extent that the conditions laid down in law for consultation are fulfilled in the particular case.

2. Without prejudice to paragraph 1, a Member State may authorize a transfer or a set of transfers of personal data to a third country which does not ensure an adequate level of protection within the meaning of Article 25(2), where the controller adduces adequate safeguards with respect to the protection of the privacy and fundamental rights and freedoms of individuals and as regards the exercise of the corresponding rights; such safeguards may in particular result from appropriate contractual clauses.

3. The Member State shall inform the Commission and the other Member States of the authorizations it grants pursuant to paragraph 2.

If a Member State or the Commission objects on justified grounds involving the protection of the privacy and fundamental rights and freedoms of individuals, the Commission shall take appropriate measures in accordance with the procedure laid down in Article 31(2).

Member States shall take the measures necessary to comply with the Commission's decision.

4. Where the Commission decides, in accordance with the procedure referred to in Article 31(2), that certain standard contractual clauses offer sufficient safeguards as required by paragraph 2, Member States shall take the necessary measures to comply with the Commission's decision.

CHAPTER V
CODES OF CONDUCT

Article 27

1. The Member States and the Commission shall encourage the drawing up of codes of conduct intended to contribute to the proper implementation of the national provisions adopted by the Member States pursuant to this Directive, taking account of the specific features of the various sectors.

2. Member States shall make provision for trade associations and other bodies representing other categories of controllers which have drawn up draft national codes or which have the intention of amending or extending existing national codes to be able to submit them to the opinion of the national authority.

Member States shall make provision for this authority to ascertain, among other things, whether the drafts submitted to it are in accordance with the national provisions adopted pursuant to this Directive. If it sees fit, the authority shall seek the views of data subjects or their representatives.

3. Draft Community codes, and amendments or extensions to existing Community codes, may be submitted to the Working Party referred to in Article 29. This Working Party shall determine, among other things, whether the drafts submitted to it are in accordance with the national provisions adopted pursuant to this Directive. If it sees fit, the authority shall seek the views of data subjects or their representatives. The Commission may ensure appropriate publicity for the codes which have been approved by the Working Party.

CHAPTER VI
SUPERVISORY AUTHORITY AND WORKING PARTY ON
THE PROTECTION OF INDIVIDUALS WITH REGARD TO
THE PROCESSING OF PERSONAL DATA

Article 28—Supervisory authority

1. Each Member State shall provide that one or more public authorities are responsible for monitoring the application within its territory of the provisions adopted by the Member States pursuant to this Directive.

These authorities shall act with complete independence in exercising the functions entrusted to them.

2. Each Member State shall provide that the supervisory authorities are consulted when drawing up administrative measures or regulations relating to the protection of individuals' rights and freedoms with regard to the processing of personal data.

3. Each authority shall in particular be endowed with:

• investigative powers, such as powers of access to data forming the subject-matter of processing operations and powers to collect all the information necessary for the performance of its supervisory duties,
• effective powers of intervention, such as, for example, that of delivering opinions before processing operations are carried out, in accordance with Article 20, and ensuring appropriate publication of such opinions, of ordering the blocking, erasure or destruction of data, of imposing a temporary or definitive ban on processing, of warning or admonishing the controller, or that of referring the matter to national parliaments or other political Institutions,
• the power to engage in legal proceedings where the national provisions adopted pursuant to this Directive have been violated or to bring these violations to the attention of the judicial authorities.

Decisions by the supervisory authority which give rise to complaints may be appealed against through the courts.

4. Each supervisory authority shall hear claims lodged by any person, or by an association representing that person, concerning the protection of his rights and freedoms in regard to the processing of personal data. The person concerned shall be informed of the outcome of the claim.

Each supervisory authority shall, in particular, hear claims for checks on the lawfulness of data processing lodged by any person when the national provisions adopted pursuant to Article 13 of this Directive apply. The person shall at any rate be informed that a check has taken place.

5. Each supervisory authority shall draw up a report on its activities at regular intervals. The report shall be made public.

6. Each supervisory authority is competent, whatever the national law applicable to the processing in question, to exercise, on the territory of its own Member State, the powers conferred on it in accordance with paragraph 3. Each authority may be requested to exercise its powers by an authority of another Member State.

The supervisory authorities shall cooperate with one another to the extent necessary for the performance of their duties, in particular by exchanging all useful information.

7. Member States shall provide that the members and staff of the supervisory authority, even after their employment has ended, are to be subject to a duty of professional secrecy with regard to confidential information to which they have access.

Article 29—Working Party on the Protection of Individuals with regard to the Processing of Personal Data

1. A Working Party on the Protection of Individuals with regard to the Processing of Personal Data, hereinafter referred to as "the Working Party", is hereby set up.

It shall have advisory status and act independently.

2. The Working Party shall be composed of a representative of the supervisory authority or authorities designated by each Member State and of a representative of the authority or authorities established for the Community institutions and bodies, and of a representative of the Commission.

Each member of the Working Party shall be designated by the institution, authority or authorities which he represents. Where a Member State has designated more than one supervisory authority, they shall nominate a joint representative. The same shall apply to the authorities established for Community institutions and bodies.

3. The Working Party shall take decisions by a simple majority of the representatives of the supervisory authorities.

4. The Working Party shall elect its chairman. The chairman's term of office shall be two years. His appointment shall be renewable.

5. The Working Party's secretariat shall be provided by the Commission.

6. The Working Party shall adopt its own rules of procedure.

7. The Working Party shall consider items placed on its agenda by its chairman, either on his own initiative or at the request of a representative of the supervisory authorities or at the Commission's request.

Article 30

1. The Working Party shall:

(a) examine any question covering the application of the national measures adopted under this Directive in order to contribute to the uniform application of such measures;

(b) give the Commission an opinion on the level of protection in the Community and in third countries;

(c) advise the Commission on any proposed amendment of this Directive, on any additional or specific measures to safeguard the rights and freedoms of natural persons with regard to the processing of personal data and on any other proposed Community measures affecting such rights and freedoms;

(d) give an opinion on codes drawn up at Community level.

2. If the Working Party finds that divergences likely to affect the equivalence of protection for persons with regard to the processing of personal data in the Community are arising between the laws or practices of Member States, it shall inform the Commission accordingly.

3. The Working Party may, on its own initiative, make recommendations on all matters relating to the protection of persons with regard to the processing of personal data in the Community.

4. The Working Party's opinions and recommendations shall be forwarded to the Commission and to the committee referred to in Article 31.

5. The Commission shall inform the Working Party of the action it has taken in response to its opinions and recommendations. It shall do so in a report which shall also be forwarded to the European Parliament and the Council. The report shall be made public.

6. The Working Party shall draw up an annual report on the situation regarding the protection of natural persons with regard to the processing of personal data in the Community and in third countries, which it shall transmit to the Commission, the European Parliament and the Council. The report shall be made public.

CHAPTER VII
COMMUNITY IMPLEMENTING MEASURES

Article 31—The Committee

1. The Commission shall be assisted by a committee composed of the representatives of the Member States and chaired by the representative of the Commission.

2. The representative of the Commission shall submit to the committee a draft of the measures to be taken. The committee shall deliver its opinion on the draft within a time limit which the chairman may lay down according to the urgency of the matter.

The opinion shall be delivered by the majority laid down in Article 148(2) of the Treaty. The votes of the representatives of the Member States within the committee shall be weighted in the manner set out in that Article. The chairman shall not vote.

The Commission shall adopt measures which shall apply immediately. However, if these measures are not in accordance with the opinion of the committee, they shall be communicated by the Commission to the Council forthwith. In that event:

• the Commission shall defer application of the measures which it has decided for a period of three months from the date of communication,
• the Council, acting by a qualified majority, may take a different decision within the time limit referred to in the first indent.

FINAL PROVISIONS

Article 32

1. Member States shall bring into force the laws, regulations and administrative provisions necessary to comply with this Directive at the latest at the end of a period of three years from the date of its adoption.

When Member States adopt these measures, they shall contain a reference to this Directive or be accompanied by such reference on the occasion of their official publication. The methods of making such reference shall be laid down by the Member States.

2. Member States shall ensure that processing already under way on the date the national provisions adopted pursuant to this

Directive enter into force, is brought into conformity with these provisions within three years of this date.

By way of derogation from the preceding subparagraph, Member States may provide that the processing of data already held in manual filing systems on the date of entry into force of the national provisions adopted in implementation of this Directive shall be brought into conformity with Articles 6, 7 and 8 of this Directive within 12 years of the date on which it is adopted. Member States shall, however, grant the data subject the right to obtain, at his request and in particular at the time of exercising his right of access, the rectification, erasure or blocking of data which are incomplete, inaccurate or stored in a way incompatible with the legitimate purposes pursued by the controller.

3. By way of derogation from paragraph 2, Member States may provide, subject to suitable safeguards, that data kept for the sole purpose of historical research need not be brought into conformity with Articles 6, 7 and 8 of this Directive.

4. Member States shall communicate to the Commission the text of the provisions of domestic law which they adopt in the field covered by this Directive.

Article 33

The Commission shall report to the Council and the European Parliament at regular intervals, starting not later than three years after the date referred to in Article 32(1), on the implementation of this Directive, attaching to its report, if necessary, suitable proposals for amendments. The report shall be made public.

The Commission shall examine, in particular, the application of this Directive to the data processing of sound and image data relating to natural persons and shall submit any appropriate proposals which prove to be necessary, taking account of developments in information technology and in the light of the state of progress in the information society.

Article 34

This Directive is addressed to the Member States.

Done at Luxembourg, 24 October 1995.

For the European Parliament   For the Council

The President   The President
K. HÄNSCH   L. ATIENZA SERNA

For the authoritative text of directive see *Official Journal of the European Community*, November 23, 1995, no. L281, p. 31.

The Privacy Principles of the Information Infrastructure Task Force

The National Information Infrastructure (NII), with its promise of a seamless web of communications networks, computers, databases, and consumer electronics, heralds the arrival of the information age. The ability to acquire, process, send, and store information at an acceptable cost has never been greater, and continuing advances in computer and telecommunications technologies will result in ever-increasing creation, use, and storage of information.

The NII promises enormous benefits. To name just a few, the NII offers the possibilities of greater citizen participation in deliberative democracy, advances in medical treatment and research, and quick verification of critical information such as a gun purchaser's criminal record. These benefits, however, do not

Reprinted from Information Infrastructure Task Force, Privacy Working Group, Information Policy Committee, *Privacy and the National Information Infrastructure: Principles for Providing and Using Personal Information*, final version, June 6, 1995 (http://nii.nist.gov/).

come without a cost: the loss of privacy. Privacy in this context means "information privacy," an individual's claim to control the terms under which personal information—information identifiable to an individual—is acquired, disclosed, and used.

Two converging trends—one social, the other technological—lead to an increased risk to privacy in the evolving NII. As a social trend, individuals will use the NII to communicate, order goods and services, and obtain information. But, unlike paying cash to buy a magazine, using the NII for such purposes will generate data documenting the transaction that can be easily stored, retrieved, analyzed, and reused. Indeed, NII transactional data may reveal who communicated with whom, when, and for how long, as well as who bought what, for what price. Significantly, this type of personal information is automatically generated, in electronic form, and is therefore especially inexpensive to store and process.

The technological trend is that the capabilities of hardware, software, and communications networks are continually increasing, while costs are continually decreasing, allowing information to be used in ways that were previously impossible or economically impractical. For example, before the NII, in order to build a profile of an individual who had lived in various states, one would have to travel from state to state and search public records for information about the individual. This process would have required filling out forms, paying fees, and waiting in line for record searches at local, state, and federal agencies, such as the departments of motor vehicles, deed record offices, electoral commissions, and county record offices. Although one could manually compile a personal profile in this manner, it would be a time-consuming and costly exercise, one that would not be undertaken unless the offsetting rewards were considerable. In sharp contrast, today, as more and more personal information appears on-line, such a profile can be built in a matter of minutes, at minimal cost.

These two converging trends guarantee that as the NII evolves, more personal information will be generated and more will be done with that information. Here lies the increased risk to privacy. This risk must be addressed both to secure the value of privacy for individuals and society and to ensure that the NII will achieve its full potential. Unless this is done, individuals may not participate in the NII for fear that the costs to their privacy will outweigh the benefits. The adoption of principles of fair information practice is a critical first step in addressing this concern.

While guidance can be found in existing laws and principles, these need to be adapted to accommodate the evolving information environment. This changing environment presents new concerns.

• No longer do governments alone acquire and use large amounts of personal information; the private sector now rivals the government in acquiring and using personal information. New principles would thus be incomplete unless they applied to both the governmental and private sectors.

• The NII promises true interactivity. Individuals will become active participants who will create volumes of data containing the content of communications as well as transactional data.

• The transport vehicles for personal information—the networks—are vulnerable to abuse; thus, the security of the network itself is critical to the NII's future success.

• The rapidly evolving information environment makes it difficult at times to know how to apply traditional ethical rules, even ones that are well understood and accepted when dealing with tangible records and documents. Consider, for example, how an individual who would never trespass into someone's home might rationalize cracking into someone's computer as an intellectual exercise. In addition, today's information environment may present questions about the use of personal information that traditional rules do not even address.

These "Principles for Providing and Using Personal Information" ("the Principles") are offered to respond to this new information environment. The Principles attempt to provide meaningful guidance, striking a balance between abstract concepts and a detailed code. They are intended to guide all NII participants and should be used by those who are drafting laws and regulations, creating industry codes of fair information practices, and designing private sector and government programs that use personal information.

The limitations inherent in any such principles must be recognized. The Principles do not have the force of law and do not create any substantive or procedural right enforceable at law. They are not designed to produce specific answers to all possible questions, nor to single-handedly govern the various sectors that use personal information. The Principles should be interpreted and applied as a whole, pragmatically and reasonably. For example, those applying these principles should consider:

• the benefits to society from the use of personal information, recognizing that privacy interests are not absolute and must be balanced by the need for legal accountability, adherence to the First Amendment, law enforcement needs, and other societal benefits recognized in law;

• the extent to which the decision to provide personal information is voluntary, and the individual's expectations regarding the use of the information (taking into account the notice and the scope of consent provided);

• the sensitivity of the information and the potential for harm to the individual that could result from a particular disclosure or use of the information;

• the cost and effort required to protect against harm to individuals, recognizing that more sensitive information may require more costly and elaborate protection procedures than less sensitive information.

Where an overly mechanical application of the Principles would be particularly unwarranted, phrases with the words "appropriate" or "reasonable" appear in the text. This flexibility, built into the Principles to address hard or unexpected cases, does not mean that the Principles need not be adhered to rigorously. Finally, the Principles are intended to be consistent with the spirit of current international guidelines, such as the OECD Guidelines,[1] regarding the use of personal information. The Principles invite further international cooperation over the development and harmonization of global privacy policies, adherence to which will bolster the ongoing development of the Global Information Infrastructure.

PREAMBLE

The United States is committed to building a National Information Infrastructure ("NII") to meet the information needs of its people. This infrastructure, created by advances in technology, is expanding the level of interactivity, enhancing communication, and allowing easier access to services. As a result, many more users are discovering new, previously unimagined ways to acquire and use personal information. In this environment, we are challenged to develop new principles to guide all NII participants in the fair use of personal information.

Existing codes of fair information practice must be adapted to a new environment in which information and communications are sent and received over networks by users who have very different capabilities, objectives, and perspectives. In this interactive, networked environment, many new relationships are being formed among individuals, communication providers, and other NII participants. New principles must acknowledge that each party has a different relationship with the individual and has different uses for personal information.

New principles should not diminish existing constitutional and statutory limitations on access to information, communications, and transactions, such as requirements for warrants and subpoenas. Such principles should ensure that access limitations keep pace with technological developments. These principles should acknowledge that all elements of our society share respon-

---

1. *See* Organization for Economic Cooperation and Development, Guidelines Governing the Protection of Privacy and Transborder Flows of Personal Data, Annex to Recommendations of the Council of 23rd September 1980.

sibility for ensuring the fair treatment of individuals in the use of personal information, whether on paper or in electronic form. Moreover, the principles should recognize that the interactive nature of the NII can empower individuals to participate in protecting information about themselves. The new principles should also make clear that this responsibility can be exercised only with openness about the process, a commitment to fairness and accountability, and continued attention to security. Finally, the principles should recognize the need to educate all participants about the new information infrastructure and how it will affect their lives.

These "Principles for Providing and Using Personal Information" ("the Principles") recognize the changing roles of government and industry in information acquisition and use. Thus, they are intended to apply to both public and private entities. The Principles are designed to guide all NII participants as well as those who are drafting legislation and crafting policy regarding the use of personal information. They provide the basic framework from which specialized principles can be developed as needed.

Trade-offs will be inevitable in implementing the Principles because privacy interests are not absolute and must be balanced against the need for accountability, the value of an unabridged flow of information, and other societal benefits recognized in law, such as lawful law enforcement activities. For example, certain decisions about the flow of personal information have already been made for us by the First Amendment, and nothing in the Principles should be read to require policies derogating the constitutionally protected freedom of speech and the press. Given these sometimes conflicting interests and public policies, the Principles must be implemented pragmatically yet conscientiously, giving due consideration to issues such as the extent to which providing personal information is voluntary, the adequacy of the notice regarding how the personal information may be used, the scope of the individual's consent, and the cost of protecting information in light of the information's sensitivity.

PRINCIPLES AND COMMENTARY

I. General Principles for All NII Participants

1. Three fundamental principles should guide all NII participants. These three principles—information privacy, information integrity, and information quality—identify the fundamental requirements necessary for the proper use of personal information, and in turn the successful implementation of the NII. All NII participants should use appropriate means to ensure that these principles are satisfied.

I.A. Information Privacy Principle

Personal information should be acquired, disclosed, and used only in ways that respect an individual's privacy.

2. The NII can flourish only if all participants respect information privacy. Information privacy is an individual's claim to control the terms under which personal information—information identifiable to an individual—is acquired, disclosed, and used. The level of privacy that must be respected is an individual's reasonable expectation, an expectation subjectively held by the individual and deemed objectively reasonable by society. Not all subjectively held expectations will be honored as reasonable. For example, an individual who posts an unencrypted personal message on a bulletin board for public postings cannot reasonably expect that personal message to be read only by the addressee.

3. What counts as a reasonable expectation of privacy under the Principles is not limited by what counts as a reasonable expectation of privacy under the Fourth Amendment of the United States Constitution. In many instances, society has deemed it reasonable to protect privacy at a level higher than that required by the Fourth Amendment. See, e.g., Electronic Communications Privacy Act, 18 U.S.C. § 2701 (1988); Right to Financial Privacy Act, 12 U.S.C. § 3401 (1988); Privacy Act, 5 U.S.C. § 552a (1988). The Information Privacy Principle fully supports such possibilities.

4. As explained in later principles and commentary, an individual's privacy can often be best respected when individuals and information users come to some mutually agreeable understanding of how personal information will be acquired, disclosed, and used. However, in certain cases—for example, if the individual lacks sufficient bargaining power—purely contractual arrangements between individuals and information users may fail to respect privacy adequately. In such instances, society should ensure privacy at some basic level in order to satisfy the Information Privacy Principle.

I.B. Information Integrity Principle

Personal information should not be improperly altered or destroyed.

5. NII participants should be able to rely on the integrity of the personal information the NII contains. Thus, personal information should be protected against improper alteration or destruction.

I.C. Information Quality Principle

Personal information should be accurate, timely, complete, and relevant for the purpose for which it is provided and used.

6. Personal information should have sufficient quality to be relied upon. This means that personal information should be accurate, timely, complete, and relevant for the purpose for which it is provided and used.

II. Principles for Users of Personal Information

II.A. Acquisition Principles

Information users should:

1. Assess the impact on privacy in deciding whether to acquire, disclose, or use personal information.

2. Acquire and keep only information reasonably expected to support current or planned activities.

7. The benefit of information lies in its use, but therein lies an often unconsidered cost: the threat to information privacy. A critical characteristic of privacy is that once it is lost, it can rarely be restored. Consider, for example, the extent to which the inappropriate release of sensitive medical information could ever be rectified by public apology.

8. Given this characteristic, privacy should not be addressed as a mere afterthought, once personal information has been acquired. Rather, information users should explicitly consider the impact on privacy in the very process of designing information systems and in deciding whether to acquire or use personal information in the first place. In assessing this impact, information users should gauge not just the effect their activities may have on the individuals about whom personal information is acquired, disclosed, and used; they should also consider other factors, such as public opinion and market forces, that may provide guidance on the appropriateness of any given activity.

9. After assessing the impact on information privacy, an information user may conclude that it is appropriate to acquire personal information in pursuit of a current or planned activity. A planned activity is one that is contemplated by the information user, with the intent to pursue such activity in the future. In all cases, the information user should acquire only that information reasonably expected to support those activities. Although information storage costs decrease continually, it is inappropriate to collect volumes of personal information simply because some of the information may, in the future, prove to be of some unanticipated value. Also, personal information that has served its purpose and is no longer reasonably expected to support any current or planned activities should not be kept.

10. The ability to acquire certain kinds of personal information does not mean that it is proper to do so. In certain cases, individuals have no choice whether to disclose personal information. For example, if the individual executes a transaction on the NII, personal information in the form of transactional data will typically be generated. In other cases, the choice may exist in

theory only. Exercising certain choices may result in the denial of a benefit that individuals need to participate fully in society—for example, obtaining a license to drive an automobile. In such cases, society should establish some basic level of privacy protection in accordance with the Information Privacy Principle (I.A.).

II.B. Notice Principle

Information users who collect personal information directly from the individual should provide adequate, relevant information about:

1. Why they are collecting the information;

2. What the information is expected to be used for;

3. What steps will be taken to protect its confidentiality, integrity, and quality;

4. The consequences of providing or withholding information; and

5. Any rights of redress.

11. Personal information can be acquired in one of two ways: it can be collected directly from the individual or obtained from some secondary source. By necessity, the principles governing these two methods of acquiring personal information differ. While notice obligations can be placed on all those who collect information directly from the individual, they cannot be imposed uniformly on entities that have no such direct relationship. If all recipients of personal information were required to notify every individual about whom they receive data, the exchange of personal information would become prohibitively burdensome, and many of the benefits of the NII would be lost.

12. For those who collect personal information directly from the individual, the Notice Principle requires the individual to be given sufficient information to make an informed decision about his or her privacy. The importance of providing this notice cannot be overstated because the terms of the notice substantially determine the individual's understanding of how personal information

will be used, an understanding that must be respected by all subsequent users of that information.

13. The Notice Principle specifically applies to personal information designated by law as a public record and to transactional data generated as a byproduct of a transaction. With respect to transactional data, this principle applies to all parties, including not only the party principally transacting with the individual in order to provide some product or service, but also to those transaction facilitators such as communication providers and electronic payment providers who help to consummate these transactions. For example, if an individual purchases flowers with a credit card through an on-line shopping mall accessed via modem, the Notice Principle applies to all parties who collect transactional data related to the purchase, not only to the florist, but also to the telephone and credit card companies. Transaction facilitators would ordinarily provide notice at the time they establish an account, or when billing the customer.

14. What counts as adequate, relevant information to satisfy the Notice Principle depends on the circumstances surrounding the collection of information. In some cases—especially where there is a continuing relationship between the individual and the information collector—notice need not be given before each instance that personal information is collected. For example, an information or communication service provider should ordinarily give notice when the individual subscribes to a particular service and perhaps periodically thereafter, not each time the individual uses the service. In other cases, the ordinary and acknowledged use of personal information is so clearly contemplated by the individual that providing formal notice is not necessary. For example, if an individual's name and address is collected by a pharmaceutical company that takes the order over interactive television simply to deliver the right medicine to the right person at the right address, no elaborate notice need precede taking the individual's order. However, should the pharmaceutical company use the information in a manner not clearly contemplated by the individual—for example, to create and sell a list of people af-

flicted with high blood pressure to health insurance companies—
then some form of notice should be provided.

15. While the Notice Principle indicates what might constitute the elements of adequate notice, it does not prescribe a
particular form for that notice. Rather, the goal of the Principle is
to ensure that the individual has sufficient information in an
understandable form to make an informed decision. Thus the
drafters of notices should be creative about informing in ways
that will help all individuals, regardless of age, literacy, and
education to achieve this goal.

16. Finally, although the Notice Principle requires information collectors to inform individuals what steps will be taken to
protect personal information, they are not required to provide
overly technical descriptions of such security measures. Indeed,
such descriptions might be unwelcome or unhelpful to the
individual. Furthermore, they may be counterproductive since
widespread disclosure of the technical security measures might
expose system vulnerabilities, in conflict with the Protection
Principle (II.C.).

II.C. Protection Principle

Information users should use appropriate technical and managerial controls to protect the confidentiality and integrity of personal information.

17. On the NII, personal information is maintained in a
networked environment, an environment that poses tremendous
risk of unauthorized access, disclosure, alteration, and destruction. Both insiders and outsiders may gain access to information
they have no right to see or may make hard-to-detect changes in
data that will then be relied upon in making critical decisions.

18. For example, our health care providers expect to become
intensive participants in the NII. Through the NII, a hospital in
a remote locale will be able to send x-rays for review by a radiolo-
gist at a teaching hospital in another part of the country. The
potential benefits are obvious. Yet, such benefits will not be
realized if individuals refuse to send such sensitive data because

they fear that the NII cannot ensure that sensitive medical data will remain confidential and unaltered.

19. In deciding what controls are appropriate, information users should recognize that personal information should be protected in accordance with the individual's understanding and in a manner commensurate with the harm that might occur if it were improperly disclosed or altered.

20. In protecting personal information, information users should adopt a multi-faceted approach that includes both technical and managerial controls. As for technical controls, information users should, for example, consider encrypting personal information, including the contents of communications and information generated from transactions. In addition, they should consider computerized audit trails, which help detect improper access by both insiders and outsiders. As for management controls, one could strive, for example, to create an organizational culture in which individuals learn about fair information practices and adopt these practices as the norm. Also, organizations could establish policies to forbid information acquired for one activity from being used for another unrelated activity.

II.D. Fairness Principle

Information users should not use personal information in ways that are incompatible with the individual's understanding of how it will be used, unless there is a compelling public interest for such use.

21. An individual's understanding encompasses the individual's objectively reasonable contemplation and scope of consent when the information was collected. As explained earlier, an individual's understanding depends principally on the notice provided by the information collector pursuant to the Notice Principle (II.B.) and obtained by the individual pursuant to the Awareness Principle (III.A.). Without a Fairness Principle, information use may know no boundaries and thus go beyond the individual's understanding.

22. If an information user seeks to use personal information in an incompatible manner, the user must first notify the individual and obtain his or her explicit or implicit consent. The nature of the incompatible use will determine whether such consent should be explicit or implicit. In some cases, the consequences to an individual may be so significant that the prospective data user should proceed only after the individual has specifically opted into the use by explicitly agreeing. In other cases, a notice offering the individual the ability to opt out of the use within a certain specified time may be adequate. Inherent in this principle is the requirement that whenever personal information is transferred from information user to user, the individual's understanding of how that personal information will be used must also be conveyed. Because all information users must abide by the Fairness Principle, both information transferor and transferee bear a responsibility to ensure that the individual's understanding is transferred along with the information.

23. In deciding whether a particular use of information is "incompatible" with an individual's understanding, information users should evaluate whether the uses are permitted explicitly in the notice or are otherwise consistent with the notice. Any use of information beyond these conditions is incompatible with the individual's understanding. What is incompatible under this Principle is not limited to what has been interpreted as incompatible under the Privacy Act. See 5 U.S.C. § 552a.

24. The Fairness Principle cannot be applied uniformly in every setting. An incompatible use is not necessarily a harmful use; in fact, it may be extremely beneficial to the individual and society. There are some incompatible uses that will produce enormous benefits and have at most a trivial effect on the individual's information privacy interest. Research and statistical studies, in which information will not be used to affect the individual, are examples. Obtaining the consent of the individual to permit new statistical uses of existing data adds cost and administrative complexity to the process and risks impairing the research project. In other cases, personal information may be used for a significant public need recognized by society in a highly formal, open

way (typically in legislation) that would be thwarted by giving the individual a chance to limit its use. One example would be the use of personal information in a law enforcement investigation for which the suspect's consent would be unlikely and even asking for such consent would be counterproductive to the investigation. Another example would be an incompatible use of personal information, made by the investigatory press, that is specifically protected and sanctioned by the First Amendment.

II.E. Education Principle

Information users should educate themselves and the public about how information privacy can be maintained.

25. The Education Principle represents a significant addition to the traditional principles of fair information practice. There are many uses of the NII for which individuals cannot rely completely on governmental or other organizational controls to protect their privacy. Although individuals often rely on such legal and institutional controls to protect their privacy, many people will engage in activities outside of these controls, especially as they engage in the informal exchange of information on the NII. Thus, individuals must be aware of the hazards of providing personal information, and must make judgments about whether providing personal information is to their benefit.

26. The full effect of the NII on the use of personal information is not readily apparent, and individuals may not recognize how their lives may be affected by networked information. Because it is important that individuals and information users appreciate how the NII affects information privacy, all information users should participate in education about the handling and use of personal information. Traditionally, governments and schools have educated the public on matters of social rights and responsibilities, and they must continue to play a lead role. However, as major builders of the NII, the private sector has as crucial a role to play. Such education, which would help individuals minimize the risks to their privacy, could involve privacy telephone hotlines, Internet privacy "help" sites, and comprehensive marketing and publicity campaigns.

III. Principles for Individuals Who Provide Personal Information

III.A. Awareness Principle

Individuals should obtain adequate, relevant information about:

1. Why the information is being collected;

2. What the information is expected to be used for;

3. What steps will be taken to protect its confidentiality, integrity, and quality;

4. The consequences of providing or withholding information; and

5. Any rights of redress.

27. Increasingly, individuals are being asked to surrender personal information about themselves. Sometimes the inquiry is straight-forward; for example, a bank will ask for personal information prior to processing a loan request. In this case, one use for the information is clear—to process the loan application. There may, however, be other uses that are not so obvious, such as using some of that information for a credit card solicitation. Indeed, individuals regularly disclose personal information without being fully aware of the many ways in which that information may ultimately be used. For example, an individual may not realize that paying for medical services with a credit card creates transactional data that could reveal the individual's state of health.

28. The Awareness Principle recognizes that although information collectors have a responsibility to inform individuals why they want personal information, individuals also have a responsibility to understand the consequences of providing personal information to others. This is especially true in an interactive realm such as the NII, in which individuals can actively shape the terms of their participation. For example, when individuals have real choices about whether and to what degree personal information should be disclosed, they should take an active role in deciding whether to disclose personal information in the first place, and under what terms.

29. Of course, if individuals are to be held responsible for making these choices, they must be given enough information to make intelligent choices. This is how the Awareness Principle works in conjunction with the Notice Principle (II.B.) and more broadly with the Education Principle (II.E) to enable individuals to take responsibility over how personal information is disclosed and used.

III.B. Empowerment Principles

Individuals should be able to safeguard their own privacy by having:

1. A means to obtain their personal information;

2. A means to correct their personal information that lacks sufficient quality to ensure fairness in its use;

3. The opportunity to use appropriate technical controls, such as encryption, to protect the confidentiality and integrity of communications and transactions; and

4. The opportunity to remain anonymous when appropriate.

30. Individuals should have a means to obtain from information users a copy of their personal information and to correct information about them that lacks sufficient quality to ensure fairness in its use. The extent to which such means are provided depends on various factors, including the seriousness of the consequences to the individual of using the personal information and any First Amendment rights held by the information user.

31. Further, if the terms of the information collection are unsatisfactory, the individual should consider various self-initiated measures to safeguard privacy. For example, to safeguard the confidentiality or integrity of a communication, the individual should have the opportunity to use appropriate tools such as encryption. Also, to avoid leaving a data trail of transactional records, individuals should have the opportunity to remain anonymous, when appropriate. For example, anonymity would be appropriate when an individual browses a public electronic library or when an individual engages in anonymous political

speech protected by the Constitution. See *McIntyre* v. *Ohio Elections Commission*, 131 L. Ed. 2d 426 (1995). In an ideal world, offering undecipherable encryption or absolute anonymity would serve to protect privacy with no negative effect. Unfortunately, in the real world, some will abuse these technologies and, in the process, harm others. It is beyond the scope of the Principles how encryption or anonymity can be offered to individuals for legitimate uses while minimizing their misuse. These issues must, however, be addressed if the NII is to achieve its full potential.

III.C. Redress Principle

Individuals should, as appropriate, have a means of redress if harmed by an improper disclosure or use of personal information.

32. Redress is required only when an individual is harmed. Designed for general applicability, the Redress Principle does not answer in any particular case whether harm has occurred at all or whether enough harm has occurred to warrant a specific form of redress. Those questions must be answered in the sectoral implementation of the Principles.

33. An improper use specifically includes a decision based on personal information of inadequate quality—information that is not accurate, timely, complete, or relevant for the purpose for which it is provided and used. The Redress Principle does not, however, set the level of culpability on the part of the information user necessary to warrant a specific form of redress.

34. When redress is appropriate, the Principles envision various forms including, but not limited to, informal complaint resolution, mediation, arbitration, civil litigation, regulatory enforcement, and criminal prosecution, in various private, local, state, and federal forums with the goal of providing relief in the most cost-effective manner possible.

General Discussion

Given the importance of the topic addressed in Fred Cate's book, Brookings organized a conference on April 9, 1997, to review Cate's manuscript, to discuss the topic in general, and to consider the larger issues raised about the appropriate legal protections for privacy in the electronic realm. Many of the nation's leading experts on privacy issues from the business sector, government, and academia attended. Senator Robert Bennett, chairman of the Financial Services and Technology Subcommittee of the Senate Banking, Housing and Urban Affairs Committee, spoke to the group during lunch. This appendix summarizes the discussion. A list of the participants appears at the end.

General Privacy Issues

Alan Westin opened the discussion by observing that privacy can be a contentious subject because it means different things to different people. Westin defined the term as "the claim of individuals, groups, or institutions to determine for themselves how, when, and to what extent information about them is communicated to others." Under this definition, individuals cannot legiti-

Views expressed in the discussion are solely those of the speakers and should not be attributed to any organizations with which they are associated.

mately expect any actions they may take that are observable in public to be treated as private. A clear problem is that in an electronic environment, it becomes hard to differentiate between a private and public place and therefore what should be protected and what should not.

Lance Hoffman argued it is unreasonable for society to subsidize the costs of individuals to maintain their privacy, pointing out that most people will choose utility over security (and thus privacy). Similarly, it is also unreasonable, Hoffman argued, for society to subsidize the costs of marketers and "junk" e-mail. In a related vein, Fred Cate suggested that privacy in many ways is like any other good: those that value it should be willing to sacrifice other goods (time, effort, and energy among them) in order to obtain it. The apparent unwillingness of many people desiring more privacy to bear the cost of that privacy, he argued, undercut their claims of valuing such additional protection. For individuals seriously interested in protecting their privacy, Cate outlined three basic tools necessary to do so: notice (to the data supplier), consent (to the consumer), and accountability.

Although accountability may be essential to ensuring privacy, it unfortunately conflicts with the anonymity privacy implies. Ron Plesser observed that on the Internet anonymity can be a big problem because it can allow individuals to infringe the copyrights of others, to defame, and engage in other unlawful conduct—all without being accountable in any way for the damage those actions may inflict. For any commerce to take place on the Internet, therefore, some level of anonymity and therefore privacy must be sacrificed. The question is how much and who will decide.

The Market for Privacy

Marc Rotenberg noted that when the European Commission adopted its privacy directive—which requires, among others, entities collecting and making use of data to register with central governments—it stated that privacy protection is a central precondition to consumers' acceptance of electronic commerce. Accordingly, a critical issue, he argued, was whether there was a "market failure" in the electronic environment that required some sort of government intervention to ensure individuals' privacy. He pointed to recent survey evidence which found that 89 percent of Americans were at least somewhat or very concerned about ensuring their privacy over the telephone or the Internet. Nonetheless, a discrepancy seems to appear between what consumers claim and how they act. Although most individuals claim to be concerned with privacy, only 2 percent take advantage of the Mail Preference Service (MPS), which allows consumers to remove their names from many national mailing lists.

Peter Swire argued that the difference between what consumers want and what they "buy" occurs because consumers do not necessarily know when organizations are collecting data from them. Even if consumers were to be educated on that subject, they would still be unable to tell what companies are doing with the data they collect. Rotenberg agreed and suggested that there is no market relationship between the data subject and the data recipient, and no opportunity to negotiate one.

Swire elaborated that two markets really exist in the collection and dissemination of data: one between the subject and the information collector and a secondary market between the subject and the person using the data. In the first market, consumers can opt out simply by not participating in activities where data are collected. They can avoid the Internet or pay cash at the supermarket. Jan Constantine opined that the existence of these options constitutes a market success.

Christopher Beshouri noted, however, that this situation presents an all-or-nothing dilemma, for if consumers allow any data to be collected, they have no bargaining power in its ultimate use. He summarized this quandary as the inability to separate one's preferences over privacy and over consumption decisions. This signifies not a market failure, but rather an incomplete market which may in time resolve itself.

Duncan MacDonald responded that privacy isn't a pure public good, and so at some point someone will have a market incentive to protect it. Nonetheless, some corporations that have tried to market their strong privacy protection have yet to see any results and have concluded that "privacy doesn't sell." Other industries have marketed privacy successfully—such as the cellular telephone industry—which could mean that the public demands for privacy are forthcoming and will eventually be profitable.

A rough consensus of the participants seemed to be that there are problems with the market for privacy, which, Deidre Mulligan suggested, might make discussing a marketplace for fair information practices a more practical exercise. Nonetheless, there are lingering concerns the market is not addressing. Swire asked, "Who, then, governs the responsibility of the information collector, or does society have to impose a sense of responsibility?"

The Role for Industry

Most attendants expressed the view that the information industry should be primarily self-regulated: the industry is changing too rapidly for government legislative solutions, and most corporations are not simply looking at the United States, but at global markets, which the U.S. government cannot regulate. This is why, Ron Plesser argued, the most effective way to address privacy issues is through industry self-regulation. Most of the participants agreed that the United States will never have the type of legislation that Europe currently has in regard to privacy. Indeed, several participants expressed the fear that any governmental attempt to oversee all U.S. data would lead to abuses by the government, while any across-the-board privacy legislation would hinder industry initiatives, especially in a fast-changing electronic environment. Leslie Byrne voiced a strong dissent from this view, arguing a need for nonsectoral, umbrella privacy legislation.

To illustrate how industry can respond to consumer needs without being told to do so, Duncan MacDonald pointed to the automobile industry's decision many years ago to create car heaters even though the government had not mandated them. He hypothesized that had heaters been left to the government, special interests would have impeded technological progress, perhaps requiring the installation of inefficient coal heaters. As a counterexample, however, Robert Litan noted that government mandated other features of the car, such as seat belts and more recently, airbags.

Nonetheless, Fred Cate noted that there are many other examples of private actors taking steps to protect disclosure of sensitive information without government encouragement or mandates. For example, lawyers maintain client-attorney privilege, doctors claim client confidentiality, and reporters protect sources. In the information technology realm, Cate noted that many companies—such as Citibank—already inform consumers that, unless told otherwise, they will disclose information to their affiliates. He suggested that a simple seal on the home page of a Web site, declaring that a company adheres to certain industry privacy standards, might ease the fears of the public and offer some level of accountability.

Alternatively, Lamar Smith suggested that the media can act as an effective watchdog, informing consumers of what information is being collected about them and how that information is being used. Leslie Byrne suggested, however, that the media have mixed objectives; while they use personal data to help write their stories, they may be reluctant to print some stories about violations of consumers' privacy because of fear of offending advertisers. Jane Kirtley responded that any suggestion that the media have a conflict of interest is incorrect and that the press has been in the forefront of alerting citizens to possible invasions of their privacy.

A number of participants suggested that large multinational companies can better negotiate for themselves across national boundaries than governments can. In the end, companies are bound by consumer demand and will check practices in collecting data that threaten this demand. Electronic commerce is unlikely to gain popularity until the issues of notice, consent, and recourse have been resolved. The market will force companies wishing to participate in this medium to address and solve those concerns.

The Role for Government

Many discussants implied or explicitly suggested that data protection is a perplexing issue for the government to face. The government has intervened previously when consumers had no relationship with data collectors, such as in the case of the Fair Credit Reporting Act, in which Congress outlined who has access to the information collected, who can use it, and how to correct it. Technology has complicated the issue, though, and Jerry Berman noted that now government must ask how, in a world of the Internet, one reconciles the objectives of protecting both privacy and the First Amendment, as well as the free flow of information.

Constantine pointed out that the public's interest in privacy is further complicated by the fact that the federal government is a great collector of personal data. Most obviously, the Internal Revenue Service collects vast quantities of detailed financial information about all taxpayers; in recent years, there have been disclosures that unauthorized individuals within the IRS have examined this information. Several participants pointed to the flap over the decision (since withdrawn) by the Social Security Administration to provide individuals' account information online. Each of these examples suggests that protecting privacy may be a greater challenge for the federal government than for the private sector.

While most discussants agreed that legislation along the lines of the European directive would be a bureaucratic nightmare if adopted in the United States, many agreed that the federal government should play a role in creating a standard for disclosure. Rotenberg went further and argued the need for a privacy agency within the United States to act as an ombudsman and to represent privacy interests so that in debates between law enforcement and industry, there is someone whose responsibility would be to protect privacy.

There also appeared to be some consensus over which sectors would require federal regulation to ensure consumer privacy. Protection of children garnered a great deal of support. Some attendants felt regulation would be necessary in banking services. During his luncheon address, Senator Robert Bennett argued for legislation to restrict disclosure of medical data. Commissioner Christine Varney argued that any legislation in this area should be as narrow as possible so as to deal with specific problems.

A few additional roles for the government seemed noncontentious. Anne Branscomb suggested that the Federal Trade Commission could clarify what is considered a public versus private domain in the electronic environment. The FTC also remains responsible for prohibiting unfair, deceptive, or fraudulent acts committed over the Internet. Varney added that the government could encourage consumers to engage in transactions anonymously when they choose, when the value of the transaction is higher for them than the cost of the disclosure. In fact, Rotenberg noted that Germany has taken this approach, informing industry that if it is going to offer business services on the Internet, it must make available a technique for anonymous payments.

Varney asked whether anyone would object to federal legislation requiring anyone who transacts business over the Internet to disclose their privacy preferences. There was no consensus among the participants on the answer. In fact, Jerry Berman warned that industry would put all its energies into fighting legislation mandating such a requirement, rather than developing technological means for making such choices possible. Scott Blackmer argued that the first approach for legislation or self-regulation should be to mandate and standardize disclosure of privacy practices, allowing users to make informed choices in a fast-evolving marketplace.

Finally, a number of the participants noted that the government—not firms in the private sector—may pose the greatest threat to individuals' privacy. After all, the government has the power to arrest people, freeze bank accounts, and collect detailed financial information from taxpayers (some of which has been looked at by unauthorized individuals).

De Facto Regulation

Whatever one may believe the appropriate role for government to be in ensuring privacy in an electronic environment, some "private regulation" is already occurring on the Internet by the computer engineers who write code and decide computer standards. In fact, Christine Varney suggested that when encryption software becomes ubiquitous it will push Internet commerce because it allows for potentially anonymous transactions, which will solve privacy issues by default.

Swire observed that while encryption will permit anonymous transactions, not all transactions—notably those involving borrowing—can be made anonymously. Swire also expressed concern that holding encryption keys is extremely risky since all value is lost if the key is forgotten or lost. This encourages spreading of risk—sharing keys with a bank or someone else in society—which detracts from anonymity. In Swire's view, encryption is very helpful in protecting the security of a message or database. But encryption provides only a limited solution to privacy concerns.

Yet another technological solution, which many of the discussants preferred, would be the Platform for Internet Content Selection (PICS) platform, which allows consumers to set some preferences about how they would like information handled if they choose to disclose it. At the same time, Deidre Mulligan pointed out, PIC technology does not at all force people to disclose information. Instead individuals can make decisions at the front end of transactions when proprietors explain what they intend to do with the data. Consumers can then decide to use the site or renegotiate what data will be used and how.

Several participants noted that the Internet Engineering Task Force (IETF) is developing default mechanisms and standards for the Internet that give individuals maximum control over their personal information. The IETF currently decides industry standards, not the government. Most discussants felt the IETF's work would be compromised if the government became involved.

"Opt In" versus "Opt Out"

One of the questions concerning the use of personal data is whether consumers should have to request becoming a data subject (opt in) or request to be removed from any data list (opt out). Currently, most companies rely on the opt-out approach.

Anne Branscomb argued that instead it would be in the interest of both companies and consumers to adopt the opt-in model. This would permit businesses to better target consumers, while individuals would be better enabled to avoid invasion of their privacy. Opt in would prevent consumers from being inundated with mail they do not want and for which they are charged by their service provider. A *USA Today* survey agrees, reporting that 90 percent of Americans believe that whoever stands to profit should bear the cost of privacy and that it is an unreasonable expectation for consumers to continually update their preferences.

A number of the discussants took a different view, suggesting that opt in is an impractical approach from a marketing standpoint and would be excessively costly for industry. In fact, several discussants questioned whether it would be less costly for consumers to opt in. Moreover Christine Varney suggested that the opt-in or out discussion ignores information about consumers that already has been captured before anything is purchased. Plesser claimed that by providing a response on a Web browser, consumers are de facto opting in.

Some discussants pointed out that the opt-out model relies on a free market assumption that may apply to the Internet, but does not apply to situations in which there may be only one or very few suppliers. When a consumer has little or no choice but to deal with a particular service provider, these discussants observed that only an opt-in model adquately ensures actual notice and actual consent. An opt-in model also advances other goals, besides privacy, that may need to be fostered in monopoly markets, such as further competition, since it puts new entrants on the same footing with incumbents.

Another option would be to have privacy preferences built into an individual's browser capabilities. Significantly, in the month after the conference was held, a group of high-tech companies announced agreement on a web-based standard that would allow consumers to interact with data collectors and inform them of what information they would be comfortable having disclosed to other parties.

Conclusions

To the extent that the meeting reached any consensus, it concerned the limited role of government and the importance for the government of the admonition given to all doctors in the words to "first, do no harm." Though premature, there is some role that government can and should play in the development of new information technologies—by enforcing contracts, regulating children's accessibility to certain material on the Internet, and encouraging discussion between consumer groups and the industry. Furthermore, as a number of participants argued, government intervention may be required to ensure that consumers know what information about them is being disclosed to other parties and to give them access to any files containing personal data to ensure that they are accurate.

At the same time, many of the participants believed that most privacy concerns are likely to be addressed in the marketplace. Companies doing business over the Internet, as well Internet service providers, have strong commercial interests in satisfying the privacy desires of consumers, to the extent those desires are strongly manifested in their purchasing decisions and consumers are aware of what information about them may be released to other parties.

Participants

Sheri Alpert, *Office of the Privacy Advocate, Internal Revenue Service*

Perry Applebaum, *Judiciary Committee, U.S. House of Representatives*

Robert F. Bennett, *U.S. Senate*

Jerry Berman, *Center for Democracy and Technology*

Jodie Bernstein, *Federal Trade Commission*

Christopher P. Beshouri, *Office of the Comptroller of the Currency*

William P. Binzel, *MasterCard International Communications*

W. Scott Blackmer, *Wilmer, Cutler, and Pickering*

Anne W. Branscomb, *Program on Information Resources Policy, Harvard University*

Leslie Byrne, *U.S. Office of Consumer Affairs*

Marilyn Cade, *Technology and Infrastructure, AT&T*

Fred H. Cate, *Indiana University School of Law–Bloomington*

Alan F. Coffey Jr., *Judiciary Committee, U.S. House of Representatives*

Jan F. Constantine, *News America Publishing, Inc.*

Manus Cooney, *Judiciary Committee, U.S. Senate*

Robert W. Crandall, *The Brookings Institution*

Mary J. Culnan, *President's Commission on Critical Infrastructure Protection*

Carol Darr, *Information Technology Industry Council*

Temma Ehrenfeld, *Newsweek*

Doris Feinsilber, *Electronic Privacy Information Center*

Peter J. Gray, *Citicorp*

Lance J. Hoffman, *Department of Electrical Engineering and Computer Science, The George Washington University*

Yury Kapgan, *Electronic Privacy Information Center*

Gene Kimmelman, *Consumers Union*

Jane Kirtley, *Reporters Committee for Freedom of the Press*

Frank Krogh, *MCI*

Jack Krumholtz, *Microsoft Corporation*

Robert E. Litan, *The Brookings Institution*

Duncan A. MacDonald, *Citicorp Credit Services, Inc.*

David Medine, *Federal Trade Commission*

Deidre Mulligan, *Center for Democracy and Technology*

Michelle Muth, *U.S. Office of Consumer Affairs*

Charlotte Newton, *MasterCard International Communications*

Ronald L. Plesser, *Piper and Marbury LLP*

Marc Rotenberg, *Electronic Privacy Information Center*

Paul M. Schwartz, *Boston College Law School*

Lamar Smith, *VISA U.S.A. Inc.*

Richard J. Srednicki, *AT&T Universal Card Services*

David A. Strauss, *University of Chicago Law School*

Peter Swire, *Ohio State University, College of Law*
Christine A. Varney, *Federal Trade Commission*
Robert N. Veeder, *Internal Revenue Service*
Miriam Wahrman, *MasterCard International Inc.*
Barbara Wellbery, *U.S. Department of Commerce*
Alan F. Westin, *Columbia University*

Bibliography

This bibliography includes recent books and articles on information privacy and major privacy studies on which this book relied. These publications offer additional, detailed information about privacy-related topics. Government and industry reports, newsletter articles, and popular press accounts concerning privacy are not included.

Electronic versions of many European legal materials concerning data protection are available from the Legal Advisory Board of the European Commission (http://www2.echo.lu/legal/en/dataprot/dataprot.html); many privacy-related U.S. government documents are available from the President's Information Infrastructure Task Force (http://iitf.nist.gov/).

A variety of periodicals and Internet web sites provide current information on privacy issues. These include *Privacy and American Business* (published by Alan Westin), *Privacy Laws and Business Newsletter* (published by Stewart Dresner), *Privacy Journal* (published by Robert Ellis Smith), *Privacy Times* (published by Evan Hendricks), and the web sites maintained by the American Civil Liberties Union (http://www.aclu.org), Center for Democracy and Technology (http://www.cdt.org), Direct Marketing Association (http://www.the-dma.org), Electronic Privacy Information Center (http://www.epic.org), Electronic Frontier Foundation (http://www.eff.org), and International Society for Measurement and Control (http://www.isa.net).

Alderman, Ellen, and Caroline Kennedy. *The Right to Privacy.* Knopf, 1995.

Bennett, Colin J. *Regulating Privacy: Data Protection and Public Policy in Europe and the United States.* Cornell University Press, 1992.

Bentley, Eric Jr., "Toward an International Fourth Amendment: Rethinking Searches and Seizures Abroad after Verdugo-Urquidez." *Vanderbilt Journal of Transnational Law* 27 (May 1994): 329–417.

BeVier, Lillian R. "Information about Individuals in the Hands of Government: Some Reflections on Mechanisms for Privacy Protection." *William and Mary Bill of Rights Journal* 4 (Winter 1995): 455–506.

Bezanson, Randall P. "The Right to Privacy Revisited: Privacy, News, and Social Change, 1890–1990." *California Law Review* 80 (October 1992): 1133–75.

Bibas, Steven A. "A Contractual Approach to Data Privacy." *Harvard Journal of Law and Public Policy* 17 (Spring 1994): 591–605.

Boehmer, Robert G., and Todd S. Palmer. "The 1992 EC Data Protection Proposal: An Examination of Its Implications for U.S. Business and U.S. Privacy Law." *American Business Law Journal* 31 (September 1993): 265–311.

Branscomb, Anne Wells. *Who Owns Information? From Privacy to Public Access.* Basic Books, 1994.

Cate, Fred H. "The EU Data Protection Directive, Information Privacy, and the Public Interest." *Iowa Law Review* 80 (March 1995): 431–44.

———. "The First Amendment and the National Information Infrastructure." *Wake Forest Law Review* 30, 1 (1995): 1–50.

———. (moderator). "From Conduit to Content: The Emergence of Information Policy and Law." *Federal Communications Law Journal* 48 (December 1995): 1–92

———. "Global Information Policymaking and Domestic Law." *Indiana Journal of Global Legal Studies* 1 (Spring 1994): 467–87.

———. "The National Information Infrastructure: Policymakers and Policymaking." *Stanford Law and Policy Review* 6 (1994): 43–59.

———, D. Annette Fields, and James K. McBain. "The Right to Privacy and the Public's Right to Know: The 'Central Purpose' of the Freedom of Information Act." *Administrative Law Review* 46 (Winter 1994): 41–74

Chlapowski, Francis S. "The Constitutional Protection of Informational Privacy." *Boston University Law Review* 71 (January 1991): 133–60.

Clark, Terence J. "Epilogue: When Privacy Rights Encounter First Amendment Freedoms." *Case Western Reserve Law Review* 41, 3 (1991): 921–28.

"The EC Privacy Directive and the Future of U.S. Business in Europe: A Panel Discussion," *Iowa Law Review* 80 (March 1995): 669–95.

Edelman, Peter B. "Free Press v. Privacy: Haunted by the Ghost of Justice Black." *Texas Law Review* 68 (May 1990): 1195–1236.

Elford, Joseph. "Trafficking in Stolen Information: A 'Hierarchy of Rights' Approach to the Private Facts Tort." *Yale Law Journal* 105 (December 1995): 727–60.

Fenrich, William J. "Common Law Protection of Individuals' Rights in Personal Information." *Fordham Law Review* 65 (December 1996): 951–1004.

Flaherty, David H. *Protecting Privacy in Surveillance Societies: The Federal Republic of Germany, Sweden, France, Canada, and the United States.* University of North Carolina Press, 1989.

Freiwald, Susan. "Uncertain Privacy: Communication Attributes after the Digital Telephony Act." *Southern California Law Review* 69 (March 1996): 949–1020.

Gellman, Robert M. "Can Privacy Be Regulated Effectively on a National Level? Thoughts on the Possible Need for International Privacy Rules." *Villanova Law Review* 41, 1 (1996): 129–72.

Gerety, Tom. "Redefining Privacy." *Harvard Civil Rights-Civil Liberties Law Review* 12 (Spring 1977): 233–96.

Gilles, Susan M. "Promises Betrayed: Breach of Confidence as a Remedy for Invasions of Privacy." *Buffalo Law Review* 43 (1995).

Goldstein, Bruce D. "Confidentiality and Dissemination of Personal Information: An Examination of State Laws Governing Data Protection." *Emory Law Journal* 41 (Fall 1992): 1185–1280.

Gormley, Ken. "One Hundred Years of Privacy." *Wisconsin Law Review* (1992): 1335–1441.

Gormley, Ken, and Rhonda G. Hartman. "Privacy and the States." *Temple Law Review* 63 (Winter 1992): 1279–1323.

Gostin, Lawrence O. "Health Information Privacy." *Cornell Law Review* 80 (March 1995): 451–528.

Hendricks, Evan, and others. "Your Right to Privacy: A Basic Guide to Legal Rights in an Information Society." (ACLU Handbook Series) (New York, 1990).

Jourard, Sidney M. "Some Psychological Aspects of Privacy." *Law and Contemporary Problems* 31 (Spring 1966): 307–18.

Kirtley, Jane E. "The EU Data Protection and the First Amendment: Why a 'Press Exemption' Won't Work." *Iowa Law Review* 80 (March 1995): 639–50.

Maxeiner, James R. "Business Information and 'Personal Data': Some Common-Law Observations about the EU Draft Data Protection Directive." *Iowa Law Review* 80 (March 1995): 619–38.

_____. "Freedom of Information and the EU Data Protection Directive." *Federal Communications Law Journal* 48 (December 1995): 93–104.

McLean, Deckle. *Privacy and Its Invasion*. Praeger, 1995.

Mei, Peter. "The EC Proposed Data Protection Law." *Law and Policy in International Business* 25, 1 (1993): 305–34.

Mell, Patricia. "Seeking Shade in a Land of Perpetual Sunlight: Privacy as Property in the Electronic Wilderness." *Berkeley Technology Law Journal* 11 (Spring 1996): 1–92.

Michael, James. *Privacy and Human Rights: An International and Comparative Study, with Special Reference to Develop-*

ments in InformationTechnology. Brookfield, Vt.: Dartmouth Publishing Co., 1994.

Miller, Arthur R. *The Assault on Privacy: Computers, Data Banks, and Dossiers*. University of Michigan Press, 1971.

Murphy, Richard S. "Property Rights in Personal Information: An Economic Defense of Privacy." *Georgetown Law Journal* 84 (July 1996): 2381–2417.

Nugter, A.C.M. "Transborder Flow of Personal Data within the EC." (Deventer, The Netherlands, 1990).

Posner, Richard A. "Privacy, Secrecy, and Reputation." *Buffalo Law Review* 28 (Winter 1979): 1–56.

———. "The Right of Privacy." *Georgia Law Review* 12 (Spring 1978): 393–422.

Prosser, William L. "Privacy." *California Law Review* 48 (August 1960): 383–423.

Prowda, Judith Beth. "A Lawyer's Ramble Down the Information Superhighway: Privacy and Security of Data." *Fordham Law Review* 64 (December 1995): 738–81.

Reidenberg, Joel R. "Privacy in the Information Economy: A Fortress or Frontier for Individual Rights?" *Federal Communications Law Journal* 44 (1992): 195–243.

———. "The Privacy Obstacle Course: Hurdling Barriers to Transnational Financial Services." *Fordham Law Review* 60 (1992): S137.

———. "Setting Standards for Fair Information Practice in the U.S. Private Sector." *Iowa Law Review* 80 (March 1995): 497–552.

Roch, Michael P. "Filling the Void of Data Protection in the United States: Following the European Example." *Computer and High Technology Law Journal* 12 (February 1996): 71–96.

Rothfeder, Jeffrey. *Privacy for Sale: How Computerization Has Made Everyone's Private Life an Open Secret*. Simon and Schuster, 1992.

Sanford, Bruce W. *Libel and Privacy*. Englewood Cliffs, N.J., 1996.

Schauer, Frederick. "Reflections on the Value of Truth." *Case Western Reserve Law Review* 41, 3 (1991): 699–724.

Schoeman, Ferdinand David, ed., *Philosophical Dimensions of Privacy: An Anthology*. Cambridge University Press, 1984.

——. *Privacy and Social Freedom*. Cambridge University Press, 1992.

Schwartz, Gary T. "Explaining and Justifying a Limited Tort of False Light Invasion of Privacy." *Case Western Reserve University Law Review* 41, 3 (1991): 885–920.

Schwartz, Paul M. "Administrative Law—The Oversight of Data Protection Law" (Book Review), *American Journal of Comparative Law* 39 (Summer 1991): 618–25.

——. "Data Processing and Government Administration: The Failure of the American Legal Response to the Computer." *Hastings Law Journal* 43 (July 1992): 1321–88.

——. "European Data Protection Law and Restrictions on International Data Flows." *Iowa Law Review* 80 (March 1995): 471–96.

——. "Privacy and Participation: Personal Information and Public Sector Regulation in the United States." *Iowa Law Review* 80 (March 1995): 553–618.

——. "The Protection of Privacy in Health Care Reform." *Vanderbilt Law Review* 48 (March 1995): 295–348.

_____, and Joel R. Reidenberg. *Data Privacy Law: A Study of United States Data Protection*. Charlottesville, Va.: Commission of the European Community under license to Michie, 1996.

Shorr, Scott. "Personal Information Contracts: How to Protect Privacy without Violating the First Amendment." *Cornell Law Review* 80 (September 1995): 1756–89.

Simitis, Spiros. "From the Market to the Polis: The EU Directive on the Protection of Personal Data." *Iowa Law Review* 80 (March 1995): 445–70.

Smith, H. Jeff. *Managing Privacy: Information Technology and Corporate America*. Chapel Hill, N.C., 1994.

Smolla, Rodney A. *Free Speech in an Open Society*. New York: Vintage Books, 1993.

Trubow, George B. ed., *Privacy Law and Practice*. New York, 1987 and updates.

———. "Protecting Informational Privacy in the Information Society." *Northern Illinois Law Review* 10 (Summer 1990): 521–42.

Westin, Alan F. *Privacy and Freedom*. New York: Atheneum, 1967.

Zimmerman, Diane L. "Requiem for a Heavyweight: A Farewell to Warren and Brandeis's Privacy Tort." *Cornell Law Review* 68 (March 1983): 291–368.

Notes

Chapter One

1. Steven A. Bibas, "A Contractual Approach to Data Privacy," *Harvard Journal of Law and Public Policy,* vol. 17 (Spring 1994), pp. 591–93; and statement of Mr. Bryan in *Congressional Record,* daily ed., September 30, 1996, p. S11868.
2. James Gleick, "Behind Closed Doors; Big Brother Is Us," *New York Times,* September 29, 1996, p. 130.
3. Ibid.

Chapter Two

1. National Telecommunications and Information Administration Fact Sheet, May 30, 1995, p. 2; and Ted Bunker, *"Is It 1984?"* LAN Magazine, August 1994, p. 40.
2. Information Infrastructure Task Force, *National Information Infrastructure Agenda for Action* 5 (Washington, 1993).
3. Anne W. Branscomb, "Global Governance of Global Networks: A Survey of Transborder Data Flow in Transition," *Vanderbilt Law Review,* vol. 36 (May 1983), pp. 985–1043, esp. p. 987; and Branscomb *Who Owns Information? From Privacy to Public Access* (Basic Books, 1994).
4. Howard Gleckman, "The Technology Payoff," *Business Week,* June 14, 1993, p. 57. See generally Fred H. Cate, "The Future of Communications Policymaking," *William and Mary Bill of Rights Journal,* vol. 3 (Summer 1994), pp. 1–28, and Larry Irving, *Equipping Our Children with the Tools to Compete Successfully in the New Economy,* remarks to the Conference on Technology and the Schools: Preparing

215

216 NOTES TO PAGES 5–8

the New Workforce for the 21st Century, Randolph Center, Vt., October 28, 1996 (http://www.ntia.doc.gov.ntiahome/speeches/ 1028961i_vermont. html).

5. Irving,"Equipping Our Children."

6. Charles Goldfinger, *La Géofinance*, p. 401 (1986).

7. Pete Engardio, "Global Banker," *Business Week*, May 24, 1993, p. 50.

8. Network Wizards, Internet Domain Survey (January 1997) (http://www.nw.com/zone/WWW/report.html.

9. Network Wizards, Number of Internet Hosts (January 1996) (http://nw.com/zone/).

10. Network Wizards, Internet Domain Survey (January 1997) (http://nw.com/zone/WWW/list-bynum.html).

11. Network Wizards, Internet Domain Survey (July 1995) (http://nw.com/zone/WWW-5607/dist-bynum.html).

12. Network Wizards, Internet Domain Survey (July 1994) (http://nw.com/zone/summary-reports/report-9407.doc).

13. Network Wizards, Domain Survey Notes (July 1994) (http://www.mit.edu/people/mkgray/net/internet-growth-raw-data.htm l).

14. The First Amendment states that "Congress shall make no law respecting an establishment of religion, or prohibiting the free exercise thereof; or abridging the freedom of speech, or of the press; or the right of the people peaceably to assemble, and to petition the Government for a redress of grievances." See also, for example, Universal Declaration of Human Rights, G.A. Res. 217A (III), U.N. GAOR, 3rd sess., U.N. Doc. A/810 (1948); European Convention for the Protection of Human Rights and Fundamental Freedoms, art. 10(1), signed November 4, 1950, 213 U.N.T.S. 221; International Covenant on Civil and Political Rights, art. 19(2), opened for signature December 19, 1966, 999 U.N.T.S. 171 (entered into force March 23, 1976); African Charter on Human and Peoples' Rights, art. 9, opened for signature June 26, 1981, 21 I.L.M. 59 (entered into force October 21, 1986); and American Convention on Human Rights, art. 13, opened for signature November 22, 1969, 1144 U.N.T.S. 123 (entered into force July 18, 1978).

15. *R.A.V.* v. *City of St. Paul*, 505 U.S. 377 (1992); and *New York Times Co.* v. *United States*, 403 U.S. 713 (1971).

16. *R.A.V.*, 505 U.S. 377; *Texas* v. *Johnson*, 491 U.S. 397 (1989); and *Consolidated Edison Co.* v. *Public Service Commission*, 447 U.S. 530 (1980).

17. *Wooley* v. *Maynard*, 430 U.S. 705 (1977); *Miami Herald Publishing Co.* v. *Tornillo*, 418 U.S. 241, 244 (1974); and *West Virginia State Board of Education* v. *Barnette*, 319 U.S. 624 (1943).

18. *Red Lion Broadcasting Co.* v. *Federal Communications Commission*, 395 U.S. 367, 386 (1969).

19. *Kouvacs* v. *Cooper,* 336 U.S. 77 (1949).

20. Ibid. at 97 (Jackson, J., concurring). See also *Turner Broadcasting System, Inc.* v. *Federal Communications Commission*, 512 U.S. 622, 637 (1994) ("In light of these fundamental technological differences between broadcast and cable transmission, application of the more relaxed standard of scrutiny adopted in *Red Lion* and the other broadcast cases is inapt when determining the First Amendment validity of cable regulation . . . . This is not to say that the unique physical characteristics of cable transmission should be ignored when determining the constitutionality of regulations affecting cable speech."); *City of Los Angeles* v. *Preferred Communications, Inc.,* 476 U.S. 488, 496 (1986) ("In assessing the First Amendment claims concerning cable access, the Court must determine whether the characteristics of cable television make it sufficiently analogous to another medium to warrant application of an already existing standard or whether those characteristics require a new analysis."); *Federal Communications Commission* v. *League of Women Voters of California,* 468 U.S. 364, 374 (1984) ("we have recognized that 'differences in the characteristics of new media justify differences in the First Amendment standards applied to them.'" (quoting 395 U.S. at 367, 386)); *Members of the City Council of Los Angeles* v. *Taxpayers for Vincent,* 466 U.S. 789, 818 (1984) ("The Court recognizes that each medium for communicating ideas and information presents its own particular problems. Our analysis of the First Amendment concerns implicated by a given medium must therefore be sensitive to these particular problems and characteristics.").

21. *ACLU* v. *Reno,* 929 F. Supp. 824 (E.D. Pa. 1996), aff'd *Reno* v. *ACLU,* __ U.S. __, 1997 U.S. Lexis 4037 (1997); and *Shea ex rel. American Reporter* v. *Reno,* 930 F. Supp. 916 (S.D.N.Y. 1996).

22. See, for example, 47 U.S.C. §§ 201–220 (1997).

23. See generally *ACLU* v. *Reno,* 929 F. Supp. at 831–32.

24. Ibid.

25. Branscomb, "Global Governance of Global Networks," pp. 987, 988. See generally Fred H. Cate, "Global Information Policymaking and Domestic Law," *Indiana Journal of Global Legal Studies,* vol. 1 (Spring 1994), p. 467.

26. Joseph N. Pelton, "The Globalization of Universal Telecommunications Services," *Annual Review of the Institute for Information Studies* (Institute for Information Studies, 1991), pp. 141, 143, 176.

27. W. Sparks, address to the Conference on World Communications, Annenberg School for Communication, University of Pennsylva-

nia, 1980, quoted in Branscomb, "Global Governance of Global Networks," p. 1006.

28. Ludwig Weber, "Postal Communications, International Regulation," *Encyclopedia of Public International Law,* vol. 5 (Max Planck Institute for Comparative Public Law and International Law, 1983), p. 238.

29. Ibid.; General Agreement on Tariffs and Trade, opened for signature January 1, 1948, 61 Stat. (5), (6), T.I.A.S. No. 1700, 55 U.N.T.S. 188.

30. Alfons Noll, "International Telecommunication Union," *Encyclopedia of Public International Law,* vol. 5 (Max Planck Institute for Comparative Public Law and International Law, 1983), p. 177.; and Peter Malanczuk, "Telecommunications, International Regulation," *Encyclopedia of Public International Law* 9 (1986), p. 367.

31. See chap. 3 in this volume.

32. The U.S. Department of State administers the International Traffic in Arms Regulations, 22 C.F.R. §§ 120.01 *et seq* (1997), under the International Security Assistance and Arms Export Control Act of 1976, P. L. 94–329, 90 Stat. 729 (1976) (codified at 22 U.S.C. §§ 2751 *et seq* (1997). The regulations require the maintenance of a list—the United States Munitions List—containing "defense articles" and "defense services," the export and import of which are restricted or prohibited. Exports of communications products, including software and technical data, with potential military applications are prohibited without a license from the State Department's Office of Munitions Control.

Chapter Three

1. Ken Gormley, "One Hundred Years of Privacy," *Wisconsin Law Review* (September-October 1992), pp. 1337–38.

2. *Silverman* v. *United States,* 365 U.S. 505 (1961).

3. *California* v. *Greenwood,* 486 U.S. 35 (1988).

4. Arnold Simmel, "Privacy," *International Encyclopedia of the Social Sciences,* vol.12 (MacMillan, 1968), p. 480.

5. Arnold Simmel, "Privacy Is Not an Isolated Freedom," *Nomos* 13: *Privacy* (1971), p. 71.

6. Randall P. Bezanson, "The Right to Privacy Revisited: Privacy, News, and Social Change, 1890–1990," *California Law Review,* vol. 80 (October 1992), pp. 1133, 1135.

7. Ibid.

8. Paul M. Schwartz, "Privacy and Participation: Personal Information and Public Sector Regulation in the United States," *Iowa Law Review,* vol. 80 (March 1995), pp. 559–60. Emphasis in original.

9. Francis S. Chlapowski, "The Constitutional Protection of Informational Privacy," *Boston University Law Review*, vol. 71 (January 1991), p. 133.

10. David H. Flaherty, *Protecting Privacy in Surveillance Societies* (University of North Carolina Press, 1989), p. 8, table 1.

11. Barrington Moore, Jr., *Privacy: Studies in Social and Cultural History* (Pantheon Books, 1984), p. 73.

12. Alan F. Westin, *Privacy and Freedom* (Atheneum,1967), p. 7.

13. Tom Gerety, "Redefining Privacy," *Harvard Civil Rights-Civil Liberties Law Review*, vol. 12 (Spring 1977), pp. 233, 262–63.

14. Karen Horney, *Our Inner Conflicts: A Constructive Theory of Neurosis* (W.W. Norton and Co., 1945), p. 76.

15. Westin, *Privacy and Freedom*, p. 33.

16. Leontine Young, *Life among the Giants* (New York, 1966).

17. Westin, *Privacy and Freedom*, p. 34.

18. Ibid., p. 35.

19. Ibid., p. 45.

20. Robert Luce, *Congress, An Explanation* (Harvard University Press, 1926), pp. 12–13.

21. Alan Bates, "Privacy—A Useful Concept?" *Social Forces*, vol. 42 (1964), pp. 429, 432–33.

22. Westin, *Privacy and Freedom*, p. 37.

23. See generally Linda Greenhouse, "Justices Guard Mystique; Anger in High Court Over Marshall Papers Is Fueled by More Than Pomp and Privacy," *New York Times*, May 27, 1993, p. 1.

24. Michael R. Beschloss, *Presidents, Television and Foreign Crises* (Washington: The Annenberg Washington Program, 1993), pp. 9, 10.

25. Westin, *Privacy and Freedom*, p. 37.

26. Richard A. Posner, "The Right of Privacy," *Georgia Law Review*, vol. 12 (Spring 1978), pp. 393–409, esp. p. 399.

27. Westin, *Privacy and Freedom*, p. 7.

28. Sidney M. Jourard, "Some Psychological Aspects of Privacy," *Law and Contemporary Problems*, vol. 31 (Spring 1966), p. 307.

29. See generally Meridith Felise Sopher, "The Best of All Possible Worlds: Balancing Victims' and Defendants' Rights in the Child Sexual Abuse Case," *Fordham Law Review*, vol. 63 (November 1994), pp. 633, 640–41.

30. It is precisely for this reason that federal law requires states to mandate that persons convicted of a sexual offense against a minor register with law enforcement officials upon their release from prison and at least annually for at least ten years thereafter. 42 U.S.C. § 14071(a) (1996). State governments may disclose registration information to the public. Ibid. § 14071(d)(3). In practice, many states require the registration, and permit the disclosure, of work address and tele-

phone number, social security number, vehicle identification or driver's license number, parents' address, and/or blood type. Some states require the registrant to provide a blood, saliva, or hair sample for use in a DNA data bank. A growing number of states permit public access to registration information via 900 numbers and the Internet. Texas even publishes the information in local newspapers whenever a registered sex offender moves into an area. Texas Revised Civil Statutes Annotated art. 6252–13c.1. See generally Michele L. Earl-Hubbard, "The Child Sex Offender Registration Laws: The Punishment, Liberty, Deprivation, and Unintended Results Associated with the Scarlet Letter Laws of the 1990s," *Northwestern University Law Review*, vol. 90 (Winter 1996), p.788.

31. Posner, "The Right of Privacy," pp. 395–96, note.

32. Ibid., pp. 395–96.

33. Westin, *Privacy and Freedom*, p. 42.

Chapter Four

1. See David H. Flaherty, *Protecting Privacy in Surveillance Societies: The Federal Republic of Germany, Sweden, France, Canada, and the United States* (University of North Carolina Press, 1989), p. 306.

2. Personal communication to the author from Scott Blackmer, April 9, 1997; "Data Protection Round-Up," *Privacy Law and Business* (January 1996), pp. 1–8. For more detailed information about national statutory protection of privacy in Europe, see Flaherty, *Protecting Privacy*, and A.C.M. Nugter, *Transborder Flow of Personal Data within the EC* (The Netherlands: Kluwer Law and Taxation Publishers, 1990).

3. European laws have also influenced recent omnibus privacy legislation outside of Europe, including in Quebec, Israel, Taiwan, and Hong Kong. Personal communication to the author from Blackmer, April 9, 1997.

4. Paul M. Schwartz, "Administrative Law—The Oversight of Data Protection Law" (Book Review), *American Journal of Comparative Law*, vol. 39 (Summer 1991), pp. 618, 619, 625.

5. Flaherty, *Protecting Privacy*, pp. 165–66.

6. Ibid.

7. Schwartz, "Administrative Law," p. 623.

8. The OECD was founded in 1960 by twenty nations, including the United States, "to promote economic and social welfare throughout the OECD area by assisting member governments in the formulation and coordination of policies; to stimulate and harmonize members' aid efforts in favor of developing nations; and to contribute to the expansion of world trade." Robert G. Boehmer and Todd S. Palmer, "The 1992 EC

Data Protection Proposal: An Examination of Its Implications for U.S. Business and U.S. Privacy Law," *American Business Law Journal*, vol. 31 (September 1993), pp. 265, 271, n. 33.

9. O.E.C.D. Doc. (C 58 final) (October 1, 1980).

10. Eur. T.S. No. 108 (January 28, 1981).

11. Ibid., arts. 5–6.

12. Ibid., art 8.

13. See "Data Protection Directive" in this chapter.

14. See generally Joel R. Reidenberg, "The Privacy Obstacle Course: Hurdling Barriers to Transnational Financial Services," *Fordham Law Review*, vol. 60 (May 1992), pp. S137, S143–48.

15. The European Commission is the administrative body of the European Union, responsible for overseeing and implementing the requirements of EU foundational treaties. The commission has 20 members, including at least one but not more than two from each member state.

16. Com(92)422 Final SYN 287 (October 15, 1992).

17. The fifteen current members of the EU are Austria, Belgium, Denmark, Finland, France, Germany, Greece, Ireland, Italy, Luxembourg, the Netherlands, Portugal, Spain, Sweden, and the United Kingdom.

18. Treaty Establishing the European Economic Community, March 25, 1957, 28 U.N.T.S. 3, art. 2 (1958), as amended by the Single European Act, O.J. L 169/1 (1987), [1987] 2 C.M.L.R. 741, and the Treaty on European Union, February 7, 1992, O.J. C 224/01 (1992), [1992] C.M.L.R. 719, reprinted in *International Legal Materials*, vol. 31 (March 1992), pp. 247–373.

19. Treaty on European Union, February 7, 1992, O.J. C 224/01 (1992), [1992] C.M.L.R. 719, reprinted in *International Legal Materials*, vol. 31 (March 1992), pp. 247–343.

20. The European Parliament is the legislative body of the EU and is composed of 624 members, who are elected through direct universal suffrage.

21. The Council of Ministers is composed of ministers from each member country; it may accept or reject, but not modify, measures proposed by the commission.

22. 1995 O.J. (C93) 1.

23. *Directive 95/46/EC of the European Parliament and of the Council on the Protection of Individuals with Regard to the Processing of Personal Data and on the Free Movement of Such Data* (Eur. O.J. 95/L281) (directive). The directive is reprinted in appendix A in this volume.

24. Ibid., art. 2(b).

25. Ibid.

26. Ibid., art 2(a). "An identifiable person is one who can be identified, directly or indirectly, in particular by reference to an identification number or to one or more factors specific to his physical, physiological, mental, economic, cultural or social identity."

27. Ibid., art. 3(2).

28. See "Basic Protections," "Disclosure to Data Subjects," "Access to, and Opportunity to Correct, Personal Data," and "Registration of Data Processing Activities" in this chapter.

29. *Directive 95/46/EC*, art. 13.

30. Ibid., art. 6(1).

31. Ibid., art. 7.

32. Ibid., art. 8.

33. Ibid., art. 11(1). The data "controller" is the person or organization who "processes personal data or causes it to be processed and who decides what is the purpose and objective of the processing, which operations are to be performed upon them and which third parties are to have access to them." Ibid., art. 2(d).

34. Ibid., art. 12(1).

35. Ibid., art. 13(1).

36. Ibid., art. 14(1).

37. Ibid., art. 13(2).

38. Ibid., art. 14(3).

39. Ibid., art. 15(1).

40. Ibid., art. 15(3).

41. Ibid., art. 17(1).

42. Ibid., art. 18(1).

43. Ibid., art. 18(2).

44. Ibid., art. 18(4).

45. Ibid., art. 19.

46. Ibid., art. 21.

47. Ibid., art. 16(1).

48. *Council Directive on the Protection of Individuals with Regard to the Processing of Personal Data and on the Free Movement of Such Data, Explanatory Memorandum*, Com(92)422 Final SYN 287, 26 (October 15, 1992).

49. Ibid.

50. Ibid.

51. *Directive 95/46/EC*, art. 13(5).

52. Ibid., art. 30(1).

53. Ibid., art. 30(2).

54. Ibid., art. 30(3).

55. Ibid., art. 23.

56. Ibid., art. 25.

57. Ibid., art. 22.

58. Ibid., art. 25(1).

59. Ibid., art. 25(2).

60. Ibid., art. 26(1).

61. Ibid., art 1(2).

62. Ibid., art. 1(1).

63. Spiros Simitis, Unpublished Address, Information Privacy and the Public Interest, Annenberg Washington Program, Washington, October 6, 1994.

64. *The Home Office Consultation Paper on the Implementation of the EU Data Protection Directive—the British Bankers' Association Response*, Annex I (Costs).

65. *Directive 95/46/EC*, art. 9.

66. Ibid., art. 8.

67. Ibid., art. 11.

68. Flaherty, *Protecting Privacy*, pp. 373–74.

69. European Convention for the Protection of Human Rights and Fundamental Freedoms, art. 10(1), signed November 4, 1950, 213 U.N.T.S. 221.

70. See, for example, Universal Declaration of Human Rights, G.A. Res. 217A (III), U.N. GAOR, 3d sess., U.N. Doc. A/810 (1948); European Convention for the Protection of Human Rights and Fundamental Freedoms, art. 10(1), signed November 4, 1950, 213 U.N.T.S. 221; International Covenant on Civil and Political Rights, art. 19(2), opened for signature December 19, 1966, 999 U.N.T.S. 171 (entered into force March 23, 1976); African Charter on Human and Peoples' Rights, art. 9, opened for signature June 26, 1981, 21 I.L.M. 59 (entered into force October 21, 1986); American Convention on Human Rights, art. 13, opened for signature November 22, 1969, 1144 U.N.T.S. 123 (entered into force July 18, 1978).

71. 32 O.J. Eur. Comm. (No. L 298) 23 (1989). See generally Fred H. Cate, *The European Broadcasting Directive*, Communications Committee, Section of International Law and Practice (American Bar Association, 1990); and Fred H. Cate, *The Continuing Battle Over the EC Broadcasting Directive*, Communications Committee, Section of International Law and Practice (American Bar Association, 1991).

72. *Directive 95/46/EC*, art. 4. "European works" are defined to include programming originating from Member States or other European states which are party to the convention, which also meet one of three conditions: (1) they are made by producers "established" in member states; (2) the production of the works is supervised and actually controlled by producers established in member states; or (3) a majority of financing for each production is supplied by EC coproducers and the coproduction is not controlled by any producer established outside of the EC. *Directive 95/46/EC*, art. 6.

"European works" may also include programming originating from European states which are neither member states nor adherents to the convention, but are produced with producers established in member states or by producers in European countries which will agree to abide by the Treaty of Rome, provided that the production must be "mainly made" with authors and workers residing in European countries.

Programming which meets none of the definitions above can still be considered a European work "to an extent corresponding to the production of the contribution of European co-producers to the total production costs," provided that the production is made "mainly" with authors and works residing in European countries.

73. *Television Broadcasting and the European Community,* Hearings before the House Committee on Energy and Commerce, Subcommittee on Telecommunications and Finance, 101 Cong. 1 sess. (Government Printing Office, 1989), p. 54 (statement of Richard Frank).

74. Paul M. Schwartz and Joel R. Reidenberg, *Data Privacy Law: A Statement of United States Data Protection* (Charlottesville, Va.: Michie, 1996), pp. 13, 15, 16.

75. Ibid., pp. 13–14.

76. Ibid., p. 15.

77. *Directive 95/46/EC* , art. 8.

78. Ibid., art. 3(2).

79. Ibid., art. 2(a).

Chapter Five

1. "The unifying theme underlying the cooperation of the nations of western Europe in the European Economic Community has been that economic union quite necessarily leads to political union, and both work in unison to preserve peace. Western Europe has become an arena of concerted economic, social, cultural, and now political union as the European Union." John P. Flaherty and Maureen E. Lally-Green, "The European Union: Where is It Now?" *Duquesne University Law Review,* vol. 34 (Summer 1996), pp. 923, 926.

2. *Clyatt* v. *United States,* 197 U.S. 207, 216–220 (1905).

3. *New York Times Co.* v. *Sullivan,* 376 U.S. 254, 265 (1964).

4. *Marsh* v. *Alabama,* 326 U.S. 501 (1946).

5. *Evans* v. *Newtown,* 382 U.S. 296 (1966).

6. "Congress shall make no law respecting an establishment of religion, or prohibiting the free exercise thereof; or abridging the freedom of speech, or of the press; or the right of the people peaceably to assemble . . . ." U.S. Const, Amend I.

7. *N.A.A.C.P.* v. *Alabama,* 357 U.S. 449 (1958).

8. Ibid. at 464–65.

9. *Breard* v. *Alexandria*, 341 U.S. 622 (1951).

10. Ibid. at 644.

11. *Kouvacs* v. *Cooper*, 336 U.S. 77 (1949).

12. Ibid. at 86–87.

13. *Rowan* v. *U.S. Post Office Dept.*, 397 U.S. 728 (1970).

14. *FCC* v. *Pacifica Foundation*, 438 U.S. 726 (1978).

15. Ibid. at 748.

16. *Frisby* v. *Schultz*, 487 U.S. 474 (1988).

17. Ibid. at 484 (quoting *Carey*, 447 U.S. at 471).

18. Ibid. (quoting *Gregory* v. *City of Chicago*, 394 U.S. 111, 125 [1969] [Black, J., concurring]).

19. 447 U.S. 455 (1980). The Court in *Carey* struck down the Illinois ordinance at issue which prohibited residential picketing, on the grounds that the ordinance excluded labor picketing.

20. Ibid. at 471.

21. 394 U.S. 557 (1969).

22. Ibid. at 568.

23. Ibid. at 564.

24. Ibid. at 565.

25. Thomas Emerson, *The System of Freedom of Expression* (Random House, 1970), p. 6.

26. *West Virginia State Board of Education* v. *Barnette*, 319 U.S. at 624.

27. Rodney A. Smolla, *Free Speech in an Open Society* (Alfred A. Knopf, 1992), p. 10.

28. Ken Gormley, "One Hundred Years of Privacy," *Wisconsin Law Review* (September-October 1992), pp. 1335, 1381.

29. Ibid.

30. *Communist Party of the U.S.* v. *Subversive Activities Control Board*, 367 U.S. 1 (1961); *Scales* v. *United States*, 367 U.S. 203 (1961); and *Noto* v. *United States*, 367 U.S. 290 (1961).

31. *Lovell* v. *City of Griffin*, 303 U.S. 444, 447 (1938); *Schneider* v. *State*, 308 U.S. 147, 163 (1939); *Staub* v. *City of Baxley*, 355 U.S. 313 (1958).

32. *Public Utilities Commission* v. *Pollak*, 343 U.S. 451 (1952).

33. *Erznoznik* v. *City of Jacksonville*, 422 U.S. 205 (1975).

34. *Cohen* v. *California*, 403 U.S. 15 (1971).

35. *Florida Star* v. *B.J.F.*, 491 U.S. 524 (1989); *Smith* v. *Daily Mail Publishing Co.*, 443 U.S. 97 (1979); *Landmark Communications Inc.* v. *Virginia*, 435 U.S. 829 (1978); *Cox Broadcasting Corp.* v. *Cohn*, 420 U.S. 469 (1975).

36. *Hustler Magazine, Inc. et al.* v. *Falwell*, 485 U.S. 46 (1988); *Time, Inc.* v. *Hill*, 385 U.S. 374 (1967).

37. The right of the people to be secure in their persons, houses, papers, and effects, against unreasonable searches and seizures, shall not be violated; and no Warrants shall issue, but upon probable cause, supported by Oath or affirmation, and particularly describing the place to be searched, and the persons or things to be seized. U.S. Const, Amend IV.

38. *Boyd* v. *United States*, 116 U.S. 616, 625–26 (1886).

39. Samuel D. Warren and Louis D. Brandeis, "The Right to Privacy," *Harvard Law Review*, vol. 4 (December 1890), p. 193.

40. 277 U.S. 438 (1928).

41. 277 U.S. at 478–79 (Brandeis, J., concurring). The Fifth Amendment provides in relevant part: "No person shall . . . be deprived of life, liberty, or property, without due process of law . . . ." U.S. Const, Amend V.

42. 389 U.S. 347 (1967).

43. Ibid. at 351.

44. Ibid. at 360–61 (Harlan, J., concurring).

45. Ibid. at 361 (Harlan, J., concurring).

46. *Terry* v. *Ohio*, 392 U.S. 1, 9 (1968); and *Smith* v. *Maryland*, 442 U.S. 735, 740 (1979).

47. See Gormley, "One Hundred Years of Privacy," pp. 1368–1370, and sources cited therein.

48. *Oliver* v. *United States*, 466 U.S. 170–97, 177–82 (*1984*); and *Smith* v. *Maryland* , 442 U.S. at 749 (1979).

49. *United States* v. *Miller*, 425 U.S. 435 (1976); and *Couch* v. *United States*, 403 U.S. 322 (1973).

50. Paul M. Schwartz and Joel R. Reidenberg, *Data Privacy Law: A Study of United States Data Protection* (Charlottesville, Va.: Michie, 1996), p. 63.

51. Gormley, "One Hundred Years of Privacy," p. 1372.

52. Schwartz and Reidenberg, *Data Privacy Law*, pp. 63–64.

53. *United States* v. *White*, 401 U.S. 745, 752 (1971) (plurality opinion).

54. *Vernonia School District 47J* v. *Acton*, 515 U.S. 646, __, 115 S. Ct. 2386, 2393 (1995).

55. 381 U.S. 479, 485–86 (1965).

56. Ibid. at 484.

57. Ibid.

58. 410 U.S. 113, 153 (1973).

59. Ibid. The Fourteenth Amendment provides, in relevant part: "No State shall make or enforce any law which shall . . . deprive any person of life, liberty, or property, without due process of law." U.S. Const, Amend XIV.

60. *Roe* v. *Wade*, 410 U.S. at 152 (quoting *Palko* v. *Connecticut*, 302 U.S. 319, 325 [1937]).

61. Ibid. at 152–53.

62. Ibid. at 155.

63. 478 U.S. 186–219 (1986).

64. 492 U.S. 490, 501, 571 (1989) (plurality).

65. Ibid. at 520.

66. Laurence H. Tribe, *Abortion: The Clash of Absolutes* (Norton, 1990), p. 23.

67. Francis S. Chlapowski, "The Constitutional Protection of Informational Privacy," *Boston University Law Review*, vol. 71 (January 1991), pp. 143–44.

68. 429 U.S. 589 (1977).

69. Ibid. at 599–600.

70. Ibid. at 599, n.23.

71. Ibid. at 603–04. The Court also explicitly rejected the application of the Fourth Amendment right of privacy, writing that Fourth Amendment cases "involve affirmative, unannounced, narrowly focused intrusions." Ibid. at 604, n.32.

72. 724 F.2d 1010 (D.C. Cir. 1984).

73. Ibid. at 1019.

74. Ibid. at 1022.

75. Ibid. at 1023.

76. *Barry* v. *City of New York*, 712 F.2d 1554, 1559 (2d Cir. 1983); *Schacter* v. *Whalen*, 581 F.2d 35, 37 (2d Cir. 1978); *Doe* v. *Southeastern Pennsylvania Transportation Authority*, 72 F.3d 1133 (3d Cir. 1995); *United States* v. *Westinghouse Electric Corporation*, 638 F.2d 570, 577 (3rd Cir. 1980); *Plante* v. *Gonzalez*, 575 F.2d 1119, 1123 (5th Cir. 1978); *Doe* v. *Attorney General*, 941 F.2d 780, 795–97 (9th Cir. 1991).

77. *Doe* v. *Attorney General*, 941 F.2d at 796.

78. 895 F.2d 188, 192 (4th Cir. 1990).

79. Ibid. at 193.

80. Ibid. at 207.

81. *J.P.* v. *DeSanti*, 653 F.2d 1080 (6th Cir. 1981).

82. 429 U.S. at 604, n.32.

83. Alan F.Westin, *Privacy and Freedom* (Atheneum, 1967), p. 7.

84. Minnesota Const, Art 1, § 10.

85. Hawaii Const, Art. 1, § 7; and Louisiana Const, Art 1, § 5.

86. Arizona Const, Art 2, § 8.

87. Florida Const, Art 1, § 23.

88. Alaska Const, Art I, § 22.

89. California Const, Art I, § 1.

90. *Hill* v. *National Collegiate Athletic Association*, 7 Cal. 4th 1, 865 P.2d 633 (1994).

91. Illinois Const, Art 1, § 6.

92. Hawaii Const, Art 1, § 6.

93. See Lyle Denniston, "Judge OKs Same-Sex Marriages," *Baltimore Sun*, December 4, 1996, p. 1A.

94. *Hill*, 7 Cal. 4th 1, 865 P.2d 633.

95. *Vernonia School District 47J*, 515 U.S. 646 (1995).

96. *NAACP et al.* v. *Claiborne Hardware Co. et. al.*, 458 U.S. 886–939, 913 (1982); see also *Carey* v. Brown, 447 U.S. 455, 467 (1980); *Mills* v. *Alabama*, 384 U.S. 214, 218–19 (1966) ("Whatever differences may exist about interpretations of the First Amendment, there is practically universal agreement that a major purpose of that Amendment was to protect the free discussion of governmental affairs."); *Garrison* v. *Louisiana*, 379 U.S. 64, 74–75 (1964); *New York Times* v. *Sullivan*, 376 U.S. 254, 269–270 (1964); *Roth* v. *United States*, 354 U.S. 476, 484 (1957) (The first amendment was "fashioned to assure unfettered interchange of ideas for the bringing about of political and social changes desired by the people."); *Stromberg* v. *California*, 283 U.S. 359, 369 (1931) ("The maintenance of the opportunity for free political discussion to the end that government may be responsive to the will of the people and that changes may be obtained by lawful means, an opportunity essential to the security of the Republic, is a fundamental principle of our constitutional system.").

97. Robert Bork, "Neutral Principles and Some First Amendment Problems," *Indiana Law Journal*, vol. 47 (Fall 1971), p. 23.

98. *New York Times Co.* v. *Sullivan*, 376 U.S. 254, 269 (1964) citing *Roth* v. *U.S.*, 354 U.S. 476, 484.

99. *Gertz* v. *Robert Welch, Inc.*, 418 U.S. 323, 339–340 (1974); see also *Whitney* v. *California*, 274 U.S. 357, 375–76 (Brandeis, J., concurring) ("the fitting remedy for evil counsels is good ones. Believing in the power of reason as applied through public discussion, they [the Framers] eschewed silence coerced by law—the argument of force in its worst form.")

100. See *Cohen* v. *California*, 403 U.S. 15 (1971); and *Hustler Magazine, Inc.* v. *Falwell*, 485 U.S. 46 (1988).

101. *Terminiello* v. *Chicago*, 337 U.S. 1, 4 (1949). Justice Brandeis wrote in *Whitney* v. *California*, that the Court has determined that "the necessity which is essential to a valid restriction does not exist unless speech would produce, or is intended to produce, a clear and imminent danger of some substantive evil which the state constitutionally may seek to prevent." 274 U.S. 357, 373 (Brandeis, J., concurring).

102. *Stanley* v. *Georgia*, 394 U.S. 557 at 566 (quoting *Kingsley International Pictures Corp.* v. *Regents*, 360 U.S. 684, 688 (1959).

103. David A. J. Richards, "Free Speech and Obscenity Law: Toward a Moral Theory of the First Amendment, *University of Pennsylvania Law Review*, vol. 123 (November 1974), p. 62.

104. *R.A.V.* v. *City of St. Paul, Minnesota* (1992), 505 U.S. 377, 436; *New York Times Co.* v. *United States*, 403 U.S. 713 (1971). See generally, Fred H. Cate, "The First Amendment and the National Information Infrastructure," *Wake Forest Law Review*, vol. 30 (Spring 1995), pp. 10–11.

105. *R.A.V.* 505 U.S. 377; *Texas* v. *Johnson*, 491 U.S. 397–439 (1989); and *Consolidated Edison Co. of New York* v. *Public Service Commission*, 447 U.S. 530–55 (1980). See generally, Cate, "The First Amendment," pp. 11–12.

106. *Wooley* v. *Maynard*, 430 U.S. 705 (1977); *Miami Herald Publishing Co.* v. *Tornillo*, 418 U.S. 241, 244 (1974); *West Virginia State Board of Education* v. *Barnette*, 319 U.S. 624 (1943). See generally, Cate, "The First Amendment," pp. 12–14.

107. *Joseph Burstyn, Inc.* v. *Wilson*, 343 U.S. 495 (1952).

108. *Philadelphia Newspapers, Inc.* v. *Hepps*, 475 U.S. 767 (1986); *Gertz* v. *Robert Welch, Inc.*, 418 U.S. 323 (1974); and *New York Times Co.* v. *Sullivan*, 376 U.S. 254 (1964). See generally, Cate, "The First Amendment," pp. 14–16.

109. *United States* v. *Eichman et al.*, 496 U.S. 310–24 (1990); and *Texas* v. *Johnson*, 491 U.S. 397 (1989). See generally, Cate, "The First Amendment," p. 16.

110. *Minneapolis Star & Tribune Co.* v. *Minnesota Commissioner of Revenue*, 460 U.S. 575–604 (1983); *First National Bank* v. *Bellotti*, 435 U.S. 765 (1978); and *Buckley* v. *Valeo*, 424 U.S. 1 (1976). See generally, Cate, "The First Amendment," pp. 16–18.

111. *New York Times Co.* v. *United States*, 403 U.S. 713 (1971).

112. *Landmark Communications, Inc.* v. *Virginia*, 435 U.S. 829 (1978).

113. *Smith* v. *Daily Mail Publishing Co.*, 443 U.S. 97 (1979).

114. *Florida Star* v. *B.J.F.*, 491 U.S. 524 (1989); *Cox Broadcasting Corp.* v. *Cohn*, 420 U.S. 469 (1975).

115. Peter B. Edelman, "Free Press v. Privacy: Haunted by the Ghost of Justice Black," *Texas Law Review*, vol. 68 (May 1990), p. 1198.

116. *New York Times Co.* v. *Sullivan*, 376 U.S. 254 (1964).

117. *Cantrell* v. *Forest City Publishing Co.*, 419 U.S. 245 (1974).

118. *Florida Star*, 491 U.S. 524.

119. *Masson* v. *New Yorker Magazine*, 501 U.S. 496 (1991).

120. *Anderson et al.* v. *Liberty Lobby, Inc. et al.*, 477 U.S. 242–73 (1986) (requiring that the standard for summary judgment motions take into account the plaintiff's burden at trial); *Bose Corp.* v. *Consumers Union of United States, Inc.*, 466 U.S. 485 (1984) (requiring independent appellant review).

121. *Philadelphia Newspapers, Inc.* v. *Hepps*, 475 U.S. 767 (1986).

122. *Monitor Patriot Co.* v. *Roy*, 401 U.S. 265 (1971).

123. *New York Times Co.* v. *Sullivan*, 376 U.S. 254; *Gertz* v. *Robert Welch, Inc.*, 418 U.S. 323 (1974).

124. *Central Hudson Gas & Electric Corp.* v. *Public Service Commission of New York*, 447 U.S. 557–606, 566 (1980); and quotation in *Board of Trustees* v. *Fox*, 492 U.S. 469, 480 (1989).

125. *Central Hudson*, 447 U.S. 557.

126. *Lowe* v. *Securities and Exchange Commission*, 472 U.S. 181 (1985).

127. "No person shall . . . be deprived of life, liberty, or property, without due process of law . . . nor shall private property be taken for public use, without just compensation." U.S. Const, Amend V.

128. *Loretto* v. *Teleprompter Manhattan CATV Corp.*, 458 U.S. 419 (1982) (only 1.5 cubic feet of private property occupied).

129. *First English Evangelical Lutheran Church of Glendale* v. *County of Los Angeles*, 482 U.S. 304 (1987) (plaintiff denied use of its property for six years).

130. *Pennsylvania Coal* Co. v. *Mahon*, 260 U.S. 393 (1922) (state abrogated right to remove coal from property).

131. See, for example, *Logan* v. *Zimmerman Brush Co.*, 455 U.S. 422 (1982) (property interest in statutorily created cause of action for discrimination against the disabled); *U.S. Trust Co.* v. *New Jersey*, 431 U.S. 1 (1977) (property interest in common law contract rights).

132. See, for example, *Mathews* v. *Eldridge*, 424 U.S. 319 (1976) (property interest in Social Security benefits).

133. See, for example, *Perry* v. *Sindermann*, 408 U.S. 593 (1972) (property interest in continued employment).

134. *Ruckelshaus* v. *Monsanto*, 467 U.S. 986 (1984).

135. *Lucas* v. *South Carolina Coastal Council*, 505 U.S. 1003, 1071 (1992).

136. Ibid. at 1016; *Agins* v. *City of Tiburon*, 447 U.S. 255, 260 (1980); *Andrus* v. *Allard*, 444 U.S. 51, 64 (1979).

137. See Jan G. Laitos, "The Takings Clause in America's Industrial States after Lucas," *University of Toledo Law Review*, vol. 24 (Winter 1993), pp. 281, 288.

138. *Lucas*, 505 U.S. at 1026.

139. Ibid. at 1027, 1029.

140. A legislature can effect a taking just as a regulatory agency can. See, for example, *Agins*, 447 U.S. 255. Both are generally referred to as "regulatory takings," although the former is actually a "legislative taking." See generally *Parking Association of Georgia, Inc.* v. *City of Atlanta*, 515 U.S. 1116 (1995) (Thomas, J., dissenting from denial of certiorari).

141. Anne W. Branscomb, *Who Owns Information? From Privacy to Public Access* (Basic Books, 1994).

142. 17 U.S.C. §§ 101–106 (1997).

143. Arthur R. Miller, "Confidentiality, Protective Orders, and Public Access to the Courts," *Harvard Law Review*, vol. 105 (December 1991), pp. 427, 469.

144. Courts are widely considered "state actors" for purposes of constitutional analysis, and the Supreme Court has recognized that the takings clause applies to the courts. In a 1967 concurrence, Justice Stewart asserted that the Fourteenth Amendment forbids a state to take property without compensation "no less through its courts than through its legislature."

Note, "Trade Secrets in Discovery: From First Amendment Disclosure to Fifth Amendment Protection," *Harvard Law Review*, vol. 104 (April 1991), pp. 1330, 1336 (citations omitted) (quoting *Hughes* v. *Washington*, 389 U.S. 290, 298 [1967] [Stewart, J., concurring]).

145. *Rakas* v. *Illinois*, 439 U.S. 128, 143–44 n.12 (1978).

146. Jeanne L. Schroeder, "Never Jam To-Day: On the Impossibility of Takings Jurisprudence," *Georgetown Law Journal*, vol. 84 (May 1996), pp. 1531–69, 1544.

147. John Locke, *Two Treatises of Government* (New American Library, 1963), p. 395.

148. Ibid. at 373.

149. Charles A. Reich, "The New Property," *Yale Law Journal*, vol. 73 (April 1964), p. 733.

150. Office of Management and Budget, Circular No. A-130, *Management of Federal Information Resources*, § 7(a), 50 *Federal Register* 52736 (December 24, 1985)

151. David H. Flaherty, *Protecting Privacy in Surveillance Societies: The Federal Republic of Germany, Sweden, France, Canada, and the United States* (University of North Carolina Press, 1989), p. 314.

152. Paul M. Schwartz, "Data Processing and Government Administration: The Failure of the American Legal Response to the Computer," *Hastings Law Journal*, vol. 43 (July 1992), 1321, 1333–34.

153. Lillian R. BeVier, "Information about Individuals in the Hands of Government: Some Reflections on Mechanisms for Privacy Protection," *William and Mary Bill of Rights Journal*, vol. 4 (Winter 1995), pp. 455–506, esp. p. 504.

154. Ibid.

155. 5 U.S.C. § 552 (1997).

156. Ibid. § 552(b)(6)-(7)(C).

157. *U.S. Department of Justice* v. *Reporters Committee for Freedom of the Press*, 489 U.S. 749, 772 (1989) (emphasis added). See generally Fred H. Cate, D. Annette Fields, and James K. McBain, "The Right to Privacy and the Public's Right to Know: The 'Central Purpose' of the

Freedom of Information Act," *Administrative Law Review*, vol. 41 (Winter 1994), p. 41.

158. Ibid. at 773, 774 (quoting *Environmental Protection Agency* v. *Mink*, 410 U.S. 73, 105 (1973) (Douglas, J., dissenting) (emphasis in original).

159. 5 U.S.C. §§ 552a(e)(1)-(5) (1997).

160. Ibid. § 552a(b).

161. Ibid. § 552a(t)(2).

162. Ibid. § 552(a)(b)(1)-(12).

163. Flaherty, *Protecting Privacy*, p. 323.

164. Paul M. Schwartz and Joel R. Reidenberg, *Data Privacy Law* (Charlottesville, Va.: Michie, 1996), p. 98.

165. P.L. 100–503, H.R. 100–802 3114 (1988) (amending 5 U.S.C. § 552a).

166. 42 U.S.C. § 1305 (1997).

167. 26 U.S.C. §§ 6103, 7431 (1997).

168. 13 U.S.C. §§ 8–9 (1994).

169. P.L. 103–322, 108 Stat. 2099–2102 (1994) (codified at 18 U.S.C. § 2721 [1997]).

170. Violent Crime Control and Law Enforcement Act of 1994, P.L. 103–322, 108 Stat. 1796 (codified at various sections throughout 18 U.S.C. [1997]).

171. 18 U.S.C. § 2721(a) (1997).

172. Ibid. § 2721(b)(1).

173. Ibid. § 2721(b)(6), (9).

174. Ibid. § 2721(b)(8).

175. Ibid. § 2721(b)(2).

176. Ibid. § 2721(b)(11).

Chapter Six

1. Paul M. Schwartz and Joel R. Reidenberg, *Data Privacy Law* (Charlottesville, Va.: Michie, 1996), p. 215.

2. For excellent, more detailed surveys of the U.S. privacy laws applicable to the private sector, see Schwartz and Reidenberg, *Data Privacy Law*, pp. 219–377; and Joel R. Reidenberg, "Privacy in the Information Economy: A Fortress or Frontier for Individual Rights?" *Federal Communications Law Journal*, vol. 44 (March 1992), pp. 195, 210–19.

3. 15 U.S.C. §§ 1681–1681t (1997).

4. Reidenberg, "Privacy in the Information Economy," p. 210.

5. 15 U.S.C. § 1681e(b) (1997).

6. Ibid. § 1681i.

7. Ibid. § 1681m.

8. Ibid. § 1681g.

9. Ibid. § 1681b.

10. Ibid. §1681c(a).

11. Ibid. §1681c(b).

12. Reidenberg, "Privacy in the Information Economy," p. 213, n.92.

13. *Department of Defense Appropriations Act, 1997*, H.R. 3610, 104th Cong., 2d sess. §§ 2401–2422 (September 30, 1996) (to be codified at 15 U.S.C. §§ 1681–1681t).

14. Ibid. § 2403(a) (to be codified at 15 U.S.C. § 1681b(a)(3)(F)).

15. Ibid. § 2403(b) (to be codified at 15 U.S.C. § 1681b(b)).

16. Ibid. § 2405 (to be codified at 15 U.S.C. § 1681b(g)).

17. Ibid. § 2404(a)(2) (to be codified at 15 U.S.C. § 1681b(c)(5)).

18. Ibid. § 2411(b) (to be codified at 15 U.S.C. § 1681m(d)).

19. Ibid. § 2406(a)(2) (to be codified at 15 U.S.C. § 1681c(b)).

20. Ibid. § 2408 (to be codified at 15 U.S.C. § 1681g(a)).

21. Ibid. § 2409 (to be codified at 15 U.S.C. § 1681i(a)).

22. Ibid. § 2413 (to be codified at 15 U.S.C. § 1681).

23. Ibid. § 2422.

24. 15 U.S.C. §§ 1681a(f), (d).

25. 15 U.S.C. §§ 1693–1693r.

26. Reidenberg, "Privacy in the Information Economy," p. 214.

27. 15 U.S.C. §§ 1693c-d.

28. Ibid. § 1693f.

29. Reidenberg, "Privacy in the Information Economy," p. 214.

30. 15 U.S.C. § 1666 (1997).

31. Reidenberg, "Privacy in the Information Economy," p. 213.

32. 15 U.S.C. § 1692c(b) (1997).

33. 18 U.S.C. §§ 2510–2520, 2701–2709 (1997).

34. Ibid. §§ 2510–11.

35. Ibid. § 2511(2)(c).

36. Ibid. § 2511.

37. Ibid. § 2511(2)(g).

38. The Federal Communications Commission regulated the disclosure of such information as a way of promoting competition among telephone companies. 47 C.F.R. § 64.702(d)(3) (1997). Under the commission's regulations, a regulated telecommunications service provider could not provide information about telecommunications transactions to its own subsidiaries who offered "enhanced" services unless the provider also disclosed that information to competitors. Ibid.

39. 18 U.S.C. § 2511(2)(h)(i) (1997).

40. P. L. 104–104, 11 Stat. 56 § 702 (to be codified at 47 U.S.C. § 222).

41. Ibid. (to be codified at 47 U.S.C. § 222(f)(1)).

42. Ibid. (to be codified at 47 U.S.C. § 222(c)(1)).
43. Ibid. (to be codified at 47 U.S.C. § 222(d)).
44. 47 U.S.C. § 551(a)(1) (1997).
45. Ibid. § 551(a).
46. Ibid. § 551(f).
47. Ibid. § 551(c)(2).
48. Ibid. 18 U.S.C. § 2710 (1997).
49. Ibid. § 2710(e).
50. Ibid. § 2710(b)(2)(E).
51. Ibid. § 2710(b)(2)(D).
52. 42 U.S.C. §§ 2000e, 2000e-2(a) (1997).
53. Ibid. §§ 3601, 3604–06.
54. 29 U.S.C. §§ 2001–2009 (1997).
55. 20 U.S.C. § 1232g (1997).
56. Ibid. §§ 1232g(a)(1)(A), 1232g(d).
57. Ibid. § 1232g(a)(2).
58. Ibid. §§ 1232g(b)(1)-(3).
59. Ibid. § 1232g(b)(3).
60. Ibid. § 1232g(e).
61. Ibid. §§ 1232g(a)(1)(B)-(C).
62. Ibid. § 1232g(a)(5).
63. Ibid. § 1232g(f).
64. See "State Constitutions."
65. Reidenberg, "Privacy in the Information Economy," pp. 227–28.
66. Massachusetts Annotated Laws ch. 214, § 1B (1996).
67. See "Tort Law."
68. Wisconsin Statutes Annotated § 895.50 (1995). See "Tort Law."
69. Ibid. § 895.50(1)(a).
70. See, for example, California Civil Code § 3344 (1996); Florida Statutes Annotated § 540.08 (1996); New York Civil Rights Law §§ 50–51 (1996). See "Tort Law."
71. See, for example, Massachusetts Annotated Laws ch. 93, §§ 50–68 (1996) (credit reporting); New York General Business Law § 380 (1996) (credit reporting); Delaware Code Annotated tit. 11, §§ 1335–36 (1996) (intrastate telephone service); Pennsylvania Consolidated Statutes Annotated §§ 5701–775 (1996) (intrastate telephone service); New Jersey Statutes Annotated § 48:5A-54 to-63 (1996) (cable subscriber information and viewing habits); California Labor Code § 1198.5 (1996) (employee personnel records); Connecticut General Statutes Annotated § 31–128e (1996) (employee personnel records).
72. Reidenberg, "Privacy in the Information Economy," p. 229.
73. Samuel D. Warren and Louis D. Brandeis, "The Right to Privacy," *Harvard Law Review*, vol. 4 (December 1890); and William L.

Prosser, "Privacy," *California Law Review*, vol. 48 (August 1960), pp. 383–423.

74. Prosser, "Privacy," p. 389.

75. Restatement (Second) of Torts § 652A (1976).

76. "One who intentionally intrudes, physically or otherwise, upon the solitude or seclusion of another or his private affairs or concerns, is subject to liability to the other for invasion of his privacy, if the intrusion would be highly offensive to a reasonable person." Ibid. at § 652B.

77. "One who appropriates to his own use or benefit the name or likeness of another is subject to liability to the other for invasion of his privacy." Ibid. at § 652C.

78. "One who gives publicity to a matter concerning the private life of another is subject to the other for invasion of his privacy, if the matter publicized is of a kind that: (a) would be highly offensive to a reasonable person, and (b) is not of legitimate concern to the public." Ibid. at § 652D; see also ibid at § 652D cmt. a).

79. *Florida Star* v. *BJF* 491 U.S. 524 (1989); and *Smith* v. *Daily Mail Publishing Co.* 443 U.S. 97 (1979); and *Cox Broadcasting Corp.* v. *Cohn*, 420 U.S. 469 (1975).

80. 475 U.S. 767, 777 (1986) (holding "a private-figure [defamation] plaintiff cannot recover damages without also showing that the statements at issue are false").

81. Susan M. Gilles, "Promises Betrayed: Breach of Confidence as a Remedy for Invasions of Privacy," *Buffalo Law Review*, vol. 43 (Spring 1995), pp. 1, 8.

82. Restatement (Second) of Torts § 652e (1976).

83. *Time Inc.* v. *Hill*, 385 U.S. 374, 387–88 (1967).

84. *Cantrell* v. *Forest City Publishing Co.*, 419 U.S. 245 (1974).

85. Bill Clinton, *A National Economic Strategy for America* (June 21, 1992) (available through U.S. Newswire).

86. The Telecommunications Policy Committee, chaired by Larry Irving, assistant secretary of commerce for communication and information and NTIA administrator, is responsible for formulating a consistent administration position on telecommunications-related NII issues. The committee is divided into four working groups: Universal Service, Reliability and Vulnerability, Legislative Drafting, and International Telecommunications. This last working group is divided into five sub-working groups: (1) Foreign Government/Foreign Corporation Participation in the NII and the Use of the NII to Open Overseas Markets; (2) Effect of Current Law on Setting Policy and Legislative Efforts to Change the Law; (3) Purposes of the United States Government Controlling the Flow of Technology Transfers; (4) United States Participation in International Organizations and Standards Setting Bodies, and (5) International Use of Research Networks.

The Information Policy Committee, chaired by Sally Katzen, administrator of the Office of Information and Regulatory Affairs in the Office of Management and Budget, is responsible for addressing information policy issues related to the NII. This committee has three working groups: Intellectual Property Rights, Privacy, and Government Information. This last working group is further divided into two subworking groups: Electronic Record FOIA Legislation, and Scientific and Technical Information.

The Applications and Technology Committee is chaired by Arati Prabhakar, director of the National Institute of Standards and Technology in the Department of Commerce, and is coordinating the administration's efforts to develop, demonstrate, and promote practical applications of information technologies. The committee is divided into three working groups: Government Information Technology Services, Technology Policy, and Health Information and Applications. The Technology Policy Working Group includes four subworking groups: Advanced Digital Video and NII, NII Roadmap, NII Services Architecture, and NII Standards. The Health Information and Applications Working Group is divided into three subworking groups: Telemedicine, Consumer Health Informatics, and Standards.

In addition, an NII Security Issues Forum coordinates so-called security issues concerning "confidentiality, integrity, and availability of information and of the systems carrying the information," and a 37-member Advisory Council on the National Information Infrastructure, created by executive order 12864, advises the task force from the perspective of information "stakeholders," including industry, labor, academia, public interest groups, and state and local governments. See generally Fred H. Cate, "Information Policymakers and Policymaking," *Stanford Law and Policy Review*, vol. 6 (1994), p. 43.

87. President's Information Infrastructure Task Force, Information Policy Committee, Privacy Working Group, *Privacy and the National Information Infrastructure: Principles for Providing and Using Personal Information* (Washington, 1995). The *Principles* are reprinted in appendix B.

88. *Personal Privacy in an Information Society: The Report of the Privacy Study Commission* (Washington, 1977).

89. Privacy Working Group, *Privacy and the National Information Infrastructure*, pp. I.A-I.C.

90. Ibid. at ¶ 2 and 4.

91. Ibid. at II.A-D.

92. Ibid. at ¶ 10.

93. Ibid. at ¶ 22.

94. Ibid. at ¶ 24.

95. Ibid. at II.E.

96. Ibid. at ¶ 25.
97. Ibid. at III.A.
98. Ibid. at III.B.
99. Ibid. at ¶ 30.
100. Ibid. at ¶ 31.
101. Ibid. at III.C.
102. Ibid. at ¶ 33.
103. Ibid. at ¶ 34.
104. U.S. Department of Commerce, National Telecommunications and Information Administration, *Privacy and the NII: Safeguarding Telecommunications-Related Personal Information* (Washington, 1995).
105. Ibid. at Introduction C and III.
106. Ibid. at III. A, III.B.
107. Ibid. at III.B.
108. *Directive 95/46/EC of the European Parliament and of the Council on the Protection of Individuals with Regard to the Processing of Personal Data and on the Free Movement of Such Data* (Eur. O.J. 95/L281), art. 8. The directive is reprinted in appendix A.

Chapter Seven

1. "Gathering of Personal Data on Internet Triggers Advent of Privacy-Approved Sites," *Daily Economic Report* (BNA), October 10, 1996, p. A23. The eTRUST site on the World Wide Web is located at http://www.etrust.org.
2. Lawrence M. Fisher, "New Data Base Ended by Lotus and Equifax," *New York Times*, January 24, 1991, p. D4.
3. Ibid.
4. Shelby Gilje, "Credit Bureau Won't Sell Names, *Seattle Times*, August 9, 1991, p. D6.
5. Kathy M. Kristof, "Deluged Lexis Purging Names from Databases," *Los Angeles Times*, November 8, 1996, p. D5. The database reportedly includes current and previous addresses, birth dates, home telephone numbers, maiden names, and aliases. Initially, Lexis was also providing social security numbers. However, in response to a storm of protest, Lexis stopped displaying social security numbers but has kept them in the data files so that requesters can search the database by social security number.
6. Ibid.
7. Direct Marketing Association, *Name Removal Services* (available at: http://www.the-dma.org/home_pages/consumer/dmasahic.html#removal).
8. 5 U.S.C. § 552 (1997).

9. 15 U.S.C. § 1681m (1997).

10. Ibid. § 1681j.

11. "BHA: Put Your Mouth Where Your Money Is," *Times-Picayune*, January 12, 1996, p. E8.

12. Ibid.

13. See "National Law."

14. See, for example, *Direct Marketing Association Guidelines for Personal Information Protection*; *Direct Marketing Association Guidelines for Ethical Business Practices*; Information Industry Association, *Fair Information Practices Guidelines*; and Direct Marketing Association and Interactive Services Association, *Principles for Unsolicited Marketing E-Mail*.

15. Steven A. Bibas, "A Contractual Approach to Data Privacy," *Harvard Journal of Law and Public Policy*, vol. 17 (Spring 1994), p. 591; and Scott Shorr, "Personal Information Contracts: How to Protect Privacy without Violating the First Amendment," *Cornell Law Review*, vol. 80 (September 1995), p. 1756.

16. Bibas, "A Contractual Approach," pp. 604–05.

17. See, for example, Paul M. Schwartz and Joel R. Reidenberg, *Data Privacy Law: A Study of United States Data Protection* (Charlottesville, Va.: Michie, 1996), pp. 307–348; and Joel R. Reidenberg, "Setting Standards for Fair Information Practice in the U.S. Private Sector," *Iowa Law Review*, vol. 80 (March 1995), pp. 497, 509–40.

18. See "Substantive Protections."

19. U.S. Department of Commerce, National Telecommunications and Information Administration, *Privacy and the NII: Safeguarding Telecommunications-Related Personal Information* (Washington, 1995), II-D. Emphasis in original.

20. *Directive 95/46/EC of the European Parliament and of the Council on the Protection of Individuals with Regard to the Processing of Personal Data and on the Free Movement of Such Data* (Eur. O.J. 95/L281).

21. See Bruce W. Sanford, *Libel and Privacy*, 2d ed. (Englewood Cliffs, N.J.: Aspen Law and Business, 1996), § 11.3.10.

22. Ibid.

23. *Directive 95/46/EC*, art. 26(1).

24. Ibid., art. 8.

25. As noted in chapter 3, it is precisely for this reason that federal law requires states to mandate that persons convicted of a sexual offense against a minor register with law enforcement officials upon their release from prison and at least annually for at least ten years thereafter. 42 U.S.C. § 14071(a) (1996).

26. Louis Harris & Associates and Alan F. Westin, *Equifax/Harris Consumer Privacy Survey* (New York: Equifax Inc., 1996), p. 3.

27. Ibid., p. 34.

28. Ibid., pp. 35, 36, 38, 39. Respondents were asked the following: "The present system in the U.S. for protecting the confidentiality of consumer information used by business combines *three* main controls: voluntary privacy practices developed by companies, individual lawsuits and court decisions, and federal and state laws in specific industries.

Some experts feel that Congress should create a *permanent federal government Privacy Commission,* as some European countries have done. This Commission would examine new technology development and could issue and enforce privacy regulations governing *all* businesses in the U.S.

Other experts believe the *present system* is flexible enough to apply those consumer privacy rights that the American public wants to have protected, and that creating a federal Commission gives too much authority to the federal government.

Which of these choices do you think is best for the U.S.?

A. Creating a federal government Privacy Commission, or

B. Using the present system to protect consumer privacy rights.

Respondents could select either option, or respond with "Neither" or "Don't Know" or they could refuse to answer the question. The placement of the question in the survey and the order in which the "A" and "B" options were presented were altered for half of the respondents. Depending upon the placement of the question and the order of the possible choices, the responses ranged from 26 to 29 percent in favor of creating a federal government Privacy Commission, 64 to 70 percent in favor of the present system, 2 to 4 percent choosing neither, 2 to 3 percent responding "Don't Know," and up to 1 percent refusing to answer the question. Equifax-Harris Consumer Privacy Survey '96 (963011/8114/July 19–96), pp. 3, 14, reprinted in *Equifax/Harris Consumer Privacy Survey.*

29. *Equifax/Harris Consumer Privacy Survey,* p. 36. Thirty-one percent of self-described privacy victims and 29 percent of privacy pessimists favored creation of a Privacy Commission.

30. Ibid., p. 37.

31. Jane E. Kirtley, "The EU Data Protection and the First Amendment: Why a 'Press Exemption' Won't Work," *Iowa Law Review,* vol. 80 (March 1995), pp. 639, 648–49.

32. Lillian R. BeVier, "Information about Individuals in the Hands of Government: Some Reflections on Mechanisms for Privacy Protection," *William and Mary Bill of Rights Journal,* vol. 4 (Winter 1995), p. 506.

33. Ibid.

34. *Directive 95/46/EC*, art. 25(1).

35. Ibid., art. 26(2).

36. Ibid., art 1(2).

37. David H. Flaherty, "Telecommunications Privacy: A Report to the Canadian Radio-Television and Telecommunications Commission" (1992), pp. 72–73.

38. Office of the [UK] Data Protection Registrar, *Seventh Annual Report* 33–34 (1990).

39. Délibération No. 89–78 du 11 juillet 1989, reprinted in Commission nationale de l'informatique et des libertés, 10e Rapport 32–34 (1989).

40. For Belgium: Délibération No. 89–98 du 26 sept. 1989 reprinted in Commission nationale de l'informatique et des libertés, 10e Rapport d'activité 35–37 (1990); for Switzerland: Joel R. Reidenberg, "Privacy in the Information Economy: A Fortress or Frontier for Individual Rights?" *Federal Communications Law Journal*, vol. 44 (March 1992), p. 199, n. 16, citing an interview with Ariane Mole, Attachée Relations Internationales, Direction Juridique de la Commission nationale de l'informatique et des libertés, Paris, France (June 6, 1991); and for the United States: Reidenberg, "Privacy in the Information Economy," p. 199.

41. Spiros Simitis, "Information Privacy and the Public Interest," Annenberg Program, unpublished address, Washington, October 6, 1994.

42. Berne Convention for the Protection of Literary and Artistic Works, September 9, 1886, revised, Paris, July 24, 1971, 828 U.N.T.S. 221.

43. Berne Convention Implementation Act of 1988, P.L. 100–568, 102 Stat 2853 (codified at 17 U.S.C. §§ 101 *et seq* (1997)).

44. Thomas Hoffman, "Citicorp Reaps Net Benefits," *Computerworld*, March 15, 1993, p.6.

45. *United States* v. *White*, 401 U.S. 745, 786 (1971) (Harlan, J., dissenting).

46. President's Information Infrastructure Task Force, Information Policy Committee, Privacy Working Group, *Privacy and the National Information Infrastructure: Principles for Providing and Using Personal Information* (Washington, 1995). The principles are reprinted in appendix B.

Index

241